ILLUSTRATED ATLAS
OF THE
WORLD

ILLUSTRATED ATLAS
OF THE
WORLD

Contents

Copyright © 1979 Vallardi Industrie Grafiche
First published in Great Britain by Purnell Books 1979
Reprinted 1988 by Macdonald & Co (Publishers) Ltd
under the Black Cat imprint

Macdonald & Co (Publishers) Ltd,
3rd Floor, Greater London House,
Hampstead Road, London NW1 7QX

a member of Maxwell Pergamon Publishing Corporation plc

ISBN 0-7481-0175-6

Printed in Italy

ILLUSTRATED ATLAS
— OF THE —
WORLD

Consultant
TREVOR MARCHINGTON M.A.

BLACK CAT

The Earth viewed from space

"It looks like a splendid jewel suspended in space." These words by the American astronaut Neil Armstrong, who became the first man to set foot on the Moon on 21 July 1969, epitomise the fascinating spectacle offered by our planet to an observer in an artificial satellite or on the Moon itself.

Unlike some planets in the solar system, such as Venus and Jupiter, which are constantly obscured by a thick mantle of clouds, the Earth is characterised by a very variable covering of cloud which often permits the actual true surface of the planet to be discerned.

The overall colour of the Earth is a bright blue, but the brilliant white of the cloud formations, the dark blue of the oceans and the deep brown of the continents can be clearly distinguished by an observer in space.

The light with which the Earth shines is due to its "albedo", the process by which all the planets reflect into space a percentage of the Sun's light which falls on them.

The Earth, owing to its mantle of clouds, the polar caps and the vast expanses of water, reflects into space about 40 per cent of the incident light from the Sun.

Naturally, if one were to travel further and further away into space, the Earth would become fainter and less visible. From Mars it would look like a star, but from Jupiter it would be practically invisible without a powerful telescope.

The Earth (above left and below)
This is how the Earth appears from the ATS artificial satellite in orbit at a height of about 35,800 km. The whole hemisphere illuminated by the Sun is visible. As shown in the map below, the South American continent with the Andes mountains and western Africa, which enclose the Atlantic Ocean, may be clearly discerned. The polar caps are obscured by clouds.

North America (left)
This photograph was taken from the Apollo 11 space vehicle at the beginning of the flight which was to carry the astronauts to the Moon in July 1969. The picture covers an area of about 2,600,000 sq km. The long, narrow peninsula of California is clearly visible in the west where a cyclone can also be seen and a sheet of cloud stretching all the way to Los Angeles. The land is almost completely clear of cloud with only tufts of white cumulus cloud indicating fine weather.

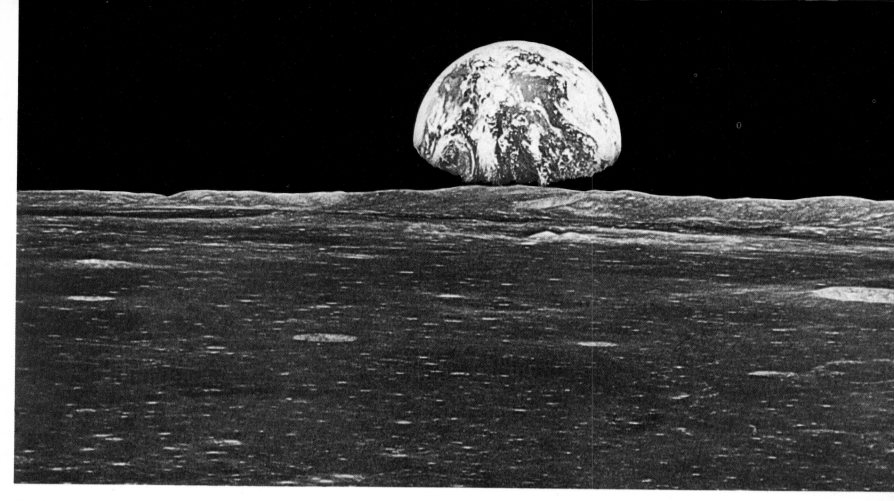

The Earth as seen from the Moon (above)

This is how the Earth looked to the crew of Apollo 10 in May 1969 while in orbit around the Moon at a height of 115 km above its surface.

The picture throws the contrast between the two worlds into sharp relief. On the one hand the Earth, the planet of life, with its atmosphere, its oceans and continents teeming with living creatures, stands out brilliantly against the dark background of space. On the other hand, the Moon with its sombre landscape coloured a monotonous yellowish brown, pockmarked with craters is devoid of any form of life. Our natural satellite, at a distance of 384,400 km from the Earth, appears utterly inhospitable. Lacking an atmosphere which by day filters the Sun's heat rays and at night retains some of the received heat, the Moon is subject to very large extremes of temperature. In order to survive under these conditions, man must recreate the climatic conditions to which he is accustomed by means of special suits like those of the astronauts or, as in science fiction, by means of huge sealed domes.

Two continents side by side (right)

Only the 25 km wide straits of Bab el Mandeb separate Asia and Africa. This photograph was taken in September 1966 from Gemini 11 from a height of about 850 km looking towards the NNE. Better than any map, the picture shows with extreme clarity one section of the largest fracture in the Earth's crust. This is the famous tectonic trench of east Africa which, starting from Mozambique, extends through the great African lake region, across Ethiopia and then divides into two branches, as the photograph clearly shows. On the left is the Red Sea and on the right the Gulf of Aden. The two opposite edges of the fracture, recent from a geological point of view, are continually evolving. Arabia and Africa are very slowly drifting apart.

In the lower part of the Arabian peninsula (at the top of the photograph) it is possible to distinguish part of the desert of Rub'-al Khali (the large yellowish-brown patch) and the mountains of the Yemen, whose line of peaks is outlined by a row of cumulus clouds. Beyond the Gulf of Aden can be seen the horn of Africa, Somalia, with the sharp Cape of Guardafui.

This photograph, taken from Apollo 9, shows the great sand sea of Edeyen Murzuq (edeyen in Berber means sandy desert). We are in Fezzan, the region of central Libya bordering on Niger. On the left, the mountains of Messak Mellet can be seen, the eastern foothills of the Hoggar mountains. The highest areas appear deeply scored and eroded. The action of the wind, together with the rare but violent rainstorms, has a continual scouring and levelling effect which is particularly effective in these areas which are completely devoid of vegetation.

At the upper right hand corner, emphasised by clusters of small cumulus clouds, the edge of the Mediterranean Sea can be seen stretching to the horizon about 1,000 km to the north. In the right hand part of the picture, where there is a vast undulating expanse, the effect of the wind on the landscape is clearly visible. These are in fact dunes, or mounds of sand heaped up by the wind which are characteristic of deserts and low sandy shore lines.

A panorama of the Earth

The advances in space travel have permitted twentieth century man to observe his own planet from a viewpoint which even the boldest and most imaginative of the explorers of the sixteenth century could probably never have conceived. In less than ten years from his first orbit of the Earth, man has set foot on his own natural satellite, realising what must have seemed an impossible dream, and is now sending probes to other planets such as Venus and Mars. Practical, scientific and prestigious motives were all relevant to those assisting with these endeavours to a greater or lesser degree. However, it was really through the unaccustomed aspect which the Earth was revealing and the photographs taken by the astronauts which were arriving back on the Earth that the variety and beauty of the landscape of this fragment of rock wandering in space, with its burning red deserts and deep blue oceans, was being rediscovered.

Lake Volta (Ghana, West Africa)
This is how Lake Volta looks from space (this photograph was taken from Apollo 6), whose dark blue waters contrast with the dark green of the forest and the white tufts of cloud. The artificial basin of Lake Volta, of which only a part is seen in the picture, has an area of 8,500 sq km and is the largest in the world. It was formed by building a large dam at Akosombo about 100 km from the mouth of the river Volta which flows into the Gulf of Guinea.

THE CONQUEST OF SPACE

4 October 1957: first satellite in orbit around the Earth. This was the Russian Sputnik 1.
4 October 1959: The Russian space probe Lunik 3 photographed the hidden side of the Moon.
12 April 1961: first man in orbit; Vostok 1 with Yuri Gagarin on board.
20 February 1962: the American John Glenn completed three Earth orbits.
18 March 1965: first "walk" in space by the Russian Alexi Leonov.
31 January 1966: first hard landing on the Moon (without crew) by the Russian space probe Lunik 9.
16 March 1966: rendezvous in space between the Gemini 8 capsule and an Agena missile.
21 July 1969: Apollo 11 mission. The American astronauts Neil Armstrong and Edwin Aldrin became the first men to set foot on the Moon. Scientific experiments were also carried out. Michael Collins remained in lunar orbit waiting for them.
14 November 1969: two other American astronauts (Apollo 12 mission) walked on the Moon.
30 May 1971: first space vehicle orbits another planet. Mariner 9 transmits thousands of photographs of the planet Mars.
14 May-22 June 1973: first Skylab mission. A space laboratory was placed in orbit to carry out a number of scientific experiments.
17 July 1975: link up in orbit between the American Apollo space capsule and the Russian Soyuz.
22 October 1975: the Russian space probe Venera 9 landed on Venus and transmitted the first photograph of this mysterious planet.
24 July 1976: the Viking probe landed on the surface of Mars and transmitted the first colour photograph.

Socotra (right)

The Isle of Socotra and to the right the small islands of Fratelli.

Socotra is about 240 km east of the easternmost point of Africa (Cape Guardafui) to which, from a geographical point of view, it belongs. The island actually consists of a base of ancient crystalline rocks covered with more recent sedimentary rocks (Mesozoic), similar to those of the high plain of Ethiopia.

Politically speaking, the island is in Asia since it is an integral part of the Popular Democratic Republic of the Yemen. This photograph was taken looking towards the south and therefore appears inverted with respect to normal maps. The colour effect is caused by reflection of the Sun in the surface of the sea and by the type of filter used. The difference between the two coasts of the island is clearly shown: the southern coast (uppermost in the photograph) descends abruptly and precipitously to the sea, while the northern coast is less barren and steep. The main town of Socotra, Hadibu, is situated close to the northern coast, near to the smaller bay to the left.

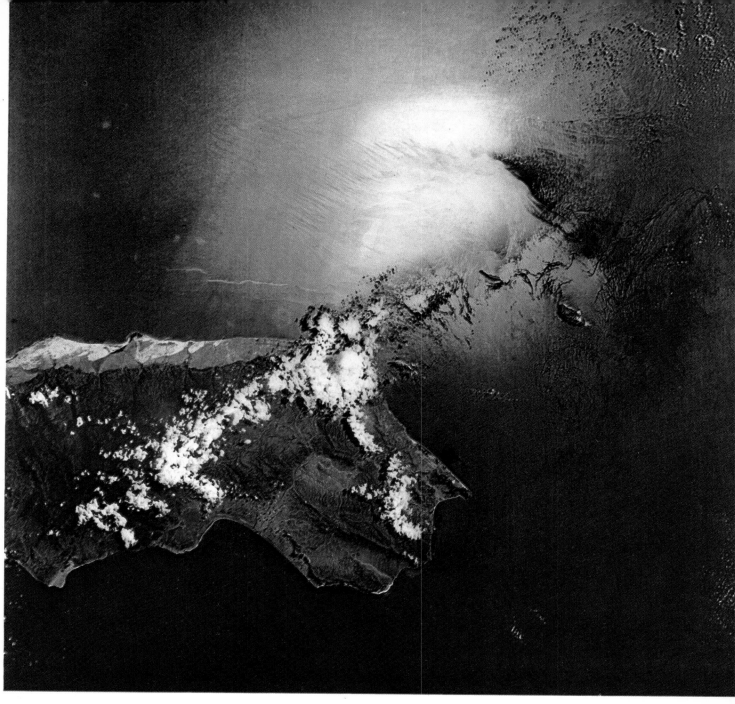

The Nile delta (right)

This is how the Nile delta appears from a height of over 300 km. The thin cloud covering fails to hide the great fan formed by the river where it flows into the Mediterranean. The whole delta appears to be highly cultivated and its blue colours seem to merge with that of the Mediterranean, but it stands out from the paler colours of the rocks and the plains of the desert. The whole of the Suez canal from Port Said to the town of Suez can also be clearly distinguished.

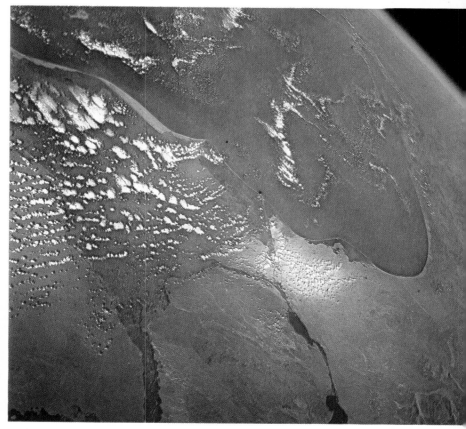

Oman (above)

Oman, the eastern point of Arabia. Both Cape al Hadd, which separates the Arabian Sea from the Gulf of Oman, and the hills of Hajar can be seen. At the lower left there is an expanse of dunes, the beginnings of the Arabian desert of Rub-al Khali.

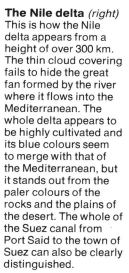

9

Space meteorology

Meteorology, the study of the physical processes and phenomena taking place in the atmosphere on which weather forecasts are based, has benefited enormously from the tremendous advances made in the field of space travel.

Photographs taken from artificial satellites and space probes supply meteorologists with a wealth of data on the Earth's atmosphere and its phenomena, even if sometimes the outlines of the continents and seas are hidden by clouds.

Photographs taken from above the atmosphere have a special practical importance since they show the early stages of development of dangerous tropical cyclones enabling their subsequent development to be followed and the necessary precautions to

be taken in those areas immediately threatened.

In particular, specially designed weather satellites with full instrumentation have contributed to a greater understanding of the distribution and location of cloud formations. Orbiting at heights of between 200 and 700 km, the satellites transmit television pictures to meteorological stations on the Earth showing the distribution, shape, type and extent of the various cloud formations.

It is thus possible to differentiate between tropical and non-tropical cyclones, characterised by their spiral shape, and jet streams, recognisable by long streaks of cloud, and high pressure areas with practically no clouds.

A cyclone over the Pacific *(above)*
This photograph was taken from Apollo 9 at a height of 130 km. The characteristic vortex structure of tropical cyclones is clearly visible. These cyclones, as distinct from the cyclones in temperate zones, are of fairly small diameter (rarely exceeding a few hundred kilometres) and have a high speed of rotation. Inside them are winds blowing anti-clockwise in the northern hemisphere at over 200 km per hour, around a central area called the "eye" where it is relatively calm. This type of cyclone originates in tropical zones in summer and in autumn when the high temperatures of the oceans combine with a very high humidity.

The structure of a cyclone
The diagram below shows the structure of a tropical cyclone (hurricane). The up-currents which form above the surface of the sea in the warmest seasons (**A**) rise rapidly and, being charged with moisture and possessing considerable energy liberated by condensation (**B**), tend to develop a rotational velocity which is anti-clockwise in the northern hemisphere (**C**). Downward currents (**E**) are found around the central nucleus, or eye (**D**).

A cyclone over Colombia *(left)*
The picture, taken from Apollo 9, shows the circular mass of clouds forming the tropical cyclone or hurricane. The name cyclone should be reserved for hurricanes in the Indian Ocean, while the term "typhoon" applies to those in Japan and "willy-willies" to those in Australia.
In the photograph, a huge area of cumulonimbus cloud can be seen rising up to a height of 6,600 m with cirrus and cumulus clouds at the outer edges.

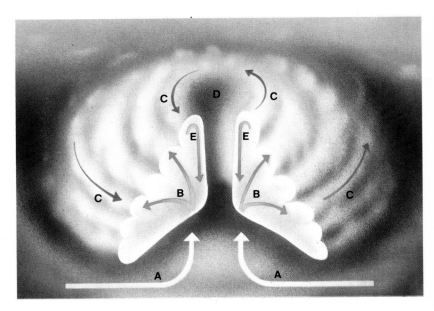

Cartography

Cartography is a very ancient occupation. It was born for obvious practical reasons (delineation of boundaries, for example) and was practised by the Egyptians and the people of Mesopotamia, but it was with the Greek civilisation that it rose to the level of a science.

One of the greatest of the cartographers of the ancient world was Claudius Ptolemy of Alexandria, who lived between 120 and 180 AD and was better known as an astronomer. He devised various types of projections (the cartographic projection is the process which allows the curved surface of the Earth to be represented on a plane surface with the minimum of distortion).

With the ending of the period of the great geographical discoveries and the development of precision optical instruments, he was able to make use of triangulation methods and produced very accurate maps for that time.

A revolution occurred with the use of aerial photographs which, by means of special instruments (such as the stereoscope), were converted into topographical maps permitting accurate representation and faster production. In this way it became possible to make more accurate maps of inaccessible regions like Antarctica.

Photographs taken from the air, however, covered only a fairly small area and therefore to produce maps of relatively large areas required much long and difficult work of co-ordination.

This problem did not arise with photographs taken from space vehicles, since a single picture could depict a very large area. Space photography is of value in other specialised fields. Infra-red pictures can provide valuable information on the state of vegetation and agriculture. Even the field of geology can benefit a good deal from space photography, especially regarding structural details, which are clearly revealed in the pictures.

The urban district of Detroit

Detroit, Michigan (USA), is one of the most important industrial centres in the United States. Situated on the right hand side of the river of the same name, Detroit is characterised by a regular grid-like urban structure as can be clearly seen in the right hand part of the photograph.

Taking photographs by infra-red light, which is emitted by everything but not perceived by the human eye, not only gives a detailed view of the urban structure but also clearly shows the green areas, the various types of crops (note the cultivated areas in the bottom left hand corner) and the nature of the wooded areas.

By infra-red light, the vegetation appears in various shades of red which reveals the extent of any pollution.

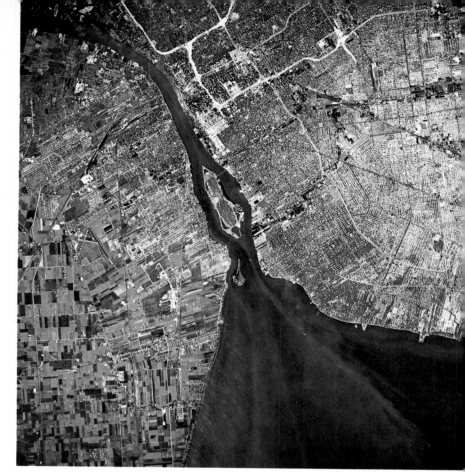

Italy seen from space (below)

Seen from an artificial satellite, the Italian peninsula clearly reveals its characteristic shape. The surface area covered is over 300,000 sq km and the distance from the Swiss lake of Neuchatel in the upper left hand corner to Cape Passero in Sicily is about 1,250 km. Using aerial photography, several thousand photographs would have been required. In the picture, the various different types of land structure are revealed: the alluvial plain of the Po and its tributaries divided into the upper Alpine regions and the Paduan trench, the sweep of the crystalline Alps with the swelling of the limestone southern Alps, the characteristic backbone of the Apennines with the upper Tyrrhenian region, the original Mesozoic Apennines and the Adriatic coast.

Space photography (above)

The diagram illustrates the value and effectiveness of a photograph taken from a body orbiting the Earth. An area can be covered by a single photograph which would have required hundreds of the traditional aerial photographs accompanied by the serious problems caused by the inevitable distortion. In order to transform the photographs into maps, it is important to provide a network of points whose co-ordinates are precisely known. For this purpose, "geodetic" satellites are used which permit rapid and exact measurement of distance, a fundamental requirement for precision map making.

Mount Etna (left)

This photograph, taken from the Skylab space laboratory orbiting the Earth, shows one section of the east coast of Sicily. The conical mass of Etna is clearly visible on the right, the highest volcano in Europe, still active, as evidenced by the thin plume of smoke issuing from the crater (A). Infra-red photography allows the different lava streams on the sides of the volcano to be distinguished; the most recent streams appear dark blue (B) and contrast clearly with the ancient streams and volcanic dust which are coloured red (C). Catania, the largest town situated at the foot of Etna, appears as a blue patch on the side on the plain of the same name (D). In the left hand part of the photograph, the beginning of the Iblei Mountains can be seen, while numerous lakes stand out because of their dark blue colour, among them Lake Pozzillo.

Volcanoes

Volcanoes, like earthquakes, are the clearest and most spectacular manifestation of the vitality and dynamism of our planet, whose crust has the task of maintaining it in equilibrium.

In fact, underneath the thin rigid crust of the lithosphere, there extends a thick region called the mantle, where the matter, which is subjected to very high temperatures and pressures, becomes plastic. It is thus quite possible for convection currents to exist in the mantle whose very slow movement (a few centimetres per year) is transferred to the overlying crust which consists of several large scales or plates.

Below the Earth's crust there is a completely or partially molten, incandescent substance called magma, made up of silicon compounds and small amounts of gas (water vapour, carbon dioxide, hydrogen sulphide, etc.). Wherever there is a local weakness in the Earth's crust, usually occurring at points where the various plates meet, the magma, because of its fluidity, is able to escape, thereby giving rise to volcanoes. The shape of volcanoes, which are typically conical, depends on the type of lava emitted and the type of volcanic material erupted (ash, lapilli or bombs). Also, the manner in which the volcano normally behaves is connected with the type of lava.

The most basic types of lava, that is to say those containing only small amounts of silica (less than 55%) but rich in magnesium and iron, are somewhat fluid. In this case, the activity of the volcano is seldom violent since the gas within the magma is able to escape easily, while the lava flows in winding rivulets which can travel considerable distances, and forms huge cones of limited steepness (shield volcanoes of the type found in the Hawaiian islands).

Acid lavas, that is those rich in silica (over 60%), are rather viscous and obstruct the emission of gases which escape with explosive force, carrying with them liquid and solid matter. These are fragments of rock, bombs, lapilli and ashes which form layers on the lava flows giving rise to the group of volcanic structures known as "composite" or "strato-volcanoes", to which nearly all of the existing great volcanoes belong.

Fountains of lava *(left)*
The Kilauea volcano in the Hawaiian islands during the 1959 eruption. A small orifice opened up on the side of a large shield volcano whose slopes extend into the Pacific Ocean to a depth of 5,000 m.

Kilimanjaro, an extinct volcano *(below)*
The peak of Kilimanjaro, whose volcanic activity is now almost totally extinct, was formed after the Cenozoic age at the same time as the opening up of the great tectonic rift of eastern Africa.

A volcanic cone *(above)*
This volcanic structure in Central America has the typical conical form. It is a layered or composite volcano formed by the building up of alternate layers of lava and volcanic material (ash and bombs). The former during periods of relative inactivity of the volcano, the latter associated with explosive activity preceded by shaking and rumbling and, as in the picture, with the ejection from the crater of a high column of gas and magmatic vapour which often spreads upwards, taking on the characteristic shape of a pine tree.

Lava streams
Lava streams winding their way down the sides of Piton de la Fournaise, a volcano on Réunion, an island in the Indian Ocean to the east of Madagascar. The lava, which is at a very high temperature (between 800 and 1,000°C) and of variable viscosity, while still in a fluid state, flows in streams and rivulets, forming cascades and complete lakes.

Types of volcanic eruption

Hawaiian type
Characterised by continuous emission of very fluid lava.

Strombolian type
Small lava flows accompanied by spasmodic explosive activity.

Vulcanian type
Violent emission of ash and larger material accompanied by a characteristic trail of smoke.

Section through a volcano *(below)*
The diagram shows a section through the lithosphere in a volcanic region. It illustrates both the fundamental elements of a volcano and the more typical aspects of volcanic terrain. The magma, which collects in the magma reservoir, reaches the surface through cracks or along the lines of least resistance. It then remains within the lithosphere and slowly cools to form a laccolith.

A) Volcanic cone composed of layers of lava and erupted material
B) Volcanic vent
C) Miscellaneous cones
D) Sedimentary rocks (sandstone, limestone, shale)
E) Metamorphic rocks
F) Magma reservoir
G) Laccolith

Santorino, the eruption which destroyed a civilisation
Santorino, which forms part of the Ciclades, a group of islands in the southern Aegean Sea, is one of the remains of the ancient land called Egeide, which linked Greece with Asia Minor. Before 1250 BC Santorino, known by the classical name of Thera, was an island on the circular perimeter where a civilisation of the Cretan-Minoan type was settled. Around 1250 BC a violent eruption destroyed the central inhabited parts of the island, which were reduced to rubble, leaving only a crescent shape and several small islets. Thus a flourishing maritime community was cut off at birth. Some archaeologists maintain that the Thera disaster explains the sudden downfall of the Cretan-Minoan civilisation. The ashes from Thera would have destroyed all vegetation and rendered the harbours of Crete non-navigable.
In recent years, the Santorino volcano, now dormant, has shown signs of reawakening. In 1956 in less than one minute 2,000 houses on the island were destroyed. In the picture the islet of Néa Kaméni is seen from the island of Santorino.

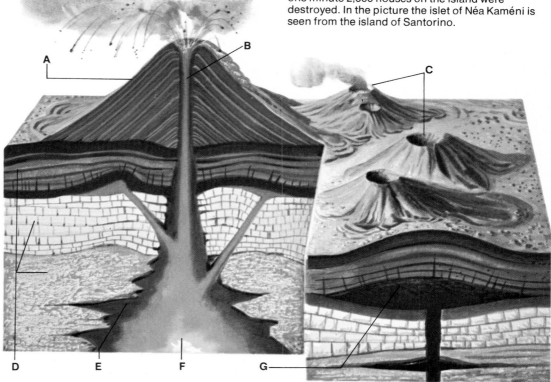

The regular cone of Mount Fuji (below)

The highest peak in the Japanese archipelago (island of Honshu, 3,776 m), worshipped as a sacred mountain and the object of pilgrimages, Fuji has been dormant since 1707, when the ashes from its eruption buried the city of Edo, now Tokyo.
Japan, which is part of the so-called "fiery ring of the Pacific", is one of the most active and unstable areas in the world where vulcanicity is concerned. Its very large number of active volcanoes mark the line of contact between the Pacific and Eurasian plates. The Pacific plate is slowly creeping under the edge of the second plate giving rise to intense volcanic activity and leading to the formation of deep trenches (the Japanese trench, the Kurili trench).

The birth of a volcanic island (above)

The island of Surtsey was formed in November 1963 by an underwater eruption. When such an eruption occurs the magma, escaping through a fissure in the floor of the ocean, is suddenly cooled on contact with the cold sea water. There follows a series of violent explosions of water vapour with outpourings of cinder which accumulates around the underwater source to form a volcanic cone which can, as in the case of Surtsey, extend above the surface of the sea. This is usually a short lived structure which is rapidly destroyed by the waves.

The crater of Vesuvius

This very famous volcano near Naples is composed of two peaks each of a quite different type. Mount Somma is the remains of an ancient crater shattered by successive explosions and the Great Cone, where lies the actual crater, reaches a maximum height of 1,277 m and is seen reflected in the bay of Naples.
The first recorded eruption was in 79 AD. This was when the nearby cities of Pompeii, Herculaneum and Stabia were destroyed and buried.

The earthquake and volcanic zones of the Earth

As can be seen from the map, there is a clear correspondence between the regions of the Earth where earthquake activity is common and those where volcanoes are located. These areas are relatively young in geological terms and therefore still unstable, and they comprise the recent great mountain chains (the Alpine-Himalayan chain and the Circumpacific chain) and the mid-ocean ridges.

DISTRIBUTION OF VOLCANIC AND EARTHQUAKE ZONES

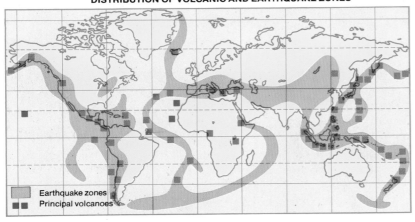

Earthquake zones
Principal volcanoes

GREAT ERUPTIONS

79 AD Vesuvius buries Pompeii, Herculaneum and Stabia.
1006 Ash from the Merapi volcano on the island of Java (Indonesia) buries the city of Baradur.
1669 Etna destroys part of Catania with flows of lava.
1783 The Asama volcano on the island of Honshu (Japan) causes thousands of deaths.
1883 Explosion of the Krakatoa volcano in Indonesia. The victims number around 40,000.
1902 The Pelée volcano on the island of Martinique destroys the city of Saint Pierre (34,000 dead).
1943 The new volcano Paricutin is born in Mexico.
1944 The last eruption of Vesuvius.
1950 The Mauna Loa volcano in Hawaii erupts lava for twenty consecutive days.
1963 The Agung volcano on the island of Bali (Indonesia) causes 2,000 deaths.
1968 In Costa Rica the Arenal volcano destroys numerous villages.
1973 On the island of Heimaey (Iceland) the Helgafell volcano destroys part of the city.

GREAT EARTHQUAKES

1693 In eastern Sicily an earthquake causes 60,000 casualties.
1755 The city of Lisbon is almost completely destroyed by a violent tremor accompanied by a tidal wave.
1906 The city of San Francisco is hit. To the destruction caused by the earthquake is added that due to the fire which followed.
1908 An earthquake and tidal wave raze Messina to the ground; 85,000 are dead.
1923 Tokyo and Yokohama are destroyed by a tremor. The dead number around 100,000.
1960 The city of Agadir in Morocco is razed to the ground.
1968 Earthquake in Belice (west Sicily). Many populated centres are destroyed.
1972 In Managua, the capital of Nicaragua, more than three quarters of the buildings are flattened. Casualties number 6,000.
1976 The Friuli earthquake. Many centres destroyed, around 1,000 dead.
1976 Very violent earthquake in China (Tangshan). One million victims.

Geysers

Geysers, fumaroles and solfataras (gas holes) belong to the group of phenomena known as "secondary volcanic activity".

Without doubt, the most spectacular of these phenomena is the geyser (the photograph above shows the spout of a geyser near West Thumb in Yellowstone National Park). Geysers are very hot springs which periodically hurl jets of water into the air which can reach a height of 50 m. They are found most frequently in New Zealand, Iceland and in the Yellowstone National Park and are caused by the heating of water from an underground spring by hot volcanic gases. Some of the water reaches boiling point and violently expels a vertical column of water, resulting in the familiar spout of the geyser.

Solfatara
The solfatara is a discharge of various gases from small craters or fissures in areas of volcanic activity. The solfatara in the picture emits gases such as hydrogen sulphide which oxidise on contact with the air, depositing the familiarly yellow-coloured sulphur.

Earthquakes

Terrae motus, trembling of the Earth. These Latin words describe exactly that startling natural event, the earthquake.

Earthquakes are felt as sudden rapid movements of the ground caused by a succession of "seismic waves" which originate in an area fairly deep down within the Earth's crust. These waves, which are usually due to a shifting of the rocks within the crust, can be divided into three types: longitudinal waves, causing up and down movement of the ground; transverse waves, which travel more slowly than the first type, causing a wave-like movement; and lastly surface waves, which travel even more slowly. The source of these waves is known as the origin or focus and the point on the Earth's surface immediately above the source is known as the epicentre. The geographical distribution of earthquakes is not random but seems to be associated particularly with those zones which are not yet completely stable (recent mountain chains, ocean trenches), and which also exhibit intense volcanic activity.

The most recent research in the field of Earth sciences tends to include earthquakes in an overall view of all the phenomena affecting the Earth's surface (vulcanism, the formation of the mountain chains and the ocean trenches and mid-ocean ridges).

Both seismic and volcanic activity are

The ruins of Gibellina
This picture conveys a very clear idea of the destructive force of an earthquake. Gibellina, a Sicilian settlement in the valley of Belice, was hit by a violent tremor in January 1968 and completely razed to the ground, resulting in many casualties.

manifestations of the release of energy occurring along the abutting edges of the many plates into which the Earth's crust is divided.

Successive phases of an earthquake
A) Rupture point
B) Seismic waves
C) Epicentre
D) Focus
E) Fracture line (fault)
F) Displacement of the edges of the fracture

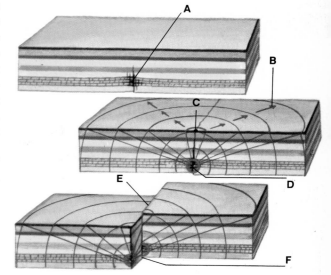

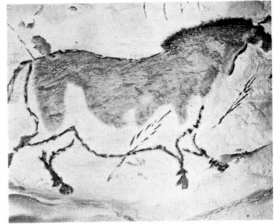

Traces of the past (above)
Prehistoric man frequently left traces of his existence on the cave walls. These were usually figures of animals engraved or painted in vivid colours as in the picture (the Lascaux cave in the Dordogne, France), probably to bring good hunting or for some other ritual purpose.

Caves and grottoes

Natural caves can result from various causes and can be found in many different types of surroundings. We find them on wave-beaten coasts, in the faces of glaciers and in solidified lava streams. The greatest and most spectacular, however, are the result of the dissolving of limestone rocks.

Limestone rocks are mostly composed of calcium carbonate which is insoluble in water. The surface water, however, contains carbon dioxide which causes the insoluble calcium carbonate to be chemically transformed into calcium bicarbonate which is water soluble and can therefore be carried away by water washing over it.

Closely related to this chemical pheno-

menon is the high degree of fissuring, either vertical (joints) or horizontal (strata or bedding planes) in limestone, which encourages the penetration of water leading to the formation of underground passages, recesses, galleries and later caves and grottoes.

The erosive action of the water and consequent structural collapse has led to the formation of caves which are sometimes of enormous size connected together by a whole system of passages, vertical shafts, and galleries, which are being systematically explored by speleologists. One of the biggest cave systems in the world is the Mammoth Caves in the United States, whose galleries stretch for 240 km.

The karst landscape
The phenomena of natural fissuring and chemical solubility typical of limestone rock give rise to a particular type of land formation known as "karst" (after the Karst plateau in Yugoslavia, where these phenomena are widely displayed), characterised by the almost complete lack of surface water features. The water actually penetrates to the depths through the numerous sinkholes and fissures and commences active erosion thereby creating the recesses, caves and grottoes as shown in the illustration.

A) Stalagmites
B) Stalactites
C) Columns
D) Sinkholes
E) Subterranean river

F) Shaft
G) Cave
H) Subterranean pool
I) Limestone rock

Stalagmites in the Tuckaleechee cave (Tennessee, USA)
The walls, vaults and floors of the caves are usually covered with calcareous accretions caused by the slow deposition of limestone by the action of the water. When the water escapes from the fissures in the cave, the carbon dioxide tends to be released because of the reduced pressure. The bicarbonate of calcium then becomes calcium carbonate which is insoluble and is deposited on the rock. This is how stalactites, which hang down, and the thicker stalagmites, which rise from the ground, are formed.

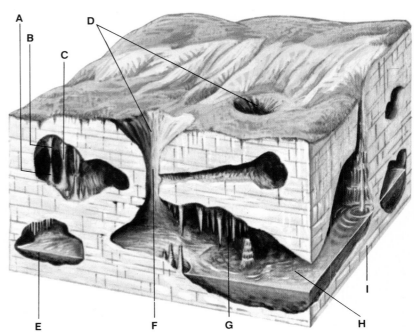

The Earth's treasures

Minerals represent a valuable gift from the Earth, whether from the scientific aspect, for their beauty (as with precious stones), or lastly for their fundamental importance and widespread utilisation in industrial fields, especially metallurgy.

The term "mineral" is applied to a homogeneous body (that is to say a substance in which each particle has the same chemical and physical properties as all the others) formed in the Earth's crust (lithosphere) by natural processes.

Many minerals are formed by the cooling and solidification of magma, others by the deposition of salts dissolved in percolating water and lastly through the phenomenon of metamorphosis, a process by which existing rocks are transformed and recrystallised by the high temperatures and pressures within the lithosphere.

Colombian Emerald. A form of beryllium (cyclosilicate of beryllium and aluminium) with a dark green colour which is one of the most precious of gems.

Gold. A natural element whose preciousness is well known. Often found in the form of threads or scales. The most prolific gold bearing zones in the world are in South Africa and the USSR.

Balangero asbestos. A phyllosilicate formed of whitish flexible fibres which is widely utilised in industry for its insulating properties.

Saxony quartz amethyst. A variety of quartz (silicon oxide) of a violet colour. Quartz is one of the most important minerals found in the various types of rock (igneous, sedimentary and metamorphic).

Diamond. A gem which has been prized from antiquity for its qualities of clarity and brilliance which can be greatly enhanced by accurate cutting.

Uranium from the Congo. Oxide of uranium, the best known mineral from which this radio-active element is extracted.

Graphite. Although, like the diamond, composed of carbon, graphite differs enormously in its physical properties. It is in fact the softest mineral known.

Magnetite with barytes. Magnetite, a translucent black colour, is one of the most useful and commonest oxides of iron found in nature. The white or colourless barytes are the commonest form of the mineral barium.

Chilean malachite. A green carbonate of copper often associated with azurite and found in large quantities in Siberia.

Calcite crystals. Calcium carbonate is widely found throughout the Earth's crust and forms the basis of the limestone rocks.

Celestine with sulphur. Celestine, colourless or slightly blue, is a sulphate of strontium often associated with sulphur.

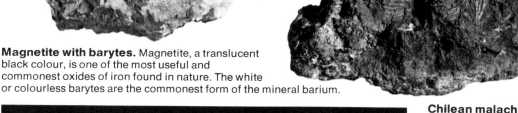

Mountains

It is undeniable that one of the most striking features of the continents is the hills and mountain ranges. These range from the giant Himalayas to the modest peaks of the Prealps, and bearing in mind the wide variety of shapes and formations found, those upward projections of the Earth's surface large enough to merit the description "mountain" can be considered to possess two characteristics in common.

The first is the well known fairly steep slope of mountainous territory (greater than 20%). This shows that erosion is at work (principally by water in its many physical states), a process of continual wearing down of these grandiose structures composed of widely differing types of rock,

sculpting, chiselling and finally flattening the mountains which were raised up by tectonic activity (mainly orogenesis and vulcanism).

The second characteristic common to all the mountains in the world is the variation in climate from the base to the peak. The air temperature is known to fall by about one degree Centigrade for every 180 m increase in height and precipitation is much heavier in the mountains than on the plains. All this has a significant effect upon vegetation and also on the settlement of man. By climbing only a few kilometres one can pass from a landscape of broad-leafed forest to pines, grasslands, arctic tundra and lastly to the region of perennial ice.

The Bernese Alps (Switzerland)
On the left can be seen the highest peak of the range, the Finsteraarhorn, which reaches a height of 4,224 m and from which the Unteraar glacier winds its way down, reaching all the way to Lake Grimsel. The landscape is typical of high Alpine mountains with a rather harsh shape, having crests and steep walls which are continuously subjected to the destructive action of freezing and thawing and to the sculpting action of many glaciers.

The Dru Needle pyramid
The Dru peak, which rises up like a slender obelisk above Chamonix in France, forms a part of the Mont Blanc range (Western Alps) and is composed of the characteristic granite known as protogine. Granite is a type of rock which originates from the cooling and solidification of a magma mass within the Earth's crust, which is then exposed and acted upon by the forces of erosion. The picture shows the vertical west wall of Petit Dru, about 1,000 m in height, characterised by huge slabs and columns of red protogine.

MOUNTAIN RANGES OF THE WORLD

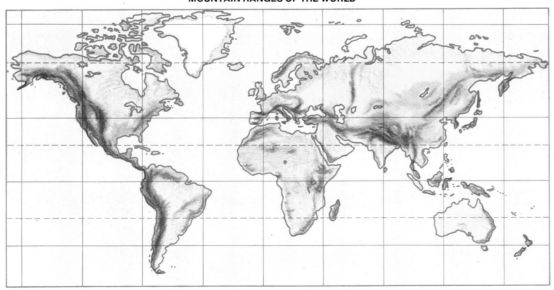

Formation of mountain ranges

The origin of mountains and uplands in general (orogenesis) has always been one of the fundamental problems facing geologists. Modern geologists, believing partly in Alfred Wegener's theory on "continental drift" dating back to 1915, maintain that it is possible to include all the phenomena occurring in the Earth's crust (mountain ranges, vulcanism, earthquakes, ocean ridges and trenches) in a single concept known as the theory of "global tectonics" or "plate tectonics". The Earth's crust (lithosphere) is said to be divided into six major rigid plates (Eurasian, African, Indian, Antarctic, Pacific and American) which float on the upper part of the mantle called the asthenosphere. The plates are subject to slow approaching, receding or tangential movement caused by subcrustal convection currents.

Over the course of the geological ages, the mutual displacement of the plates has carried the continents to many different positions (see below). This phenomenon was and still is always accompanied by the formation of ocean ridges (where two plates are receding) and by orogenesis (when two plates are colliding and their edges tend to become corrugated, forming mountains).

The birth of the continents
Ridges (green), fractures (black), direction of movement (red)

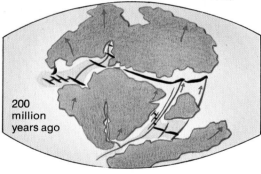

200 million years ago

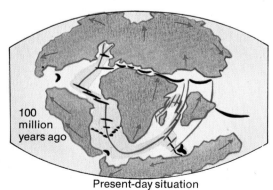

100 million years ago

Present-day situation

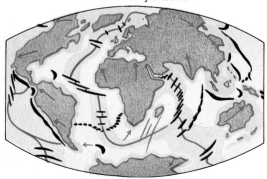

Orogenesis from the collision of two plates

The movement of two plates of the lithosphere towards each other can give rise to the formation of mountain ranges. This occurs when the approach velocity is limited (less than 6 cm per year) and the force of impact can therefore be absorbed by means of folding of the two edges of the plates.

In the other case (when the velocity is greater than 6 cm per year) we have the phenomenon of subduction, where one plate dives beneath the other and re-enters the mantle where it again becomes molten.

The drawings on the right show the principal phases in the formation of the Himalayan mountain range. The Asiatic and Indian plates are moving together slowly owing to subcrustal convection currents, causing corrugation of both edges of the plates. The accumulated sedimentary deposits in the basin dividing the two plates become compressed and forced upwards, while part of the crust is reabsorbed and remelted into the mantle. At the point of contact of the two plates there is thus massive deformation of the crust which, compressed and folded, gives rise to new mountain ranges such as that of the Himalayas.

Successive stages of orogénesis *(right)*
A) Two plates of the lithosphere (1) are approaching each other because of convection currents (arrows) in the mantle (2).
B) The edges of the two plates and the sedimentary deposits between them are compressed (3) and become corrugated.
C) The compression continues and leads to the elevation of the mountain range.

The Himalayas seen from space
The central part of Asia's huge mountain range looked like this to the astronauts in the Apollo 9 space capsule. The picture clearly shows the corrugation caused by the collision of the Indian plate (on the right, where the Ganges plain can be faintly seen) and the Asiatic plate on the left (part of the plain of Tibet can be seen). The Himalayas, which boasts the highest land on Earth (there are at least ten peaks there which exceed 8,000 m in height), is a tectonic structure of recent origin. Its formation dates back in fact to the Tertiary age and is contemporary with the birth of the Alps.

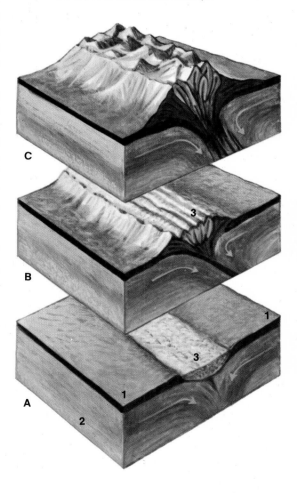

At the summit of Mount Maudit
(Western Alps) *(left)*
Mount Maudit, 4,468 m in height, is one of the highest peaks in the granite mountains of Mont Blanc. Beyond the summit, from which cornices of snow formed by the wind project into space, can be seen the summit of the Grandes Jorasses.

The amazing trinity of Lavaredo
(Dolomites) *(below)*
The Three Peaks of Lavaredo have overhanging northern walls. The Peaks of Lavaredo are composed of three blocks of basic dolomite, a rock which was formed millions of years ago by the accumulation of sediments on the ocean bed and hence called sedimentary rock.

Mountains of the world

Man has always been fascinated by mountains but for century upon century "the cathedrals of the Earth", as John Ruskin called them, were cloaked in a veil of mystery and fear. For many people the mountain was a point of contact with God, or indeed the very seat of God; from Mount Olympus, home of the classical Greek gods, to the prehistoric shrines of Monte Bego in the Maritime Alps and to those of Mount

Fuji on the island of Honshu in Japan.

For centuries considered either as points of contact among the people or as inconvenient obstacles by the commercial world, only since the end of the eighteenth century have mountains been appreciated for the scientific curiosity which they arouse and for their fascinating beauty, often wild and bleak, which is well illustrated in the pictures appearing on these two pages.

K2 in the Karakoram *(below)*
The majestic pyramid of rock, K2, rises from the Godwin Austen glacier. On the right can be seen the south-east ridge called the Abruzzi Ridge, along which the first ascent of the mountain was made (by Achille Compagnoni and Lino Lacedelli in 1954). K2, with a height of 8,611 m, is the second highest mountain in the world. It is in the Karakoram, a mighty Asian mountain range situated north-west of the Himalayas at the border between India, Pakistan and China, and is composed of extremely dense granitic gneiss. The name K2 comes from the classification assigned by the Indian geodetic service and means Peak no. 2 of the Karakoram.

Everest, the roof of the world
(Himalayas) *(left)*
The highest peak in the world (8,848 m) stands out darkly on the left, while in the foreground can be seen the pointed pyramid of Nuptse which reaches the respectable height of 7,879 m. Everest rises from the Himalayas at the borders between Nepal and Tibet which form the most spectacular mountains on the surface of the Earth. The whole structure was formed by Tertiary orogenesis which also caused the formation of the Alps. The name Everest commemorates Sir George Everest who between 1823 and 1842 was head of the Indian geodetic service. The Tibetan name, Chomolungma, is much more poetic, meaning Goddess Mother of the Earth.

Glaciers at the Equator: Mount Kenya *(right)*
Together with Kilimanjaro and Ruwenzori, Mount Kenya (5,199 m) makes up the great trio of African mountains. Situated just south of the Equator in the African state of the same name, Mount Kenya is the remains of an ancient volcanic structure which has been severely weathered and carved by erosion. The many glaciers have contributed to the sculpturing of this massive structure which, as can be seen in the picture, dominates the high valley of Teleki. Only a small distance from the mountain's perennial glaciers, appear groups of seneci, herbaceous plants which, owing to the particular climate of Kenya, can reach a height of as much as 15 metres.

McKinley, the giant of Alaska *(left)*
At 6,193 m McKinley is the highest peak in the whole North American continent. Situated in the Alaskan Range, it rises imposingly in isolation above the tundra, its sides hidden by glaciers. Visible from a great distance, it was discovered by George Vancouver, the navigator, in 1794, but the summit was not reached until 1913.

Grand Teton, the "Matterhorn of the United States" *(right)*
It is given this name because its slanting strata are vaguely reminiscent of the famous Alpine peak. Grand Teton (4,190 m) is the highest peak in the granite Teton mountains (Teton Range) in the central part of the Rocky Mountains (Wyoming). The area surrounding Teton has been declared a national park.

Cerro Torre, Patagonian Andes *(left)*
The rocky spire of Cerro Torre (3,128 m), with its near vertical granite walls, seems to offer a challenge of nature to the courage of mankind. Continually struck by blizzards from the Pacific Ocean, Torre is covered with a layer of unstable and soft ice ready to turn into a terrifying avalanche.

Aconcagua, the father of the Andes *(right)*
Aconcagua, which reaches a height of 6,960 m, is the highest peak in the whole of both North and South America. It is in the Andean chain in the far west of Argentina. The mountain, which is of volcanic origin, is composed of lava from the Tertiary era (and therefore a contemporary of the Alpine orogenesis), which was deposited on top of older marine sediment. The picture on the right shows the south-east face with the Lower Horcones glacier.

21

The Morteratsch Glacier (Swiss side of the Piz Bernina) *(left)*
This picture clearly shows the two parts into which a glacier can be divided. The collecting basin, or source, at the highest point and covered with snow even during the summer, and the trunk which, free of snow, consists of a mass of moving ice which tends to flow downwards. From the end of the trunk, called the snout of the glacier, there flows the glacial stream which races noisily down to lower levels.

Crevasses
In the foreground can be seen some deep cracks in the ice, or crevasses. These are fractures of the ice mass whose depth varies from a few metres to 50 metres or so. Crevasses are formed when the ice flow, in its descent, encounters a slope that is too steep and which tends to stretch or compress it, thereby exceeding the elastic limit of the ice.

Glaciers

Confined in small basins called "cirques", squeezed between rocky walls, or flowing in a great frozen mass like a solidified river, glaciers owe their origin to a slow process of transformation of the snow.

Above a certain altitude (known as the limit of permanent snow), which is around 2,700 m in the Alps, the snow which falls in the coldest months does not completely melt in the summer. The snow therefore accumulates from year to year and is slowly transformed by the gradual expulsion of air due to the increasing pressure first into granular snow and then eventually into compacted ice.

The resulting mass of ice does not remain static but, owing to gravity, tends to slide over the ground with a velocity which varies between a few tens and a few hundreds of metres per year. The glacier will be halted naturally in its downstream movement at the height at which the increasing temperature is high enough to melt it. The survival of a glacier therefore is related to the balance between the accumulation of snow in the coldest months of the year and its melting or ablation in the warm summer months.

If over a number of years the snowfall is heavy and the summer temperature is low, the glacier will tend to lengthen and in the opposite case it will tend to shorten.

The Colory Glacier in Alaska
The glaciers of Alaska, which together cover an area of over 50,000 sq m, are of the piedmont type. As they flow out of the valleys, their trunks merge into one giant ice flow which sometimes, as in the photograph, reaches all the way to the sea. The dark winding line which appears to divide the glacier is a moraine, which consists of rock debris torn from the mountain face and carried along by the movement of the glacier.

Longitudinal section of a valley glacier

A) Glacial cirques
B) Lateral moraine
C) Glacial stream
D) Base moraine
E) Transverse crevasses
F) Longitudinal crevasse
G) Glacial trunk
H) Central moraine
I) Terminal moraine

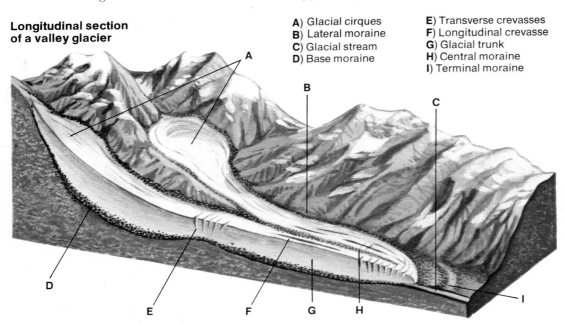

The Aletsch, the greatest glacier in the Alps *(right)*
The Aletsch glacier is in Switzerland, in the Finsteraarhorn mountains. It is a compound valley type glacier, that is it is formed by the confluence of several single valley glaciers (those glaciers where a single trunk flows down from the collecting basin and occupies the upper part of a valley). The Aletsch glacier is over 20 km in length and covers an area of more than 100 sq km.

The face of an Antarctic glacier
Antarctica is almost totally covered by an ice sheet from which many glaciers flow to the sea. In the picture there can be seen areas which are not covered with ice. Near the valleys without glaciers there is in fact one of the few Antarctic regions almost totally devoid of snow.

The Baltoro Glacier (Karakoram)
In the great Karakoram and Himalayan ranges in Asia there are many glaciers which fill entire valley systems. Among the biggest of these is Baltoro which is about 60 km in length and covers over 700 sq km in area.

The great Quaternary ice ages

Continental (inland) glaciers and the glaciers of the various mountain ranges on the Earth cover at the present time an area of around 15 million sq km, which represents 10% of the land area. Ice covers nearly all (96%) of the great Antarctic region (12,600,000 sq km) and the island of Greenland (1,800,000 sq km).

By the beginning of the last century several studies had already shown that at one time the glaciers occupied a much larger area. Evidence for this theory were the scattered boulders, the scoured rocks and above all the corries and moraines found well outside the Alpine valleys. Today it is agreed that between one million and 12,000 years ago there were several ice ages when the ice coverage increased to around 47 million sq km, about three times bigger than now. Great ice caps formed, outside Antarctica and Greenland, in North America, Scandinavia and in Central Siberia. The Alps themselves have been invaded by massive rivers of ice at least four times, reaching right down to the plains.

Much study has been devoted to discovering the cause of the ice ages of the Quaternary era, which were clearly linked with climatic changes. Nowadays some people believe that the climatic oscillations may have been due to variations in the amount of thermal energy coming from the Sun, resulting from the changes in the eccentricity of the Earth's orbit and the variations in inclination of the Earth's axis.

The expansion of the ice caps during the Quaternary era
The illustration shows the limits reached by the ice during the great Quaternary ice ages when ice covered a large part of North America and Europe.

The Ganges, sacred river of India
The picture on the left shows the plain of the Ganges as it looks from a height of 230 km (the photograph was taken in October 1968 from Apollo 7). On the left, covered by cloud, part of the great Himalayan range can be seen where the Ganges rises in the north at a point about 4,500 m high. After flowing 2,700 km through large cities such as Allahabad and Benares (the photograph above shows the Ganges at Benares), the Ganges discharges into the Bay of Bengal in a delta having an area of 75,000 sq km.

A bend of the Rio Grande
Called by the Mexicans Rio Bravo del Norte, the Rio Grande marks the boundary over a long distance from El Paso to the Gulf of Mexico, between the United States and Mexico.

Rivers

To an observer in an aircraft, the land appears to be frequently covered with winding silver threads of varying width which here and there flow together forming a complex network. These are the water courses, rivers and streams which are fundamental elements in the evolution of the landscape which they alter by erosion and silting but which are also indispensable to man to whom they bring the precious gift of water.

In order for an area to be provided with water courses, certain requirements must be met such as a sufficient quantity of water, which may come from atmospheric precipitation or from the melting of snow and ice, a suitable gradient to enable the water to flow towards other rivers and thence to lakes or to the sea and a low surface permeability so that the water is not lost as it flows over the ground.

The water which is not absorbed by the ground first runs down slopes then collects in rivulets, some of which, having greater erosive power, excavate deeper beds and annexe nearby streams. Thus a stream is born which grows ever larger until eventually it becomes a river.

The Zaire river *(below left)*
Completely surrounded by dense equatorial forest, the Zaire winds slowly, through sweeping curves, down to the Atlantic Ocean. These bends are characteristic of slow running lowland rivers and some valley rivers. To the sides of the river can also be seen some isolated bends, remains of more highly developed bends which have been abandoned as small lakes in the typical horseshoe shape. Considered to be among the greatest rivers in the world on account of its length (4,200 km), the Zaire, formerly called the Congo river, is second to the Amazon in the area of its basin (3,822,000 sq km).

The course of a river

A) Upper course	1) Valley	4) Cut off
B) Middle course	2) Alluvial fan	5) Delta
C) Lower course	3) Meander	6) Sea

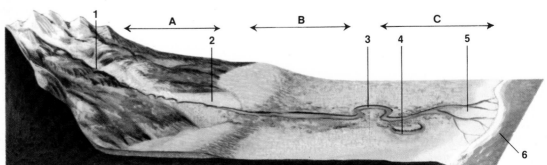

The Amazon

The Spaniards gave the river this name when, in the sixteenth century, they first entered the equatorial forests and were attacked by Indians with long hair whom they mistook for female warriors, like the Amazons of Greek mythology. With a length of 6,280 km, which puts it in second place among the great rivers of the Earth, the Amazon has no rivals where flow rate is concerned. At about 600 km from the ocean, its flow rate is over 200,000 cu m of water per second. Before discharging into the Atlantic, the river divides into a number of branches separated by sandy islands which are continually reshaped by material transported by the river and deposited at the mouth.

Log flotation on the Si-Kiang (left)

There are several important rivers in China. Two of the largest are the Yangtse-Kiang and the Hwang Ho (Yellow River). The Hwang Ho is so called because of the large amount of yellowish alluvial material carried by its waters. In fact the river flows across some plains covered with loess, a very soft yellow rock formed by the accumulation of fine desert dust carried by the wind and deposited on the plains.

The Rhine (above)

The Rhine, which flows through several European countries, is essentially a German river which has always figured in the history and economy of Germany.

The falls of the Blue Nile (left)

Rising in Lake Tana in Ethiopia, the Blue Nile then joins the White Nile at Khartoum to form the Nile proper. The Egyptian civilisation grew up along this river which boasts a length of 6,680 km.

The Mississippi, father of all rivers (below)

So called by the American Indians, the Mississippi and its tributary, the Missouri, reaches a length of 6,260 km and is a most significant feature of the United States landscape from the Rocky Mountains to the Gulf of Mexico.

Lakes

Among the most beautiful and picturesque features of the Earth's landscape are lakes; so often associated with an idyllic serenity. A lake is simply a basin filled with water which has no immediate means of flowing to the sea. In keeping with this definition, lakes, which can be filled either by rivers and streams which flow into them or by precipitation, may have a wide variety of different origins.

The most common criterion of classification relates to the origin of the basin, distinguishing between lakes formed by obstruction of water and those formed in original or existing basins.

In the first case, the lake is formed when an obstruction of some kind blocks the normal flow of water which, in order to continue on its way to the valley, obviously has first to fill up the existing hollow upstream of the obstruction. This obstruction may consist of a landslide (as in the case of Lake Alleghe, for example), a glacial moraine, a glacier, a coastal ridge or a dune.

Among those lakes whose basins are original and not due to some obstruction are crater lakes (for example Crater Lake, Oregon) and tectonic lakes, which fill great fissures in the Earth's crust like those of eastern central Africa (Lake Edward, Lake Tanganyika, Lake Malawi, etc.). There are also karst lakes, formed from caves and sinkholes, glacial lakes formed by the eroding action of flowing ice, and lakes in meteorite craters.

Lake Saimaa *(left)*
Lake Saimaa, one of the largest in Finland (1,300 sq km), owes its existence to the expansion of the ice caps which occurred during the Quaternary age which at various times covered the whole of Scandinavia and the Baltic. In Finland, aptly called "land of the 10,000 lakes", the erosive action of the ice has given rise to a very large number of lakes (totalling over 50,000) which cover about one tenth of the land area. The lakes are mostly of irregular outline, dotted with small islands covered with coniferous forest and of a depth which rarely exceeds ten metres.

Crater Lake
Situated in the Cascade Mountains (Oregon, USA), Crater Lake is a typical example of a volcanic or crater lake. This one fills the base of an enormous crater or basin (its diameter exceeds eight kilometres and its depth 800 metres) and it was formed by the subsidence of the upper part of a volcano into the magma reservoir below.

Lake Band-i-Amir
The picture shows two of the Band-i-Amir lakes in Afghanistan. This is a system of seven lakes in the Valley of Band-i-Amir in Hazarajat (Koh-i-Baba mountains). The lakes occur along a fissure line, visible evidence of which can be seen in the often vertical rocky walls enclosing them which are one of the edges of this fissure. These lakes are therefore tectonic in origin, that is, they are formed by the filling up of rifts resulting from movements of the Earth's crust.

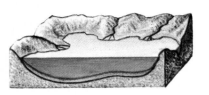

The inflowing rivers of a lake begin to deposit alluvial material on the bottom and to form deltas.

In the intermediate phases, the deposits on the bottom reach a significant thickness and the deltas continue to extend.

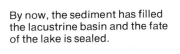

By now, the sediment has filled the lacustrine basin and the fate of the lake is sealed.

The stages in the sedimentation of a lake *(left)*
Lakes are but transitory features of the Earth's landscape, and from a geological point of view have an extremely short life, especially when they are of limited size and depth. The inevitable disappearance of a lake follows the filling up of its basin with alluvial material from the rivers which flow into it, forming deltas which continually advance towards each other until they unite, as illustrated in the drawings on the left.

Lake Baikal *(above)*
Lake Baikal in eastern Siberia also has its origins in tectonic phenomena of the Earth's crust and fills a deep, asymmetrical fissure between two mountain ranges.
Like the great tectonic lakes of east Africa, the most pronounced characteristic of Lake Baikal is its length rather than its width. With a depth reaching 1,740 metres, Lake Baikal is the deepest lake on Earth.

The Brianza lakes *(above)*
The three small stretches of water of Alserio, Pusiano and Annone appear blue among the gently rolling hills of Brianza (Lombardy). Of shallow depth (a maximum of ten metres) and limited area (the largest is Annone with 5.7 sq km), these lakes can be described as morainic, as they were formed behind the successive moraines deposited by the ancient ice.

Lake Titicaca *(above)*
Politically divided between Bolivia and Peru, Lake Titicaca is the largest lake in South America (8,300 sq km) and also one of the highest in the world at a height of 3,800 metres.

Lake Nakuru *(above)*
Thousands of pink flamingoes inhabit the banks of Lake Nakuru, which with its surrounding land forms one of the national parks of Kenya.
Lake Nakuru is situated in the eastern branch of the Rift Valley, that great fissure that opened up during the Tertiary and Quaternary eras stretching for thousands of kilometres across eastern Africa and containing numerous lakes of widely varying sizes.

Lake filled region in New Zealand *(below)*
Enclosed between steep mountain sides clothed with vegetation, the lakes of the South Island of New Zealand are reminiscent of the great lakes in the foothills of the northern Italian and Swiss Alps. New Zealand has also been subjected to intensive glacial erosion, the most visible evidence of which is in the elongated lake basins carved out during the ice ages by the ice masses.

The oceans

The name "Earth" for our planet does not seem very appropriate when we consider that over 70% of its surface is covered by seas and oceans which comprise a single connected system to which various names have been given by geographers. These include the Pacific Ocean (this is the largest, covering an area of 180 million sq km), the Atlantic Ocean and the Indian Ocean together with a number of minor seas. Over the centuries man has learnt to travel over and chart these vast expanses of water, but only recently have some of the secrets been revealed that are hidden below the waves. The massive submarine mountain ridges, submarine volcanoes, the mid-ocean ridges crossed by fissures and the movement of the

sea bed are discoveries of contemporary science.

Despite the fact that modern technology has enabled the enormous depths of the ocean trenches to be explored (the bathyscaphe Trieste reached a depth of 11,000 metres in 1960 in the Mariana trench in the Pacific), our knowledge of the underwater world is still very limited. The future of mankind may well depend upon the expansion of our knowledge in this area. In an overpopulated world which is rashly wasting some of its natural resources, the oceans, with their immense supplies of water, food, minerals and energy could very well play an important part in the determination of our future.

The Cape of Good Hope
Although it is not Africa's most southern promontory, the Cape of Good Hope is an essential point of reference on the route linking the Atlantic to the Indian Ocean.

The topography of the world beneath the sea
The illustration shows a section through a typical ocean bed in which can be seen the various features which comprise the underwater scene and which are usually hidden by the water.

A) Granite continental mass
B) Continental shelf
C) Basaltic crust
D) Ocean trench
E) Mantle
F) Mid-ocean ridge
G) Guyot (underwater mountain with flat top)
H) Volcano
I) Ocean islands

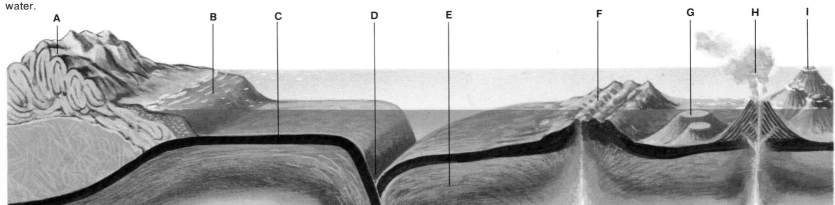

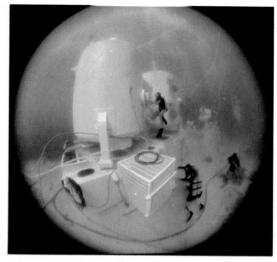

Man and the Sea

Oceanography, the study of the chemical, physical, geological and biological characteristics of the oceans, is a very young science. Today many people are studying this subject. Some are able to remain for long periods in special submarine laboratories (photograph above) and to carry out experiments on the possibility of exploiting the depths.

Submarine exploration
1) Beebe-Barton bathysphere (932 m). **2)** Frogman. **3)** Research submarine Ben Franklin (down to 1,000 m). **4)** Alvin submersible (1,200 m). **5)** FNRS III bathyscaphe (2,300 m). **6)** Deepstar submersible (4,000 m). **7)** Bathyscaphe Trieste (10,911 m).

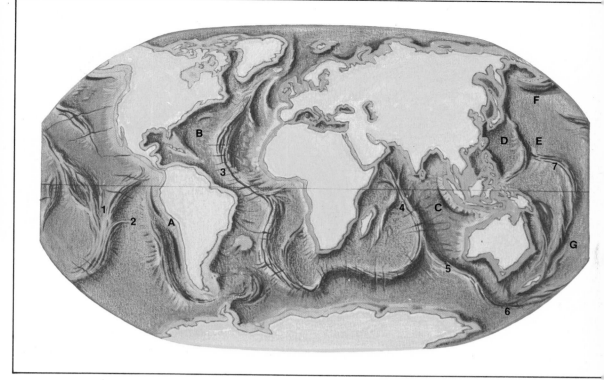

The ocean beds
Contrary to what was thought for centuries, the floor of the oceans is anything but flat and smooth. Modern hydrographic measurements have shown that the beds of the seas and oceans have an extremely varied topography in which, as shown in the map, imposing mountain ranges (ridges) lie alongside deep valleys and trenches.

Ocean ridges
1) Pasque Island
2) Eastern Pacific
3) Mid Atlantic
4) Indian
5) Antarctic Indian
6) Pacific Antarctic
7) Hawaiian

Ocean trenches
A) Chilean-Peruvian
B) Puerto Rican
C) Andaman
D) Philippine
E) Mariana
F) Aleutian
G) Kermadec

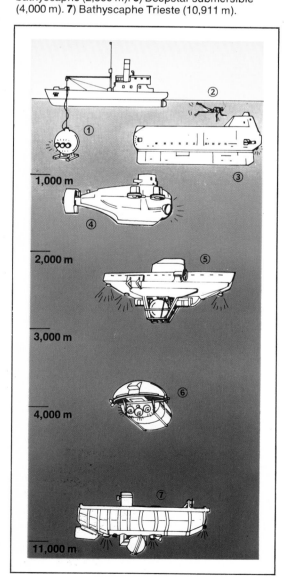

Ocean currents
Caused by the motions of trade winds and the Earth's rotation, to which is added the variation of thermal characteristics of density and salinity different from the waters surrounding them, these currents are like vast rivers moving about in the oceans. Among the best known is the Gulf Stream whose favourable effects are so far-reaching as to be felt even in the coastal areas of north-western Europe.

Ocean currents
(cold currents shown blue and warm currents red)
1) North Pacific
2) North Equatorial
3) East Countercurrent
4) South Equatorial
5) Peruvian
6) Antarctic
7) Cape Horn
8) Brasilian
9) Benguela
10) Canaries
11) Gulf Stream
12) North Atlantic
13) Mozambique
14) Indian Countercurrent
15) Monsoon

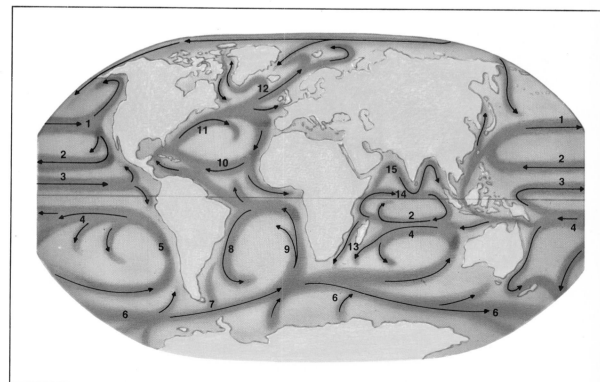

Waves

The surface of the seas and oceans is rarely flat and calm. More often there are undulations or waves to be seen which, in open waters, do not usually exceed a height of ten metres. Waves are usually caused by the action of the wind which, even if not very strong, always exerts a frictional force on the upper layers of water.

In exceptional cases, waves are caused by submarine volcanic action or earthquakes

which are extremely dangerous for inhabited coastal regions for these waves can reach very high velocities of the order of 800 km per hour and a height of over 25 m. These are known as tidal waves or "tsunami".

An observer of the waves on the surface of the sea would notice an apparent forward movement of the waves; this is only an illusion. In deep water, there is no actual forward movement of water, but only movement of energy. The particles of water actually move in closed paths, assuming a circular motion in deep water when the wave only affects a limited depth of water. This motion becomes elliptical, however, when the wave approaches the shore and is slowed down by friction with the bottom.

Breakers (left)
When the oscillatory motion of a wave meets the bottom of a gently sloping shore, the water particles are slowed down by friction with the bottom and take on an elliptical movement (see diagram below). Travelling on towards the shore, their orbital path is broken and the crest of the wave falls forward resulting in breakers which exert considerable forces on the shore and harbour installations.

Tides

Tides are periodical fluctuations of the level of the seas and oceans. Every day, or rather every 24 hours and 50 minutes, there are two rises in the level (flowing of the tide) followed by two reductions (ebbing). The principal cause of this phenomenon is the attraction exerted by the Moon on the mass of water on the Earth (see drawing below). In the middle of the oceans and the landlocked seas, the tide is scarcely noticeable (for example, in the Mediterranean it is less than one metre). In bays and estuaries the increase in the water level reaches quite high values and has a significant effect on navigation (the highest tides, 20 metres, have been recorded in the Bay of Fundy in Canada).

The cause of the tides
The principal cause of the tides is lunar gravitational attraction, but the Sun's gravitational pull also has an effect. The highest tides occur when, as shown in the diagram, the Earth, the Moon and the Sun are in line (syzygy). The Sun and Moon combine then to give the highest high tides and lowest low tides, called spring tides. On the opposite side of the Earth, owing to the reduced gravity, there is a further raising of the tide.

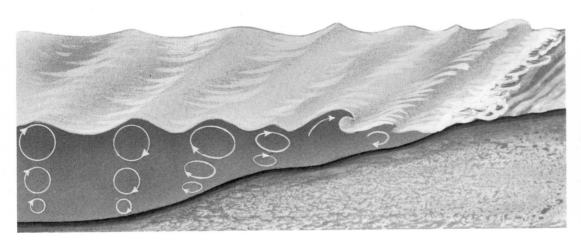

Coastlines

The coast, where the land meets the oceans and the seas, can take on many different aspects which change with time. Its position can change owing to variations in sea level (eustatic phenomena, typical of the Quaternary era which saw the formation and melting of enormous glaciers) or because of tectonic movements (caused by the shifting of plates) or isostatic movements (rise or fall of the land when, for example, an ice sheet accumulates or melts upon it).

The coast is also continually subjected to reshaping, either through erosion or by the accumulation and deposition of material. Erosion, the effect of which naturally depends on the type and characteristics of the rocks forming the coast, is principally caused by the waves which, because of the pressure of the water and the materials contained in it (sand and shingle) are capable of slowly breaking up the coast which is occasionally protected from being completely eroded away by the accumulation of debris. The waves and the tides can actually deposit suspended materials and thus form beaches or offshore bars.

Different types of coastline
Coasts, whose shapes are due to the effects of erosion and deposition acting alternately, are usually divided into two groups: those with high cliffs and those with low beaches. The photographs on the right, from top to bottom, show three types of high cliffs.

The first shows true cliffs, typical of the French coast of the Channel, steep and sheer, carved in the sedimentary rocks of the Secondary era.

The second picture shows the Australian coast north of Perth, where the action of the waves has left a series of spurs projecting into the ocean and exposed the various layers of sandstone.

The third photograph shows the coastline of Esterel in Provence (southern France), composed of resistant red porphyry.

The low coast at Oahu (left)
The narrow beach of Oahu, the most important island in the Hawaiian archipelago, is composed of sand and volcanic material, resulting from erosion or the wearing down of ancient volcanic structures.

31

Islands

Isolated stretches of land of various sizes, but always smaller than a continent, islands are scattered not only in the seas and oceans but also in lakes and rivers. Taking account of their geographical location and neglecting islands and islets in lakes and rivers, islands can be divided into two principal categories: continental and oceanic.

The first type form part of a continent (the British Isles are an example of this) in that they rise from the same base structure as the main continental mass and in past ages were often joined with the main continent.

Oceanic islands, which are mostly volcanic in origin, rise straight from the ocean floor. The Hawaiian islands are oceanic islands.

Islands can also be classified according to their origins. Thus there are, among others, volcanic islands, such as Surtsey in Iceland which is of very recent origin; and coral islands, common in tropical seas, built by living organisms.

The Isle of Levant (above)
Situated a short distance from Trapani and included in the Egadi group, the Isle of Levant is one of the western outcrops of Sicilian territory. It is formed of limestone and dolomite rock and this gives the coastline its often harsh and precipitous appearance.

Continental islands off the coast of China
This photograph, taken from a satellite, shows a stretch of the east coast of China in the straits of Taiwan (Formosa) near the city of Foochow. As well as the mouths of the Min Chiang, numerous islands and islets can be seen rising from the same foundations as the Asian continent from which they are separated by narrow and often quite shallow stretches of water. Islands of this type were often united with the main continent quite recently in geological terms owing to eustatic, tectonic or isostatic movements (see main text).

THE LARGEST ISLANDS	
Greenland	2,175,600 sq km
New Guinea	785,000 sq km
Borneo	736,000 sq km
Madagascar	587,000 sq km
Baffin	476,065 sq km
Sumatra	420,000 sq km
Great Britain	229,885 sq km
Honshu	227,414 sq km
Victoria (Canada)	212,198 sq km
Celebes	172,000 sq km
South Island (New Zealand)	150,461 sq km
Java	125,900 sq km
Newfoundland	112,300 sq km
Cuba	105,007 sq km
Luzon	104,687 sq km
Iceland	102,820 sq km
Sicily	25,426 sq km

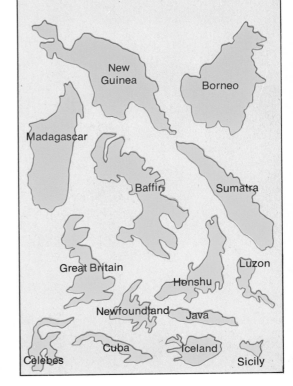

An atoll in the Maldives (Indian Ocean)
The Maldive Islands form a long archipelago between the Arabian Sea and the Indian Ocean to the west of Ceylon. There are over 2,000 islands and islets, all formed of natural coral following the slow and gradual sinking of the underwater shelf (subsidence). Most of the islands are surrounded by a coral reef in the shape of a ring covered with foam from the breaking ocean waves.

The birth of an atoll

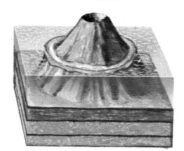

Coral grows around a volcanic island which is slowly sinking.

The island continues sinking while the coral structures grow up towards the surface.

The island has completely submerged. Vegetation appears on the coral reef.

An islet in New Caledonia
New Caledonia (French Oceania) comprises the principal island which gives its name to the group and an indefinite number of small islets. These are generally surrounded by a coral reef, which can be clearly seen in the picture.
Within the reef, the waters are calm and lap over a narrow beach of very white sand.

Atolls

The process by which atolls were formed has always posed an interesting scientific problem, made more complex by the special conditions necessary for the life of the organisms of which they are constructed (water temperature over 20°C, depth at the bottom less than 40 metres, continual submersion, and clear water with a high salinity). Yet today Darwin's theory seems to be correct, at least in general terms. He postulated a slow sinking of the rock base on which the first coral colonies had formed and a consequent upward growth of these colonies which could not survive at the increased depth (see drawings on the left).

The island of Bora Bora (above)
The principal features of the landscape of Bora Bora, an island in the Polynesian archipelago of Society, are the volcanic rocks, sculptured by erosion, the palm trees and the coral reef over which break the waves of the Pacific.

The archipelago of Tuamotu (below)
This photograph was taken from a height of about 250 km. The islands of the archipelago, which forms part of Polynesia, reveal their origin because of their characteristic shape. They are atolls, forming a circular or elliptical coral reef enclosing a lake. From the right, some of the larger atolls can be distinguished: Apotaki, Toau and Fakarawa with the little settlement of Rotoava. The inner lake, which looks the same colour as the surrounding ocean in this picture, is in reality very shallow (one hundred metres maximum).

33

Cirrus. High clouds (from 6,000 to 12,000 metres, the limit of the troposphere). They are shaped like tufts or thin fibres and are formed from tiny needles of ice which barely obscure the light of the sun. When, as in the picture, cirrus clouds are broken up, this is caused by high winds.

Cumulus. Clouds with very clear outlines which grow vertically up to quite great heights and have dome-shaped tops with white, rounded protuberances. They are convection clouds, caused by upward air currents, and usually indicate fine weather until they tower to great altitudes.

Atmospheric phenomena

Rain, snow and wind together with temperature variations (collectively known as atmospheric phenomena) are the clearest evidence of the way in which the physical characteristics (humidity, pressure and temperature) of the troposphere, that is those layers of the atmosphere between the Earth's surface and an average height of 12 kilometres, change and combine together in different ways.

In particular, rain is associated with the process of condensation of water vapour in the atmosphere which is the result of the phenomenon of evaporation. The amount of water vapour that can be absorbed by a mass of air is not unlimited, but is a function of the temperature. At 0°C for example, one cubic metre of air cannot absorb more than five grammes of water vapour, while at 30°C it can absorb more than 30 grammes. Clearly a reduction in the temperature will cause separation of the excess water vapour, which condenses in minute water droplets.

The rains, as can be seen in the map below, are not distributed uniformly over the surface of the Earth, but depend on the location of areas of high and low pressures. The most significant rainfall occurs in the equatorial belt where large masses of warm, humid air converge.

Cumulonimbus. Clouds rising to a great height with a very broad upper region. They are accompanied by storms with violent rain and lightning. They are typical of areas where warm and cold air masses meet (fronts) and the cold air drives a wedge under the warm air.

ANNUAL RAINFALL

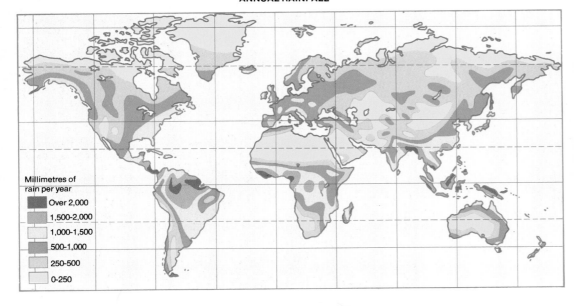

Millimetres of rain per year

- Over 2,000
- 1,500-2,000
- 1,000-1,500
- 500-1,000
- 250-500
- 0-250

Lightning. This is an electrical discharge occurring during thunderstorms between the base of the cloud and the ground or between two clouds. It is due to the potential difference between parts of the atmosphere which have accumulated electrical charges.

Snow
Snow is also the result of the condensation of water. This phenomenon occurs when the temperature is below freezing point and the water vapour passes from the gaseous state to the solid state to form tiny ice crystals which, if the temperature of the lower layers of the atmosphere is low enough, can reach the ground without melting.

Drops of dew on a leaf
During the night the ground loses heat by radiation and the layer of air in contact with the surface is cooled. The water vapour in the air condenses in minute droplets and is deposited on the vegetation.

Wind

The wind, which is usually defined as a mass of air moving parallel to the surface of the Earth, is a phenomenon caused by the variations of pressure occurring in the atmosphere. The pressure, or force exerted by the air, is measured in millibars or millimetres of mercury and varies with height, humidity and temperature.

The air masses tend to move away from areas of high pressure (anticyclones) towards those of low pressure (cyclones, or depressions) like a river which flows from the highest to the lowest level. The winds are known as constant if they always blow in the same direction (like the Trade Winds which blow from the north-east in the northern hemisphere) or periodic when they blow alternately from two opposite directions (like the monsoons).

Windmills
Over the centuries, wind has been a valuable source of energy for man.

A bank of fog forming
Fog, which only affects the lower layers of the atmosphere, is formed of minute water droplets suspended in banks of varying density which can seriously reduce visibility. Near large industrial and urban centres the fog, combining with smoke, can easily become smog.

The prevailing winds
The map shows the directions of the principal prevailing winds. The so-called Trade Winds can be seen blowing towards the Equator from 30° NE and SE as can the westerly winds blowing towards the poles and the polar winds.

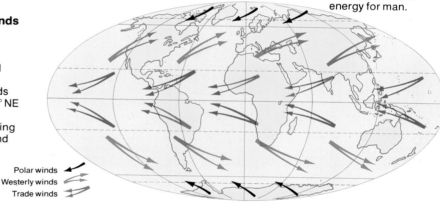

Polar winds
Westerly winds
Trade winds

Temperature

The temperature of the air is determined by the luminous and ultraviolet radiation emitted by the Sun which is transformed into thermal radiation by the Earth and radiated into the atmosphere. Like rainfall, thermal energy is not spread evenly over the Earth. The spherical shape of the planet, its rotation and revolution around the Sun with its axis always oriented in the same direction prevent this. The temperature is further influenced by altitude, cloudiness and by the distribution of the oceans and continents.

Sunlit tropical beaches
The areas between the Tropics are the hottest. The rays of the Sun reach these areas with the minimum obliquity and there is the least variation in the lengths of the day and night.

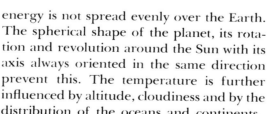

DISTRIBUTION OF TEMPERATURE ZONES

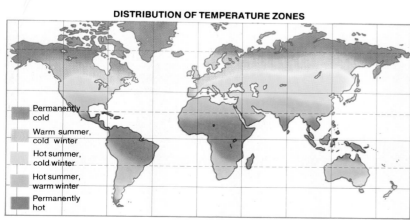

Permanently cold

Warm summer, cold winter

Hot summer, cold winter

Hot summer, warm winter

Permanently hot

Houses of ice beyond the Arctic Circle
The area above the Arctic Circle is constantly subjected to low temperatures. There the Sun's rays are at their maximum inclination and the difference between the length of the day and of the night is greatest.

Climate and vegetation

The net effect of the atmospheric phenomena (rain, wind and temperature) which are associated with a region for a long period of time constitutes the climate, as opposed to the weather which can be defined as the temporary combination of these phenomena. The climate can therefore be said to describe the average weather conditions for a region.

It is obvious that the climate plays an important part in the shaping of the landscape, in determining the type of vegetation (compare the map on this page with the one on the opposite page) and in man's way of life.

There are several factors which, to a greater or lesser extent, can affect the climate, and thereby also the type and distribution of vegetation, by altering the established balance between temperature, humidity and pressure. Such factors, for example, as latitude, exposure to the sun, closeness to the sea, varying height and the existence of a certain wind or sea current. It is known, for example, that the eastern coasts of the Atlantic Ocean in winter are warmer than the western coasts so that while in New York the Hudson is often blocked by ice, at Narvik in Norway, which is not far from the Arctic Circle, shipping is virtually unaffected. This is due to the warming effect of the Gulf Stream which, originating between Florida and Cuba, bathes Nothern Europe with one of its offshoots (the North Atlantic Drift). There are many different systems of classifying the various types of climate. Among the most useful are those of the geographers Köppen and Trewartha.

In the rain forest
In the warm and humid tropical zones the typical vegetation is the rain forest, whose prolific growth is due to the high temperatures and above all the amount (over 2,000 mm per year) and regularity of the annual rainfall.

Towards the tundra
The gradual disappearance of the pine and birch trees signals the transition from the cold sub-arctic climate to the polar climate of the tundra, where because of the very low temperatures (falling as low as −40°C) only mosses and lichens can survive.

THE CLIMATIC ZONES

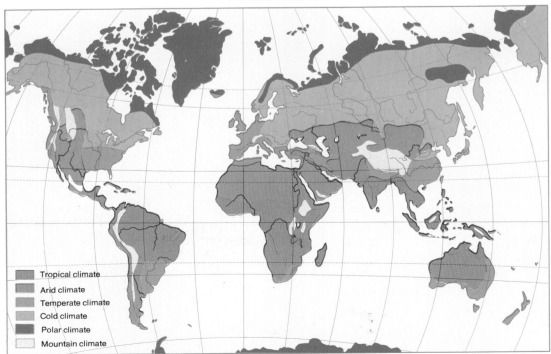

Tropical climate
Arid climate
Temperate climate
Cold climate
Polar climate
Mountain climate

Broad leafed forest (above)
This is the typical vegetation of temperate climates, which are further subdivided into oceanic and continental climates based on their distance from the oceans.

Desert vegetation (below)
Despite the very high temperatures reached in summer (up to 55°C) and the almost complete lack of rain, in the desert of the Valley of Death (USA) tiny plants manage to survive.

The grasslands (right)
The grassland, typical of continents with temperate climates, is characterised by vast expanses of grass. The establishment of herbaceous vegetation rather than trees is encouraged by the shortage of rainfall (less than 500 mm per year).

The savannah (far right)
The savannah, vegetation typical of tropical zones with two seasons, is composed of grasses with the addition of a few trees, either singly or in small groups (tree-bearing savannah).

Alpine mountain sides (above)
This picture of the Retiche Alps (Mount Piazzi, 3,439 m), shows the effect of altitude on the climate and hence on the vegetation. Several zones can be distinguished (forest, grassland and snow) whose sequence is similar to that found when passing from temperate to polar regions. In fact either increasing latitude or increasing altitude causes an overall reduction in temperature which is reflected in the vegetation.

VEGETATION

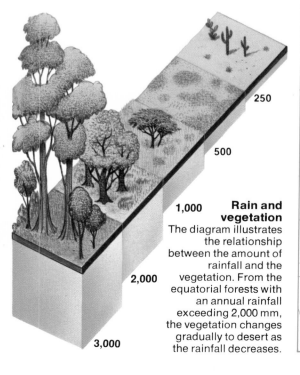

250

500

1,000

Rain and vegetation
The diagram illustrates the relationship between the amount of rainfall and the vegetation. From the equatorial forests with an annual rainfall exceeding 2,000 mm, the vegetation changes gradually to desert as the rainfall decreases.

2,000

3,000

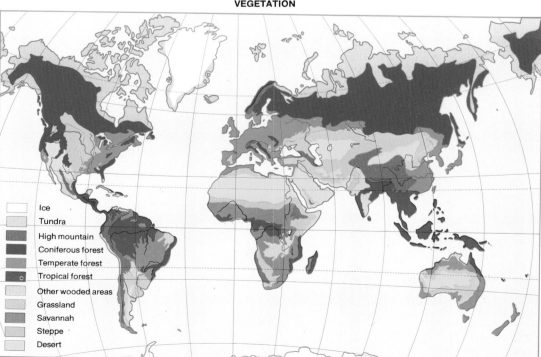

- Ice
- Tundra
- High mountain
- Coniferous forest
- Temperate forest
- Tropical forest
- Other wooded areas
- Grassland
- Savannah
- Steppe
- Desert

The Arctic

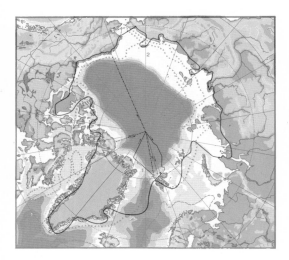

Petrel

Steller's albatross

Ice fulmar

Birds of the Arctic
In the milder season many species of birds, attracted by the tranquillity and plentiful supplies of food, reach the Arctic to nest. These are generally species of flighted birds such as the albatross, petrel and fulmar which spend most of their lives at sea.

Vegetation
In spring, after the thaw, the water-laden soil of the Arctic is covered with mosses and lichens.

Icebergs
In the northern hemisphere the icebergs come mainly from glaciers in Greenland.

The Arctic includes the North Pole and the region beyond the Arctic Circle (latitude 66°32' North). Besides the polar cap, it includes the northern parts of the New and Old Continents as well as numerous islands.

• Polar bear

Carnivores
The largest Arctic carnivore is the polar bear, which wanders restlessly in search of prey. The arctic wolf too is a tireless hunter, whose insatiable appetite makes him very daring.

Arctic wolf

Walrus

The seals
Seals, sea-lions and walruses visit the shores only during the breeding season. Thanks to a thick layer of subcutaneous fat they are able to survive the low temperatures of the polar regions.

Ringed seal

Sperm whale

Narwhal

The cetaceans
Whales, dolphins and sperm whales are mammals which have undergone various changes to adapt them to marine life. Their limbs have been transformed into fins, their skin is smooth and waterproof and their bodies have taken on hydrodynamic shapes. A thick layer of subcutaneous fat helps these animals, which spend many months of the year in polar waters, to maintain an even body temperature.

White dolphin

Killer whale

Herring

Sparidae

Cod

The poles are among the coldest places on Earth, since they receive the least heat from the Sun whose rays there are tangential to the surface of the Earth. In addition the glaciers reflect the solar energy like a mirror, dispersing it in space. The poles differ considerably from each other, for while the North Pole is in the frozen Arctic Ocean, covered with perpetual ice and surrounded by the northern boundaries of the Old and New Continents, the South Pole is a circular shaped continent which is also covered by perpetual ice. The covering of ice has an uneven surface due to the effect of the strong winds blowing from the Arctic Ocean, and is 2 to 4 metres thick.

The fish
The abundance of life in the polar seas depends on the phytoplankton, which are comparable to huge marine prairies. On these feed the zooplankton, a collection of unicellular animals and fish larvae which forms the diet of numerous species of fish, which in turn are preyed upon by larger animals.

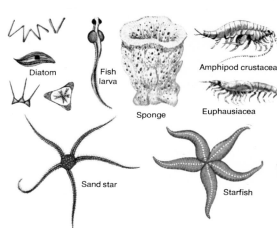

Diatom

Fish larva

Sponge

Amphipod crustacean

Euphausiacea

Sand star

Starfish

The Antarctic

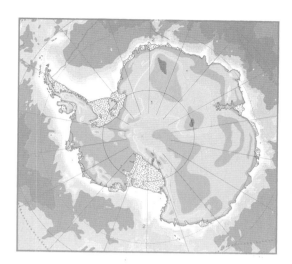

The vegetation
Animal and vegetable life in the Antarctic is restricted by the lack of water and warmth. In the centre of the continent in the brief period of thaw, the only vegetation present is in the form of lichen. By the coasts and on the islands there are also mosses and liverworts. Life is more abundant on the Antarctic Peninsula and on the islands where the only land animals are tiny invertebrates, mites and insects which live on tufts of grass. Many other animals however, like some penguins, visit the islands and Antarctic coasts each year at breeding time.

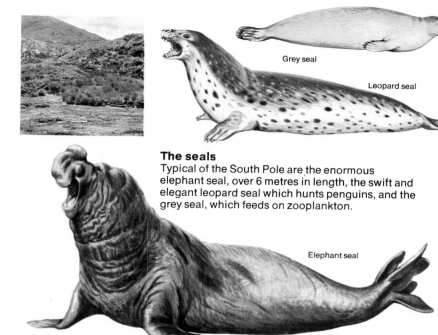

Grey seal

Leopard seal

The seals
Typical of the South Pole are the enormous elephant seal, over 6 metres in length, the swift and elegant leopard seal which hunts penguins, and the grey seal, which feeds on zooplankton.

Elephant seal

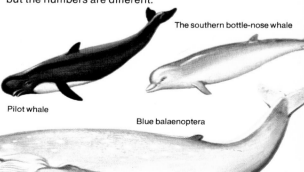

The penguins
In the Antarctic and subantarctic regions, dense colonies of penguins collect at breeding time. These birds are remarkably well adapted to aquatic life in the cold polar regions. Adélie penguins enter the continent to build their nests.

In spite of the basic differences, the two extreme ends of the world have one thing in common. For six months of the year the length of darkness greatly exceeds the length of daylight, and vice versa, and for several weeks of the year there is continuous daylight or continuous darkness. Also at both poles strange luminous phenomena, called auroras, can be seen which paint the polar sky with colour. Much of the Antarctic has never been seen, but it is known to be the most desolate continent in the world. The lowest temperatures in the world are found here (90°C below zero) and the worst climate. 90% of the world's ice is found in the Antarctic and in some places the ice is 3,000 metres thick.

The cetaceans
The cetaceans of the southern seas include the majority of the species of the northern hemisphere but the numbers are different.

The invertebrates
Sponges, riccia, starfish and numerous species of molluscs and crustaceans enrich the fauna of the Antarctic.

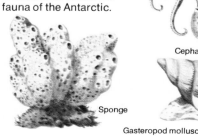

Cephalopod mollusc

Sponge

Gasteropod mollusc

A rich sea
The large amounts of sunlight during the summer months enables a high rate of photosynthesis to be sustained by which the plants containing chlorophyll (phytoplankton) convert inorganic substances into organic substances. That is to say, carbon dioxide and various mineral salts are converted, by means of the solar energy stored in the chlorophyll, into sugars, amides, fats and proteins. Thus the food supply chain begins with plants, on which herbivores live who, in turn, are prey to predators.

The southern bottle-nose whale

Pilot whale

Blue balaenoptera

The tundra

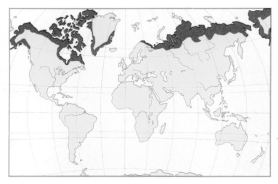

The tundra is a zone without any actual groups of trees, which stretches between the taiga – the band of conifers in the northern hemisphere – and the polar region. There is no equivalent zone in the southern hemisphere where at the same latitude (60°–70°) there is no dry land.

The rodents
In spite of the rigours of the climate, many animals spend the whole year in the tundra. Rodents like the pica (*above left*), the lemming (*left*) and the marmot (*above right*) pass the long winter underground.

Snowy owl

The tundra is characterised by low temperatures (the average in the warmest month is + 10°C) and soil which is frozen for most of the year. Even in the brief summer, the soil only thaws on the surface, the lower layer remaining permanently frozen (permafrost).

During the long winter the action of the snow and frost breaks up the rocks, altering the appearance of the terrain and making the growth of vegetation difficult. With the arrival of summer, the snow melts to form marshy areas. Thanks to the moisture and the Sun, which shines for longer each day and for 24 hours a day at the height of summer, the tundra is clothed with mosses and lichens. Animal life is made difficult by the dark and severe winter.

Hibernation and migration
A few mammals merely become lethargic but many hibernate. Others migrate, among them many birds, reindeer and caribou and all animals which obtain their food from rivers and lakes which are frozen for many months of the year. The lynx (*right*) and the arctic fox (*far right*).

The taiga

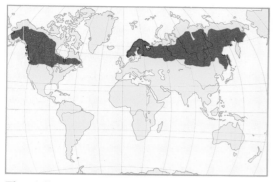

The trees
The white spruce has a conical shape with needles and light grey bark. The red spruce has branches which bend downwards, short needles and reddish brown bark. The larch is deciduous with short, soft needles and thick bark. The pine has long slender needles.

White spruce

Red spruce

Larch

Pine

The soil
The damp, cold climate of the taiga encourages the accumulation of dead organic material in the upper layer of the soil (1); the formation of humus is slow. Bacteria and earthworms are rare and so decomposition is retarded. Rain washes essential minerals such as iron and aluminium down to lower levels. (2) Compact layer resting on the bed-rock (3).

In the coniferous woods
Only specially adapted birds survive in this environment. The turkey (left), like other similar birds, feeds on pine needles. The elk (below) occurs throughout the polar regions and there are many similar species.

The taiga is found south of the tundra in continental countries which experience long severe winters such as eastern Europe, Siberia and North America. The main varieties of trees are coniferous and include spruce, larch and, near water, mountain maples, poplars, willow and birch. The coniferous forests cover a huge area and the trees are closly spaced. The undergrowth, brambles and bushes, is not very dense. The soil is poor and at times marshy. In spite of the relative poverty of the environment, it still provides food the year round and the fauna are varied. There are wolves, bears, foxes, badgers, beavers, marmots, ermine, martens, lynxes, elk, squirrels, hares, crossbills, eagles, jays and many others.

The birds of prey
The great birds of prey of the taiga hunt in the forest glades, where they dive on their prey and carry it off.

Royal eagle

The great hunters
The numerous rodents, reptiles and birds of the taiga are the usual prey of the weasel family (polecats (left), weasels, ermine, etc.). The great carnivores, bears and wolves (far left), hunt stags, elk and deer, but are content with smaller prey if they cannot find sufficient larger prey to meet their needs.

The temperate forests

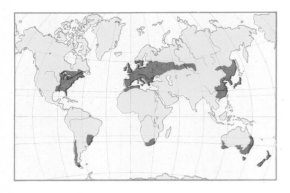

The leaves fall
The biological cycle of the trees is determined more by variation of temperature than by rain. Summer leaves absorb the maximum amount of light from the Sun, but because of their delicate structure cannot survive the rigours of the autumn and fall to the ground. In the winter, the tree lives on its reserves.

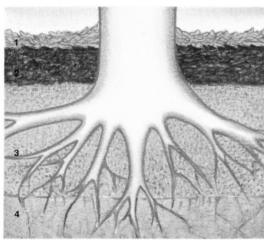

The soil
There are four layers in the cross section through the soil of a broad-leaved forest: **1)** the surface layer, consisting of animal debris (excrement and carrion) and vegetable matter (dead leaves, etc.); **2)** humus; **3)** intermediate layer, with a little decomposed organic material in small particles and a great deal of inorganic matter; **4)** base layer of rock and sand where the true geological substrata begins. The mass of leaves falling on the ground is attacked first of all by the annelida and arthropods, then by bacteria of decomposition which transform it into inorganic material.

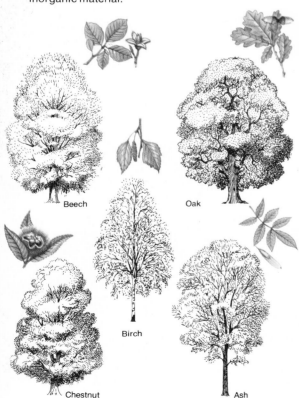

Beech

Oak

Birch

Chestnut

Ash

Deciduous forests occur in the temperate zones where the humidity is constant all the year round and the winters, though short, are severe enough to slow down the biological cycle of the trees. In the cold season, the trees shed their leaves which, falling on the ground, are broken down first of all by worms, woodlice and other creatures, and are then decomposed by bacteria to form mineral salts which enrich the soil, making possible the growth of rich undergrowth. Man's intervention in this region has considerably reduced its original area. At one time the forest covered a large part of North America, central Europe, central Asia, Japan, Chile and the Argentine.

Australian forest
The geographical isolation of Australia has influenced the evolution of animals and vegetation. The temperate forest consists almost exclusively of varieties of the Eucalyptus. Numerous marsupials live there (*left:* koala bear), and also many birds (*right:* lyre bird).

The tree, a world of its own

A large number of animal species find their ecological niche in the giant oak tree. There are three separate habitats: the roots, the trunk and the branches. Among the roots live many animals which are of great benefit to the tree. These include worms which aerate the soil with their tunnels and carry small pieces of leaf into the subsoil where fungi and bacteria transform them into mineral salts which serve to nourish the tree. Predators collect in the root region in search of prey. The trunk is mainly inhabited by insects. Squirrels and birds build their nests in hollow trunks. The branches form the richest habitat and give shelter to wasps, butterflies, caterpillars, spiders and many varieties of birds.

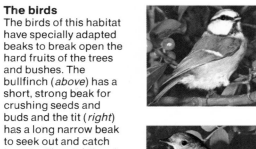

The insects

Many of the insects of this habitat are harmful, like the butterfly larvae which eat the leaves or the aphids which suck the sap. Others are very useful, like the ladybird (*left*) which feeds on parasites, or the bees (*below*) which pollinate the tree.

The herbivores

The forest offers the numerous herbivores a different diet each season; buds and leaves in spring, fruit in summer and dry fruit and berries in autumn. (*Above:* deer).

The birds

The birds of this habitat have specially adapted beaks to break open the hard fruits of the trees and bushes. The bullfinch (*above*) has a short, strong beak for crushing seeds and buds and the tit (*right*) has a long narrow beak to seek out and catch insects. The nightingale (*lower right*) feeds on both insects and fruit and berries.

The predators

The predators are usually of small size, like the fox, weasel, wild cat and several kinds of snake such as the Austrian coronella (*below*) and numerous birds of prey including kestrels, falcons and owls. Their prey consists mainly of rodents, birds and frogs. With the huge number of insects there are also many animals which feed on them, among them various species of bat (*right*), hedgehogs, green lizards (*below*) frogs and toads.

In the bamboo forest

In the bamboo forests of China lives the lesser panda. It feeds exclusively on the stalks and leaves of the bamboo (*left*).

The raccoon

The raccoon is an inhabitant of the temperate forests of North America. It is skilful at catching crayfish and other aquatic creatures and also eats fruit, berries, eggs and insects.

43

The tropical forests

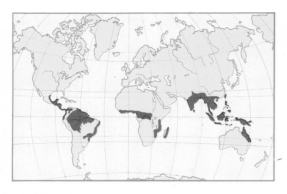

The undergrowth
Many varieties of fern grow in the dark, dense undergrowth shown above. There are also numerous multi-coloured flowers, including several species of orchid. Carnivorous plants (*left*) have strong scents to attract insects. The insects are then trapped and digested.

The insect world
Because of the constant very high humidity in this region those insects and invertebrates without mechanisms for controlling body fluid level can flourish. Their metabolism is also greatly accelerated by the high temperature so that many species reach a considerable size. Butterflies, dragonflies, spiders, worms, etc. of exceptional size live in the tropical forests. There are also large numbers of amphibians. Many of these live in the water which collects in plants whose leaves grow to form a receptacle.

A tropical forest region always has a hot and humid climate but other features may vary. Tropical forests can be found in mountainous or low-lying areas, and the rainfall may be constant all the year round or seasonal, as in monsoon areas. Mangroves sometimes grow in coastal swamps.

The vegetation which has no annual dormant period grows very rapidly. Among the many varieties of trees, very tall palms and hardwoods predominate, such as mahogany, teak and ebony, with heights between 30 and 70 metres. With the abundance and variety of food at every season of the year, this region is rich in animal species.

Life in the trees
Many reptiles and mammals are adapted to tree life and never descend on to the ground. On the left is a gibbon which is an expert at travelling through the trees.

The vegetation
The vegetation in this region is divided into five different height groups, each of which occupies its own habitat. The upper layer includes the branches of the tallest trees which project above the canopy, beneath these are the shorter trees, a layer of bushes and the soil covered with plants.

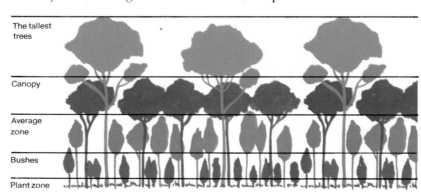

The tallest trees

Canopy

Average zone

Bushes

Plant zone

Above the canopy of the forest, numerous birds of prey seize birds and small mammals which venture on to the highest branches in search of food.

The food offered by the forest – mostly flowers and fruit – is found almost exclusively on the trees. For this reason, the animals have developed certain adaptations to tree life. The most numerous species are those that are confined to the branches of the canopy, where the food is richest. They generally have bright colours which harmonise with their restricted surroundings, and slender shapes necessary for agile movement. The South American monkeys have prehensile tails and the flying squirrels have a membrane attached to their limbs to form a kind of parachute. The beaks of the birds have different shapes according to their food: long and slim in the humming-bird which feeds on nectar, hooked and strong in the parrots which eat hard foods. The creatures drink water which collects in the leaves.

Just as the majority of the animals of the tropical forest live in the trees, so the predators are adapted to tree life. Besides the many snakes which live on birds, small mammals, amphibians and eggs, leopards and wildcats pursue their prey into the trees, restricting themselves mainly to the lower parts where the branches can bear their weight.

The animals which live on the ground, where little light penetrates, generally have subdued colours. Here live stags, antelopes, buffalo and wild boar, tapirs and porcupines. There are many varieties of snake including poisonous ones. Among the predators, the tiger is the largest and most ferocious. Also on the ground live those birds not adapted to much flying, such as the sultana bird and many species of pheasant and peacock. Groups of rodents, insects, molluscs, millipedes and worms live in the damp subsoil.

Common in the forests of South America, the crested eagle is a large bird of prey which feeds exclusively on monkeys.

On the left, from the top: toucan, swallow-tail butterfly, gibbon and humming-bird
Above: Vampire bat
Below: flying squirrel
Right: tarsier

Above: emerald green boa
Right: chimpanzees

Left: leopard, Indian elephant
Above: millipede
Below: cobra
Right: gorilla, tiger

The grasslands

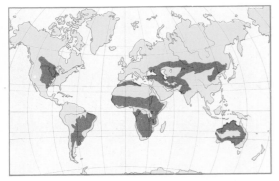

The grasslands
The grasslands are the zones of transition between the forests and the deserts. With a few trees near the forest edge, they become progressively more arid near the deserts. There are two types of grassland: temperate, and tropical or savannah. The temperate grasslands of the northern hemisphere are located within the continents and therefore far from the influence of the rich moisture bearing winds from the sea. They experience cold winters and hot summers with very little rain the whole year round. The grasslands of the southern hemisphere too are affected by dry winds for a large part of the year and are therefore somewhat arid. In contrast, the tropical grasslands experience high temperatures all the year and heavy rain in the summer owing to the seasonal swing of the overhead Sun and the rain belt associated with it.

The temperate prairies have only a brief period of summer rain, during which the plants and trees flourish, but their growth is halted with the arrival of the dry period and the icy winter which follows. In these regions the soil is mainly covered with a continuous carpet of short grass. The prairies of Eurasia, North America, the South American pampas, the South African veldt and the lowlands of Australia belong to this category. In the savannah, however, the soil is often covered with longer grass, sometimes over 3 metres high and there are the characteristic flat-topped trees. The African (above), Indian and north Australian savannah and the grasslands of the Brazilian Highlands belong to this type.

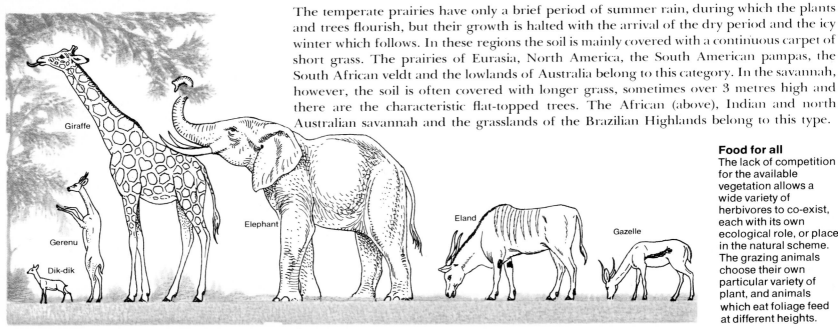

Giraffe

Gerenu

Dik-dik

Elephant

Eland

Gazelle

Food for all
The lack of competition for the available vegetation allows a wide variety of herbivores to co-exist, each with its own ecological role, or place in the natural scheme. The grazing animals choose their own particular variety of plant, and animals which eat foliage feed at different heights.

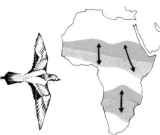

Migration
With the coming of the dry season many animals, including gnus, zebras, antelopes and numerous birds, leave the savannah and migrate to more hospitable areas. The African bee-eater crosses the Equator during its migration.

African bee-eater

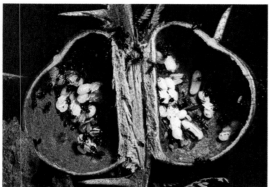

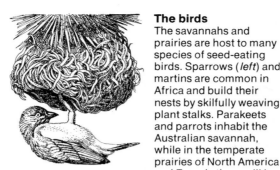

The insects
The innumerable types of insect, notably locusts, ants (*left*) and termites, play an important role in the development of animal and vegetable life. In the temperate zones, the worms do the work of nourishing the soil. In the savannah, this work is performed by termites.

The birds
The savannahs and prairies are host to many species of seed-eating birds. Sparrows (*left*) and martins are common in Africa and build their nests by skilfully weaving plant stalks. Parakeets and parrots inhabit the Australian savannah, while in the temperate prairies of North America and Eurasia there will be found capercailzie (*right*).

Dung beetle

Natural fertilisers
Fire converts vegetation into ash, water vapour and carbon dioxide, which enriches the soil. The dung-beetles (*left*) bury enormous quantities of the excrement of herbivores in the form of pellets, in which they lay their eggs, thereby contributing to the fertilisation of the soil.

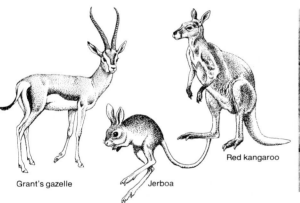

The great herbivores
The largest herbivores and the swiftest predators live in the vast spaces of the grasslands. The antelopes, zebra, buffalo and wildebeast, form into numerous herds which is one of the best means of defence against predators. Elephants (*right*) and rhinoceros (*left*) defend themselves by means of their imposing tusks and enormous strength. The herbivores feed on various types of couch-grass. Their teeth, which are adapted for grinding down plant stems, are subjected to continuous wear and therefore continuous growth. These creatures, like all vertebrates, cannot digest cellulose and the bacteria and protozoa present in their intestines perform this function. They usually have imitative colours which merge into their surroundings.

The lion
Unlike most cats, the lion (*left*) lives in groups called "prides". This has many advantages, such as the ability to bring up their young in a community.

Slave birds
These birds (*above*) have taken on the unusual task of freeing the elephant from the parasites infesting it.

Grant's gazelle

Jerboa

Red kangaroo

Safety in flight
Running is one of the commonest and most effective means of defence among animals of the savannah. Some, like the kangaroo, hare and wallaby, are also excellent jumpers. Ostriches, emus and nandus, which are flightless birds, can match the fastest herbivores at running. Other species, such as the armadillo and anteater, or of small size like the many rodents, hide in holes.

Ostrich

Anteater

Armadillo

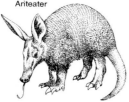

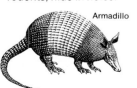

The carnivores
There is not much competition for food among the carnivores either. Gnu and zebra are the preferred prey of the lions, leopards (*right*) and wild dogs, while the swift cheetah pursues the gazelle. The great cats feed from the entrails of their prey, from which they obtain substances such as vitamin A which they cannot produce themselves. Hyenas, jackals, vultures and marabou feed on carrion. Insects eat the remainder, while bacteria and fungi, the agents of decomposition, reduce the organic matter in the scraps to inorganic materials which fertilise the soil.

The deserts

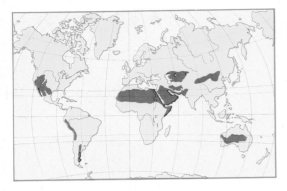

The deserts are distributed along two discontinuous bands, one to the north and one to the south of the Equator, and they are generally found in the interior of the continents. In Africa there are the Sahara (*below right*), the Kalahari and the Namib deserts. Then there are the Arabian desert and the deserts of Turkestan, the Gobi, the Indian Thar and the Chinese Takla Makan. In the Americas there are the Great Basin and the deserts of Mojave, Sonora, Chihuahua, the Grand Canyon, Patagonia and Atacama. Finally there is the great Australian desert. The deserts are

The flowering desert
Heavy rains transform the desert briefly into a flowering garden, causing multi-coloured corollas to bloom on the succulent plants and the germination of seeds which may have lain dormant for years.

arid and inhospitable regions of many different appearances characterised by an annual rainfall of less than 250 mm. Because of the cloudless skies, the earth absorbs 90% of the Sun's heat, creating very high daily temperatures. At night, the heat is lost and the temperature may fall below zero.

Many factors contributed to the formation of the deserts and dryness was undoubtedly the most important of these. This is a direct consequence of the distribution of the air masses which carry moisture, scattering it in the form of rain. For example, the high pressure areas which form over the hot deserts cause currents of hot air which absorb moisture rather than provide it. In the coastal deserts of Peru and Chile in South America and Namibia in Africa, the cold Antarctic currents condense the moisture in off-shore clouds which yield little water for the land. In other cases there are high mountain ranges which hold back the moist winds from the sea as in the cold Asian deserts.

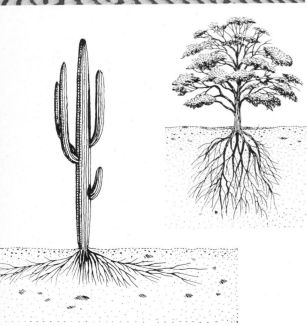

The vegetation
Plant life has developed many adaptations to the dryness. Some have an enormous root system in order to collect the maximum amount of water; others store water in roots and tubers; the fleshy plants, however, collect water in their tissue. Still others store water in their waxy leaves.

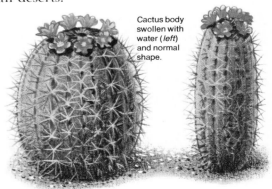

Cactus body swollen with water (*left*) and normal shape.

48

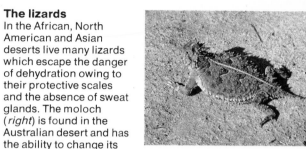

The antelopes
Among the many African varieties of antelope in the desert is the addax (*left*), which can run very fast on the sand owing to its very large hooves which give a good grip. The wild asses too (*below:* an Asian onager) withstand the drought well and can lose over 30% of their body weight through dehydration.

The problem of water
The supply of water is of vital importance. Most of the desert is covered with sand and stones, and although not totally absent, nearly all of the water is found in the oases and the wells which form after the rains. Furthermore the wells dry up in a very short time. The herbivores obtain most of their water from the vegetation on which they feed. The carnivores, insects and reptiles extract it from their prey. The hard shells of the insects and spiders and the scales and carapaces of the reptiles are of great help in minimising the loss of water. Reptiles, birds and many mammals drop highly concentrated excreta. Kangaroo rats, for example (*below*), can live without drinking.

The carnivores
Only small carnivores like foxes and wild cats are natives of the desert. Jackals (*above*) and cheetahs (*above right*) are occasional visitors and only venture into the desert in search of prey. In general, they live in the savannah, which is less arid and richer in their natural prey: animals such as the gazelle.

The lizards
In the African, North American and Asian deserts live many lizards which escape the danger of dehydration owing to their protective scales and the absence of sweat glands. The moloch (*right*) is found in the Australian desert and has the ability to change its colour according to its state of mind or to the ambient temperature. The heloderma (*right*), a venomous lizard of the North American deserts, feeds on rodents and birds.

The snakes
The rattlesnake (*left*) also lives in the American deserts and prairies. It catches rodents, which it locates using heat sensitive organs between the eyes and nostrils which can detect the temperature variations produced by the body of its prey.

Similar to the great migale, the American tarantula snares its prey and lives in holes in the ground.

Found in the African deserts, the dung-beetle makes pellets of dung in which it lays its eggs, then buries them in the soil.

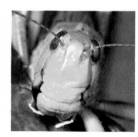

Under certain conditions, locusts multiply excessively, damaging the vegetation in the whole area.

Life in the desert
For the animals of the hot deserts, another way of limiting water loss is to avoid exposure to the scorching rays of the sun and confine their activities to the night. They pass the hottest hours of the day in holes made usually in the ground. Foxes do this, and small rodents, reptiles and even some birds, like the sand owl and the wheatear. Other birds, however, like the nightjar, the swifts and humming birds, escape excessive heat by lapsing into a sort of lethargy. The Gila woodpecker and the elf, a tiny owl, carve their hideouts in saguaros (giant cactus). Another method used by some animals to dissipate excessive body heat is to speed up their respiration rate. Many reptiles, birds and some mammals do this. There are also some morphological adaptations useful for heat dissipation: the huge eyes of the fennec, a small fox of the Sahara, act as radiators to disperse excess body heat.

Elf owl

Gila woodpecker

Pigmy fox

Sand owl

Kangaroo mouse

Desert rat

White-footed mouse

The mountains

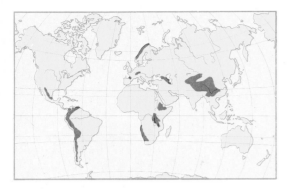

The mountains play an important role with regard to the climate, influencing the direction of the prevailing wind and therefore the rainfall. The wind and rain also erode the slopes, depositing the soil in which the vegetation grows. On the left is a chamois and on the right ibex.

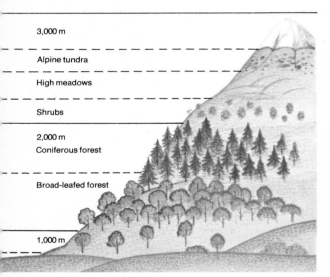

3,000 m

Alpine tundra

High meadows

Shrubs

2,000 m
Coniferous forest

Broad-leafed forest

1,000 m

The vegetation
Ascending the slope of a mountain from the temperate zone, we first come to a strip of deciduous forest, followed by a belt of mixed broad-leaf and coniferous forest. After this we find true coniferous forest which continues up to the limit of tree growth. Before reaching the zone of perennial ice, there is a zone of shrubs, meadows and, finally, a belt of lichen and heather, called the alpine tundra. Latitude has a similar effect to altitude on the distribution of vegetation on the land. In fact, as one travels further from the Equator and moves towards the poles, one passes from the equatorial and tropical rain forests through the temperate forests, the mixed forests and the coniferous forests before finally reaching the Arctic tundra. At the Equator, the upper limit for trees is about 4,500 m while in the Alps, it is about 2,000 m.

The mountain environment varies greatly according to the height and temperature as well as the direction of the prevailing wind. As one climbs the slopes, the temperature falls about 1°C every 150 metres and the soil becomes poorer. The mountains force the winds to rise, so that they are cooled and their water vapour condenses into clouds. As a result, the rain falls on the side of the mountain exposed to the winds. Only dry winds blow down the opposite side and vegetation is therefore scarcer. In Asia, for example, the monsoons which blow from the sea towards the land are cooled by the Himalayas and heavy rains fall on the mountains themselves, while to the north of the range stretch the deserts.

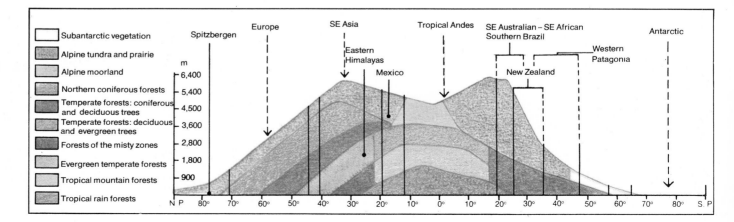

☐	Subantarctic vegetation
▦	Alpine tundra and prairie
▦	Alpine moorland
▦	Northern coniferous forests
▦	Temperate forests: coniferous and deciduous trees
▦	Temperate forests: deciduous and evergreen trees
▦	Forests of the misty zones
▦	Evergreen temperate forests
☐	Tropical mountain forests
▦	Tropical rain forests

m
6,400
5,400
4,500
3,600
2,800
1,800
900

Spitzbergen — Europe — SE Asia — Eastern Himalayas — Mexico — Tropical Andes — SE Australian – SE African Southern Brazil — New Zealand — Western Patagonia — Antarctic

N P 80° 70° 60° 50° 40° 30° 20° 10° 0° 10° 20° 30° 40° 50° 60° 70° 80° S. P

50

Life at high altitude

Life for animals above the tree line is made more difficult by their isolation. High mountain ranges actually form natural barriers to migration. The rarefied atmosphere causes certain environmental problems. The air is less rich in oxygen (the gas used by all animals to release energy by the combustion of food); the thin atmosphere allows more ultra-violet rays to penetrate; the soil absorbs more heat with respect to the surrounding air and gives it up more rapidly. Furthermore, the rarefied air is able to absorb less moisture.

The animals have developed certain adaptations to their surroundings. Compared with similar species from the plains, the vertebrates have more developed hearts and lungs and their blood contains more red corpuscles whose haemoglobin stores more oxygen. To give additional protection from ultra-violet rays and the cold, many animals have very thick coats. Others have darker colours to absorb the ultra-violet and protect the underlying tissue. Some animals hibernate during the winter, like the marmot (*right*) or the viper (*left*). Others, such as the stags, descend to the valleys, and others, like the Tibetan magpie, hide away in holes supplied with food.

Alpaca

Yak

Moufflon sheep

Mountain goat

The herbivores

Herbivores living at high altitudes have very thick coats which protect them from the cold and the harmful ultra-violet rays. They also have hooves which give the best grip on the very uneven ground of their habitat.

The insects

Above the tree line, the most numerous creatures are the invertebrates (insects, spiders, etc.), which survive the severe winter by sheltering under the ground where the snow protects them from the frost and ultra-violet radiation and also prevents dehydration. The strong winds make flying difficult for the insects so most (over 60%) have no wings. Many butterflies are found at high altitudes and the Apollo (*left*) is found at heights up to 2,000 m.

The birds

Most of the mountain birds are birds of prey (eagles, falcons and vultures), which are strong flyers capable of overcoming the high winds, and members of the sparrow family which fly close to the ground and manage to survive on the available supplies of food. Some small humming birds live in the South American Andes at heights of between 2,000 and 5,000 metres.

The giant panda

In the bamboo forests of China, at a height of over 2,000 metres, lives the giant panda (*above*). It lives a lonely existence, feeding almost exclusively on bamboo buds and shoots.

The carnivores

The carnivore which reaches the greatest height, 6,000 m, is the snow leopard, found in the Himalayas. There are pumas (*above*), lynxes and various species of bear (*left*, a brown bear), foxes (*right*) and several species of stoats and martens (mink, ermine and polecats (*below*). The carnivores play a vital role in maintaining the balance of life by eliminating old and sick animals and preventing the proliferation of herbivores which would destroy the vegetation.

Fresh water

The fresh or inland waters include stretches of water (from the smallest pools to the great lakes), rivers and streams. Stagnant waters are rich in floating plant life offering shelter and food to many animals. The small photographs show two examples of aquatic plants. The large photograph shows a great heron among the lilies of a pond.

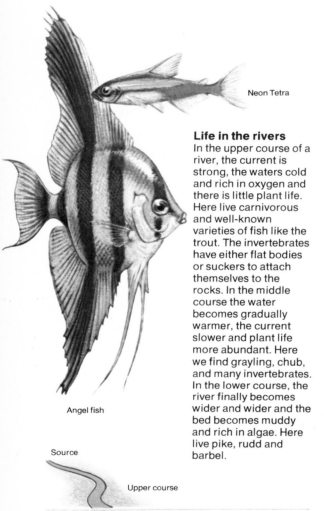

Neon Tetra

Life in the rivers
In the upper course of a river, the current is strong, the waters cold and rich in oxygen and there is little plant life. Here live carnivorous and well-known varieties of fish like the trout. The invertebrates have either flat bodies or suckers to attach themselves to the rocks. In the middle course the water becomes gradually warmer, the current slower and plant life more abundant. Here we find grayling, chub, and many invertebrates. In the lower course, the river finally becomes wider and wider and the bed becomes muddy and rich in algae. Here live pike, rudd and barbel.

Angel fish

Source

Upper course

Middle course

Lower course

Mouth

Inland waters offer a great variety of habitats. Rivers flow in all latitudes and in all types of climate. The young, or oligotrophic, lakes are deep and lacking in nutrient salts, consequently there is little plant life and limited animal life. The eutrophic lakes, on the other hand, have gentle slopes and are rich in nutrients and plant and animal life. The older, or dystrophic, lakes are rich in nutrients but lacking in oxygen and have gradually been transformed into marshes. The lake fauna too, like that of the sea, is subdivided into littoral (sponges, crustaceans, molluscs, larvae, insects and fish), pelagic (including well-known fish like trout and grayling) and deep, or benthonic (molluscs and insect larvae).

Trout

'Cobitidae

Sea scorpion

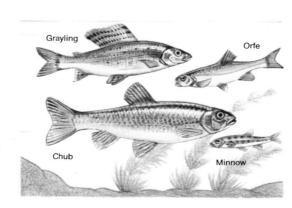

Grayling

Orfe

Chub

Minnow

Pike

Rudd

Perch

Barbel

The aquatic birds found on the shores of lakes and ponds occupy various positions in the ecological spectrum and find their food in many different ways. The waders (1) wait for their prey to approach the shore, while the ducks on the surface (2) feed on what they can reach by shallow diving. The web-footed divers (3) swim under the water to catch their prey. Finally, other birds like the kingfisher (4) dive on the water, seize their prey and fly away.

Fighting fish

A male fighting fish in its mating colours (*above*), so called because during the mating season, it engages in furious struggles with other males of the same species. A pair of sticklebacks (*below*). The male (red) builds a nest of plant material where the female lives prior to laying her eggs.

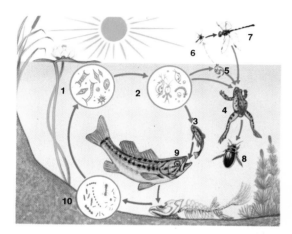

Although they are land insects, dragonflies undergo their larval period in the water. For the amphibians (frogs, toads and newts) water is essential for the growth of their eggs.

Tree frog

Many species of reptile live in fresh water, such as the water snake, which spends its whole life in water. *Above:* a North American terrapin.

Pond life
The water in a pond is usually still and is subject to considerable temperature variations. Furthermore, light does not easily penetrate the water. The abundant plant life offers food and shelter to many amphibians, birds, aquatic mammals and invertebrates. From the surface, rich in plankton, insects and larvae, to the muddy bottom which is host to bivalves, molluscs, crustaceans, worms and larvae there is great activity. The life cycle begins with primary producers (1), that is plants and phytoplankton, which convert inorganic substances into organic materials using the Sun's energy. The zooplankton (2) feed on phytoplankton and both form the diet of small fishes (3) and other vertebrates. These, like the frog (4) eat larvae (5) and insects such as the mosquito (6) and dragonfly (7). The water beetle (8) is a predator, preying on animals much larger than itself. The great predators like the trout (9) complete the feeding cycle. Animal and plant remains are converted into inorganic substances by bacteria of decompositon (10).

Fresh water mammals
There are several species of fresh water mammal, including hippopotami, shrews, coypu, otters and beavers. They are usually good swimmers who catch their food in the water. The largest aquatic mammal is the hippopotamus, found in Africa (*below*). It is a herbivore and spends most of its life in the water from which only its eyes and nostrils protrude.

Fresh water invertebrates and fish
Invertebrates are the commonest animals found in fresh water. Their presence is a necessary prerequisite for the existence of fish and other aquatic vertebrates. Many land insects, such as the dragonfly, complete their larval development in water. About one third of the known species of fish (over 25,000) live in fresh water. These are usually bony fish. Some, like the eels and salmon, are temporary visitors. Among the cartilaginous fish there are only rays and some species of shark, which occur in estuaries.

The principal fresh water fish and invertebrates

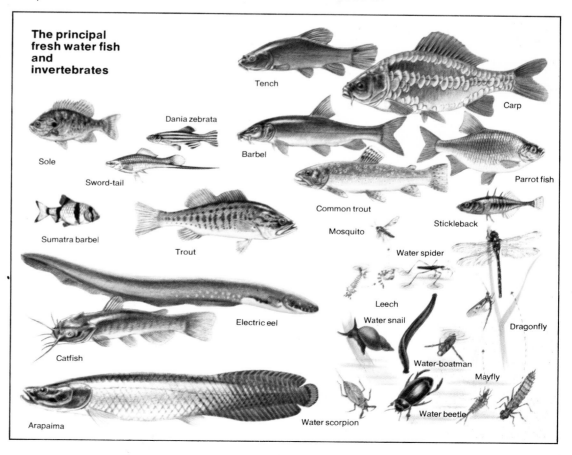

Tench
Sole
Dania zebrata
Carp
Sword-tail
Barbel
Parrot fish
Sumatra barbel
Common trout
Stickleback
Mosquito
Trout
Water spider
Electric eel
Leech
Water snail
Dragonfly
Catfish
Water-boatman
Mayfly
Arapaima
Water scorpion
Water beetle

The seas and oceans

The body of water comprising the seas and oceans which cover 360 million sq km of the Earth's surface, equal to 71% of the total area, almost constitutes a single entity since most of the seas are in communication with each other. There also exist numerous ecosystems, caused by differences in temperature, salinity and depth, which form barriers to the movement of species.

Phytoplankton and zooplankton
The largest group of marine flora is the phytoplankton, a collection of tiny floating algae, including the diatoms (*above*). The distribution of phytoplankton is not uniform and depends mainly on sunlight and the presence of mineral salts. Small quantities of the latter are carried to the seas by rivers but the larger part comes from rising sea currents which agitate the water and bring nutritive substances to the surface. Phytoplankton is the food of zooplankton, which is composed of unicellular creatures and the larvae of fish and invertebrates. Radiolaria (*above left*), Copepoda (*left*).

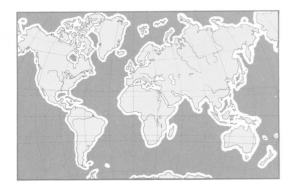

The shores
There are three different types of sea shore, rocky, sandy and muddy. Along the rocky coasts live sea anemones, sponges, sea urchins, mussels, limpets, crayfish and fish which have adapted themselves for survival at low tide. Many sea birds nest on the shores. (*Above:* a cormorant.)

The starfish (*above*) is a benthonic creature, that is one which lives on the sea bed. It is a carnivore and feeds on bivalves, among other things, whose valves it can open.

The polychaeta (*below left*) lives on sandy bottoms and feeds on micro-organisms. The seahorse (*below*) can attach itself to seaweed and coral with its prehensile tail.

The first characteristic of the sea bed is the continental shelf, which extends from the land for about 70 km with a depth of up to 200 metres. In the open sea, the gradient increases rapidly on the continental slope, reaching the bottom of the ocean in a very short distance at a depth of 2,000 metres. The ocean beds are crossed by huge mountain ranges, called ridges, dividing the oceans into several basins. There are also numerous deep trenches. The waters on the shelf comprise the neritic zone and are the home of the littoral fauna, while the waters on the slopes and the ocean bed form the ocean zone, where the pelagic fauna have their existence.

Protective mimicry among fish
For both predators and their prey, it is essential to attract as little attention as possible. For this purpose, these creatures have developed many adaptations in the course of a long evolution. Deep sea fish are dark coloured on top, so they are not conspicuous when viewed from above, and light coloured underneath so that, when viewed from below, they blend into the sunlit water. But the real mime artists are the littoral species and, in particular, those of the coral reefs. The octopus can change its colour suddenly to match the bottom over which it is moving. Other species have unusual shapes and many different colours which, against the variegated background of their habitat, makes them practically invisible. (*Right:* sea cucumber.)

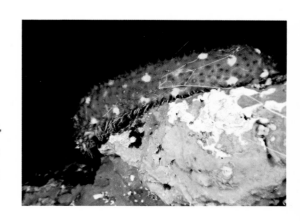

In the pelagic region, that is in the open sea, there is life everywhere, from the surface to the depths. The density of life is, however, much less than in the littoral zone. This is because in the open sea, the surface water, where penetrating sunlight permits the photosynthesis of chlorophyll, contains few mineral salts. These salts are present in large quantities in deeper waters where sunlight, however, cannot reach. Sunlight can only penetrate to a depth of 200 metres.

In consequence, plant life, the first link in the feeding chain, is limited and concentrated in areas where ascending currents carry mineral salts to the surface. The creatures of the deep sea have developed special adaptations in order to survive in this habitat where there is no cover. For example, tunnyfish, swordfish and squid swim very fast; herrings and anchovies form dense shoals; others, such as the flying fish, squid and mantas, leap out of the water to escape their predators.

The intermediate, or bathypelagic, zone lies between 2,000 and 3,000 metres. The temperature in this region falls from 10°C to 4°C towards the bottom. As the depth increases, the amount of sunlight decreases and the water pressure increases.

The creatures of the bathypelagic zone are fish, crustaceans and cephalopods, whose body fluids are at the same hydrostatic pressure as the surrounding water.

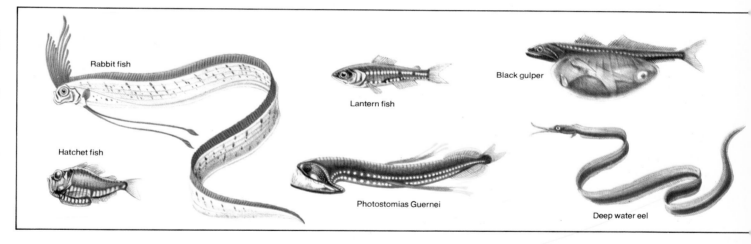

Below 3,000 metres lie the abysses. Here there is total darkness, intense cold and enormous hydrostatic pressure. At 10,000 metres, the pressure exceeds one tonne per sq cm. There is a total absence of vegetation and food is scarce. Because of this, many small fish and some invertebrates rise towards the surface in search of food or develop special modifications to a meagre diet. Others feed on the waste matter which falls to the sea bed. Because of the lack of light, the deep water fish are generally dark in colour. Many species are equipped with light cells, called photophores.

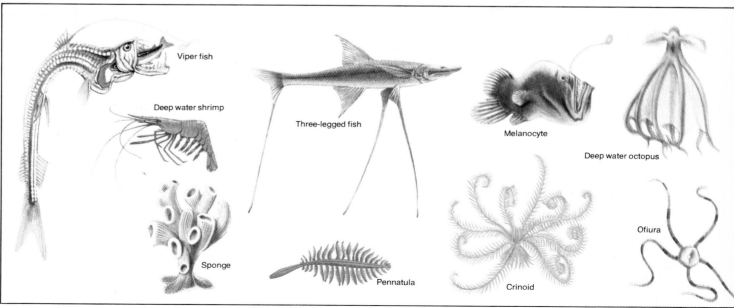

The inhabited world

Compared with the age of the Earth, which according to the most recent determination is around five thousand million years, mankind has existed for only a very brief period.

The first hominids actually appeared only twenty million years ago and about three million years ago, they began to use primitive stone tools. Finally, a little over 70,000 years ago, there appeared Neanderthal man, the direct ancestor of homo sapiens, who spread over nearly all the planet, cultivating the soil and domesticating the animals.

Thus began the wearisome and troubled history of man, whose intelligence caused him to stand apart from all other animals and who, with his science and technology, could bend the very forces of nature to his own wishes and turn his gaze towards the other planets and the stars. The distribution of man over the Earth was never uniform and still is not. As can be seen from the map of population density (below) there are numerous completely uninhabited zones (the oceans, the poles, the deserts, the forests and the highest mountains), covering an area of about 30 million sq km. The remaining 120 million constitute the inhabited areas.

Among the inhabited areas, there are some zones with a high density of population, mostly located in temperate zones in the northern hemisphere (southern Japan, the plain of the Ganges, central southern China, Western and Central Europe and the United States). This particular population distribution has either been encouraged by natural conditions (climate, relief or type of soil) or by historical, political or economic considerations.

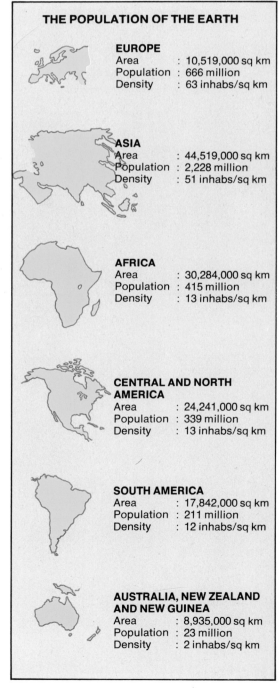

THE POPULATION OF THE EARTH

EUROPE
Area : 10,519,000 sq km
Population : 666 million
Density : 63 inhabs/sq km

ASIA
Area : 44,519,000 sq km
Population : 2,228 million
Density : 51 inhabs/sq km

AFRICA
Area : 30,284,000 sq km
Population : 415 million
Density : 13 inhabs/sq km

CENTRAL AND NORTH AMERICA
Area : 24,241,000 sq km
Population : 339 million
Density : 13 inhabs/sq km

SOUTH AMERICA
Area : 17,842,000 sq km
Population : 211 million
Density : 12 inhabs/sq km

AUSTRALIA, NEW ZEALAND AND NEW GUINEA
Area : 8,935,000 sq km
Population : 23 million
Density : 2 inhabs/sq km

POPULATION DENSITY

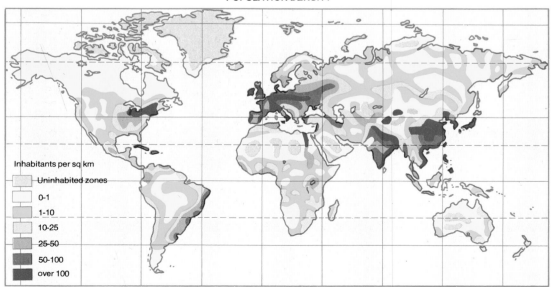

Inhabitants per sq km
Uninhabited zones
0-1
1-10
10-25
25-50
50-100
over 100

Nomadism and urbanisation
Two contrasting life styles in the world today. Nomadism (*left:* nomads in the Algerian desert), which is found among certain peoples who breed animals, is a way of life which is now followed by a very limited portion of the population of the world. Such nomads are continually reducing in number because of the heavy and widespread development of industrialisation and urbanisation (*right*).

Agriculture and commerce in the developing countries
Agriculture based on the plough, which is often made of wood (*above:* an Indian peasant in Orisa), clearly shows the primitive technology and low productivity of many peoples. In such areas, trading in goods (*right:* a market in Rwanda) takes place only in limited areas or not at all, since often agricultural produce barely sustains those who produce it.

The population problem

In 1650 the world population reached 500 million, growing to 1,000 million by 1830. In mid-1975 a UN survey estimated that it had reached 3,967 million, an increase of 77,000,000 over the previous twelve months. This shows how the world's population has dramatically increased since the nineteenth century as science and technology have developed. If the present rate of increase is maintained, the population will double by 2014.

The population explosion is largely due to the reduction in the mortality rate (especially among children), owing to progress in medicine and improvement in the standard of living. Clearly, this population increase poses enormous problems to the various nations. Many solutions have been put forward, but a real answer has yet to be found. It is clear, however, that the planet will eventually be unable to support its ever-increasing population.

Modern industrial installations
Since the second half of the eighteenth century, Western Europe has been undergoing the so-called Industrial Revolution which caused the Earth to be divided into two blocks from an economic point of view (on one side, the economically advanced countries, such as some European countries together with the United States, Japan and Australia, and on the other, the many developing countries).

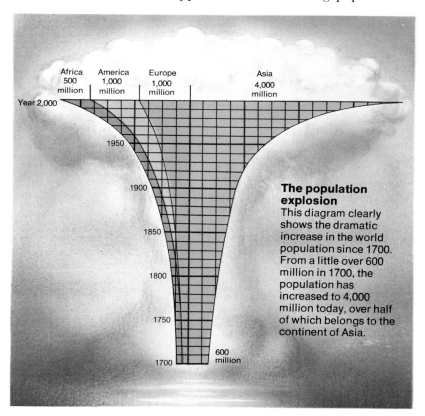

The population explosion
This diagram clearly shows the dramatic increase in the world population since 1700. From a little over 600 million in 1700, the population has increased to 4,000 million today, over half of which belongs to the continent of Asia.

The many races

The map shows the principal zones occupied by the three major racial groups. As can be seen, the mongoloid group occupies the larger part of Asia, and some areas of America and eastern Madagascar. The caucasians occupy the whole of Europe, part of Asia, the northern part of Africa and its southern tip in addition to enormous areas of America. The negroid group is found in Africa, part of Madagascar and a small area of the American continent.
It is a situation which is continually changing; there have been numerous and massive population movements (remember the negro slave trade and the white immigration in America).

Mongoloid
Caucasian
Negroid

Homo sapiens, who thousands of years ago gained ascendancy over the other species, today has many different outward appearances from one group to another. One can meet very tall people with white skin, blue eyes and fair hair like the inhabitants of northern Europe, and short people with dark skin and hair like the pigmies of Africa. Taking account of these and other physical differences, anthropologists divide humans into three major groups or races: caucasians, mongoloids and negroids, in proximity with whom however there are often people with intermediate characteristics.

Mongoloids
The classic mongoloids have yellowish skin, straight hair and the typical slanting eyes. They are found throughout Asia (with the exception of part of India and western Asia) and in the eastern part of Madagascar.

Negroids
Living in central and southern Africa, the western part of Madagascar, Australia, the Philippines and the Indonesian islands, they usually have dark skins and curly hair.

Caucasians
Found throughout Europe, Arabia, India and northern Africa, the caucasians have many different outward appearances. For example, the colour of their skin varies from whitish to brown, while their hair may be either fair, brown or black.

The Eskimos
Spread along the shores of Alaska and Canada, the Eskimos are small in size and have yellowish skins.

The Samburu
The Samburu are a tribe in northern Kenya similar to the Masai, with dark brown skin and tall stature.

The Albanians
The Albanians exhibit characteristics of the Dinaric and Alpine peoples which spread from France to Russia.

The Tibetans
Springing from a mixture of Mongolians and an ancient white people, the Tibetans have slightly narrow, mongoloid faces.

The Bushmen
Small in height, the Bushmen once occupied a large part of southern Africa. Now found in the Kalahari desert, they are becoming extinct.

The Indians
The Indians are one of the largest groups in the world. They have brown skins and slender physiques.

The American Indians
The American Indians are descended from mongoloid groups who reached the New World about 25,000 years ago.

The Papuans
Having come from Asia across the Malay peninsula and Papua, they have very dark skins, curly hair and are found in New Guinea.

The Tuareg
The Tuareg, who belong to the Berber people, live in the Sahara and have dark skins and tall stature.

Religions

If one excludes the religious beliefs in spirits of the primitive peoples, which are still found among people living close to nature, modern religions are found far outside the geographical boundaries within which they originated. Whether monotheistic or polytheistic, throughout history the many religious faiths have been propagated widely among millions of people through evangelism and conversion.

In particular, Christianity and Islam (or Mohammedanism), both monotheistic religions, believe it to be their sacred mission to convert all mankind and they are found in practically every continent.

Judaism is another monotheistic religion, from which both Christianity and Islam have drawn inspiration, and it has grown in strength following the re-establishment of the state of Israel after the Second World War. The great eastern religions, however, are polytheistic like Hinduism (or Brahminism), an Indian religion which worships a large number of gods or Buddhism, based on the teaching of Gautama Buddha.

RELIGIONS

- Christian
- Moslem
- Hindu
- Buddhist
- Spirit worship

Christianity
This is the religion with the largest number of followers at the present time (*above:* an orthodox ceremony). There are over 960 million Christians, subdivided into Catholics, Protestants and Orthodox. Christianity is based on the doctrine of Jesus of Nazareth who lived in Palestine almost two thousand years ago.

Islam
There are today over 500 million followers of Islam. The founder was Mohammed who lived in Arabia between the sixth and seventh centuries AD. *Right:* a place of worship (mosque).

Hinduism
Found almost entirely in the Indian peninsula (*left:* ritual bathing in the sacred Ganges), Hinduism is practised by over 480 million followers.

Buddhism
There are now over 220 million Buddhists found mainly in China, Japan, Sri Lanka and Indochina (*right:* a statue of Buddha).

Spirit worship
The worship of spirits is a form of religion found among primitive peoples who believe that every object around them represents a good or evil spirit, which must be propitiated or driven off by special rituals. There are about 100 million spirit worshippers.

Languages

Language is another factor which distinguishes the inhabitants of the world. It is difficult to establish how many different languages there are because it is not always possible to differentiate between languages and dialects. It is believed, however, that there are over 2,500 languages, some spoken by small groups like the Basques, others used daily by millions of people like English. The classification criterion is generally historical, that is those languages with a common origin are grouped at various levels. For example, Italian, Spanish, Portuguese and French form the neo-Latin group since they are all derived from Latin.

LANGUAGES

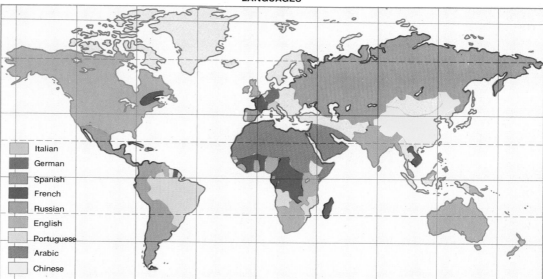

- Italian
- German
- Spanish
- French
- Russian
- English
- Portuguese
- Arabic
- Chinese

The city

The birth of the city is not a phenomenon exclusive to the present age, neither is it confined to the economically developed countries.

Long before the Industrial Revolution, which since the eighteenth century has affected many European countries, there were few areas on our planet without cities. One can speak of a complete urban revolution starting in the fourth millennium before Christ in Sumeria, Egypt, and the Indus valley when from a primitive economic form based on hunting, fishing and agriculture, it progressed to a more complete form which required differentiation of tasks between different members of the group. It is clear that co-ordination and guidance of the various groups could only be achieved if the controlling bodies were concentrated in one well defined area which could form a point of reference for the surrounding region. Thus then was born an

urban settlement in an easily accessible position (usually along rivers or on the coasts) which provided services to the remainder of the territory from which, in turn, it received its supplies.

This is how the great settlements developed, like Babylon which 3,000 years before Christ contained 100,000 inhabitants; Athens, dominated by the hill of the Acropolis; or Rome which at the height of its splendour boasted over half a million inhabitants.

One had to wait, however, for the Industrial Revolution of the eighteenth century before this way of life became characteristic of a large proportion of the population and cities with over a million inhabitants developed. In the urban areas of Europe, North America and Japan, this phenomenon was linked to industrial development, while in continental Asia it was due above all to the development of trading centres.

Palmanova
This aerial view reveals the characteristic polygonal layout of Palmanova, the centre of Friuli which was built as a city-fortress by the Venetians at the end of the fifteenth century and whose ramparts and ditches are still intact.

A street walk in Barcelona
The dense crowd strolling along the avenues where there are bars and shops (in Barcelona these avenues are called Ramblas) is perhaps one of the most typical marks of the modern way of life.

THE GREAT URBAN AREAS

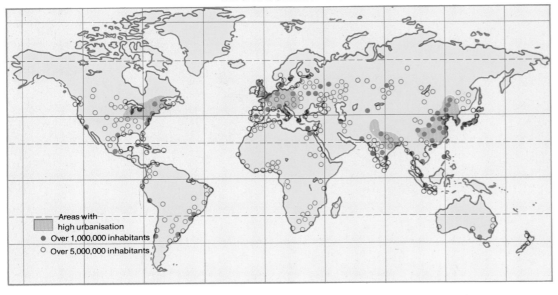

Areas with high urbanisation
● Over 1,000,000 inhabitants
○ Over 5,000,000 inhabitants

THE CITIES WITH THE LARGEST POPULATIONS IN EACH CONTINENT

EUROPE:		AFRICA:	
Paris	9,108,000	Cairo	5,126,000
Moscow	7,400,000	Alexandria	2,032,000
London	7,168,000	Kinshasa	1,991,000
Leningrad	4,133,000	Casablanca	1,753,000
Madrid	3,146,000	Lagos	1,476,000
Rome	2,875,000	Johannesburg	1,434,000
Athens	2,540,000	**AMERICA:**	
Budapest	2,065,000	New York City	11,570,000
West Berlin	2,048,000	Mexico City	10,220,000
Vienna	1,860,000	Buenos Aires	8,925,000
Kiev	1,830,000	Rio de Janeiro	7,094,000
ASIA:		Los Angeles	7,032,000
Tokyo	11,580,000	Chicago	6,979,000
Shanghai	10,820,000	São Paulo	5,241,000
Peking	7,570,000	Philadelphia	4,818,000
Calcutta	7,030,000	Detroit	4,430,000
Bombay	5,970,000	Santiago	3,263,000
Seoul	5,536,000	Lima	3,158,000
Djakarta	4,576,000	San Francisco	3,109,000
Tehran	3,858,000	**OCEANIA:**	
Delhi	3,630,000	Sydney	2,874,000
Tientsin	3,600,000	Melbourne	2,584,000

A village in Kenya
Around the cities where millions of people live, the phenomenon of settlements occurs all over the Earth in the form of villages (the photograph shows a Kikuyu village). The village consists of a group of thatched huts whose inhabitants devote their entire lives to agriculture in order to support themselves.

Pueblo village in New Mexico (USA)
The villages of the Pueblos in the southern part of the Rocky Mountains are usually built under rocky shelters with dwellings reached by flights of steps.

Floating city in Hong Kong *(left)*
Shortage of space on land and the extreme poverty have led to the growth near a number of cities in eastern Asia (for example Hong Kong, Singapore, Bangkok) of actual cities on the water where boats have taken the place of houses.

The problems of urbanisation

Although the birth of the city took place centuries ago, it is only in recent times that the problems of living in large conurbations have appeared. While urban life offers numerous advantages with respect to rural life (the work is usually better paid, there are many opportunities for recreation and meeting people and there are numerous services of which to avail oneself), there are also many disadvantages, frequently associated with the urban areas of industrially and economically developed regions and with those of underdeveloped zones. You only have to think of the noise, the pollution, the traffic congestion, the rising cost of living and the continual influx of people from the country who find it harder and harder to find work and who are forced to live on the outskirts of the city, often in very poor accommodation.

The development of London

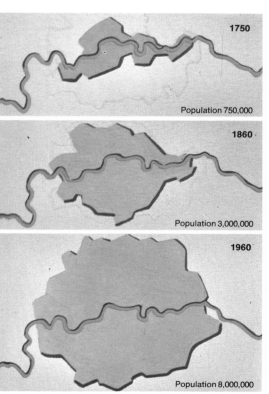

1750
Population 750,000

1860
Population 3,000,000

1960
Population 8,000,000

Tokyo, the easternmost city in Asia
The photograph shows the commercial centre and the streets of Ginza (one of the most central parts of the city) teeming with dense and fast-moving traffic.

Agriculture

Agriculture has been the centre of human activity through the centuries. When man passed from a nomadic life to a sedentary one, he abandoned the simple picking of the fruits provided by nature, realising that the land would provide more abundant and more secure nutrition if he lavished some care on it.

Thus developed the idea of sowing and fertilising, which today is still at the heart of all agriculture. Men began to take a greater and more positive control of nature as they sowed, tended and reaped the crops they needed in the best possible conditions. Following the significant progress of the classical era (the Romans used the rotation of crops and perfected many agricultural implements), and the decline of the Middle Ages and subsequent recovery, it was due to the great scientific discoveries of the nineteenth century that agriculture took a decisive step forward with a complete overhaul of the traditional methods of cultivation.

The most important developments were in the field of mechanical and chemical engineering, which overcame man's fatigue in the fields through large scale mechanisation and led to the maximum growth of the various crops through adequate fertilisation.

In spite of the enormous developments in industry which have taken place since the eighteenth century, today still about half of those in business are involved with agriculture. The percentage of activity in this sector varies significantly from country to country and from region to region.

We travel from countries where there is intensive mechanisation with high productivity and a low percentage of the people employed in agriculture (in the United States 3.5%, in Belgium 4% and in Canada 5.5%, for example) to countries where mechanisation is almost non-existent, and the entire agricultural output often only supports the population with nothing left over for export. In such countries the percentage of those engaged in agriculture is very high. In Burundi, for example, 95% of the population is involved in agriculture, in Tanzania 94% and in Nepal 92%.

Wheat *(above)*
Known by the common name of "grain" and now grown all over the world, wheat originated in south-west Asia. (*Right:* barley.)

Rice
The traditional and sometimes the only food of many people in Asia, rice requires high temperatures and plenty of moisture.

Maize
Also known as Indian corn, maize is a herbaceous plant from central South America. In many countries, much of the production is destined for livestock feeding.

CROPS

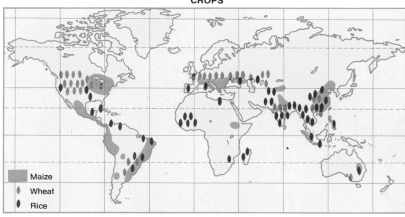

- Maize
- Wheat
- Rice

The olive
Among the most characteristic oil bearing trees, the olive is typical of the Mediterranean area and is well adapted to rather poor and harsh soil.

Vines
Vines are woody plants, usually climbing, whose fruit is either eaten fresh (usually a little over 10%) or used for wine making.

Fishing

An activity as old as man himself, fishing has been affected over the centuries by technical limitations and by eating habits which prevented greater expansion. Today, fishing provides only a little over 5% of the food consumed by the entire population of the world and is in a phase of rapid development (the most active country is Japan with over 10 million tonnes of fish landed annually) which could make it one of the decisive factors in the struggle against hunger which affects such a large proportion of mankind.

Tuna fishing
The tuna, which is much sought after for its tender and tasty flesh, lives at considerable depths. In spring they collect in shoals for breeding and come to the surface where many of them are caught by tuna fishermen. The fishermen use a collection of nets across which the fish must pass to the last net, called the death chamber, where they are finally caught.

Rearing livestock

The rearing of livestock is an old and well-established part of the agriculture and economy of many countries of the world. Only since the eighteenth century has significant technical progress been made in Europe leading to the enrichment of the diet of the larger animals and improvement of the breed.

Today there are two kinds of animal breeding. The first is the European method, which has benefited from the notable progress in agriculture (rotation of crops, cultivation of fodder crops) and from the techniques of conservation and commercialisation. This type of animal breeding is found all over Europe and also in parts of America and Australia where it is run as a vast business concern.

The second type of breeding is what may be called non-European and is characterised by a lack of rationalisation in the areas of animal feeding and breeding by selection. This is generally carried on on a small scale. A particular case of this type of animal husbandry is India which has the largest population of cattle (about 180 million) but cannot exploit these resources for religious reasons.

Flocks of sheep in Australia
In Australia, the country with the largest number of sheep, this type of livestock breeding is used for the production of wool and meat.

Pigs
The pig is very suitable for small breeders, and is found in large numbers in China.

ANIMAL BREEDING AND FISHING

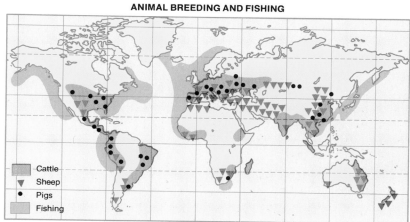

Cattle
Sheep
Pigs
Fishing

Energy and raw materials

In ancient times most energy was produced by manpower. In the Middle Ages man began to harness the energy of animals, the wind and water, which is still used today in developing countries.

Coal, from which thermal and mechanical energy is obtained, has only become important since the eighteenth century. This was followed by rapid development of water power, which was converted into electrical energy, and the exploitation of hydrocarbons, particularly petroleum (the photograph above shows an oil-field in Iraq). At the beginning of the twentieth century almost nine tenths of the world production of energy was based on coal, but within sixty years the percentage fell to less than 40%,

while the percentage for hydrocarbons rose to over 60%. The upward surge in the use of petroleum energy since the second world war is dependent on either existing resources or on the exploitation of new deposits, especially in the Middle East and the Sahara.

The continued growth in demand for energy and the fact that oil is only found in certain countries is leading to the increasing research into alternative energy, and also the use of nuclear energy, which at the beginning of the seventies accounted for a little over 2% of all the energy produced. The amount of energy consumed per head in a country is a reliable guide to the level of development attained (see map below).

Iron mine in the USA
Together with fossil carbon and petroleum, iron is one of the essential raw materials in industry and the economy in general of any country. Iron is extracted from many minerals, including magnetite and haematite, and is widely used in metallurgy as well as the iron industry. Often, as in the photograph, the mines are opencast. At the present time, about 500 million tonnes of iron per annum are produced throughout the world.

ENERGY CONSUMPTION

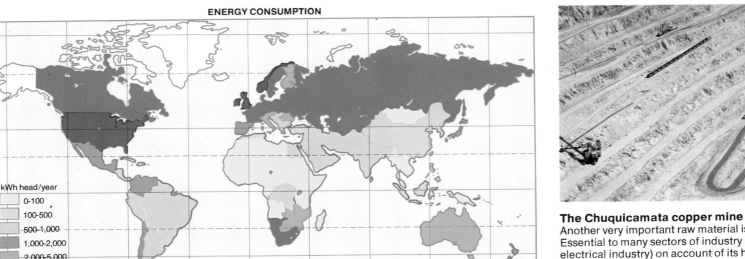

kWh head/year
- 0-100
- 100-500
- 500-1,000
- 1,000-2,000
- 2,000-5,000
- 5,000-10,000
- over 10,000

The Chuquicamata copper mine in Chile
Another very important raw material is copper. Essential to many sectors of industry (especially the electrical industry) on account of its high electrical and thermal conductivity, copper is extracted in large quantities from mines in the United States, the USSR and Chile.

COAL DEPOSITS

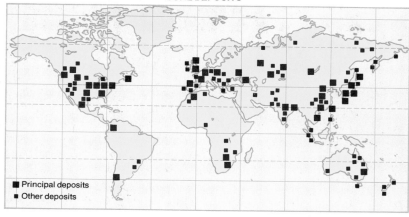

■ Principal deposits
▪ Other deposits

Coal

Used long ago by the Chinese to produce thermal energy, fossil coal became fundamental to world, and particularly European, economy after the discovery of the steam engine. Heavy concentration of industry occurred in the mining areas (the Ruhr in Germany, the Pittsburgh area in the United States and the Donetz in the USSR), and the production of coal only slowed down after the introduction of the internal combustion engine, which was fuelled by petroleum products (the photograph on the right shows coal being extracted in an Australian mine). Today coal remains an indispensable raw material in the iron industry, many sectors of the chemical industry and for the generation of electricity.

OIL RESERVOIRS

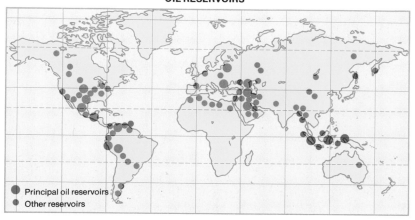

● Principal oil reservoirs
• Other reservoirs

Oil

Oil, which is an extremely important raw material in modern life, is a natural mixture of hydrocarbons. These hydrocarbons are produced by the transformation by bacteria of a mud layer rich in organic substances deposited on the sea bed or in marshes.
Oil is only found in reservoirs consisting of porous and permeable rock, called mother rock, which is impregnated with the precious fluid. World oil production exceeds two thousand million tonnes per year.
The oil producing countries can be divided into three groups: the American group with the United States, Venezuela and Canada, North Africa and the Far East which has only begun to develop its resources, and the socialist countries including the USSR and Romania. Britain should be self-sufficient by 1980.

Drilling for oil

The methods and techniques for the extraction of oil have today been perfected. Drilling is preceded by a complete geological survey in order to minimise the risk of dry wells and the resultant unnecessary expenditure. The drilling installation consists of a metal derrick supporting the drill (*above right:* an oil installation in the Libyan Desert), which is fitted with a rapidly rotating bit which can penetrate to a depth of 6,000–7,000 metres. By means of special platforms (*right:* an exploration drilling platform in the Adriatic) it is possible to drill wells under water. The oil is then piped to the refineries which are on land.

Electrical energy

Electrical energy has to be produced from other forms of energy (mechanical, thermal or nuclear). Electricity offers many advantages over other forms of energy because of its ease of distribution (this applies in practically every case) and its many uses. Electricity can be produced from the energy stored in water in hydroelectric power stations (the photograph below shows the dam of the Aswan station in Egypt) or from the thermal energy of fossil fuels in thermoelectric power stations (the photograph on the left shows the Piacenza thermoelectric power station).

Nuclear energy

Electricity can also be produced from the energy released by nuclear reaction, in particular the fission of uranium (the photograph below shows the Avoine nuclear power station in France).
Uranium is an element which is relatively plentiful in the Earth's crust, but its extraction is fairly costly and complicated and therefore requires advanced technology as do the power stations themselves. At the present time, the electricity produced by nuclear power stations is more expensive than that produced by either hydroelectric or thermoelectric power stations.

A changing world

The works of nature

To one who has not studied natural phenomena, the surface of the Earth seems changeless and immutable but it is in reality continually undergoing changes. Where man once built busy cities, corals now flourish and where the highest mountain peaks now rise up, were plains inhabited by strange animals of which there are few remains.

These were changes which occurred very slowly, at a rate almost inconceivable by the human mind, being measured in terms of tens of millions of years. Only in exceptional cases (subsidence, earthquakes and the silting up of lakes, for example) can man observe this continual evolution which is forever changing the morphology of the Earth's crust. Many different agents contribute to this transformation, in particular rivers, wind, glaciers and the sea.

The waters
Channelled water constitutes one of the most active agents that change the landscape in temperate climates. Its action may be explained in terms of erosion, transportation and deposition. In mountain stretches, where the slope is steep, rivers have considerable erosive power which is in proportion to their mass, velocity, the amount of abrasive material in suspension and the friability of the rocks on which they act. Thus we have the excavation of a valley with the typical V-shaped cross section (*above:* channels cut by streams in the soft rock of the Goreme in Turkey). It is a slow process of destruction of the mountain started, especially at great heights and in high latitudes, by the disintegration of the rock brought about by the freezing and thawing of water. When the energy of the river has been dissipated, the suspended particles are deposited, which raises the level of the plains and fills up the seas.

The wind
The action of the wind is clearly seen in areas deprived of vegetation whose surface is covered with very fine material (sand and dust) produced by the crumbling of rocks owing to temperature variations. Wind action therefore occurs in desert areas and is a form of abrasion called "corrasion" caused by the wind, carrying particles of sand, scouring the rocks which become rounded and smooth (the photograph on the right shows an arch in the Rocky Mountains, USA, formed by wind erosion).
When the wind encounters an obstruction, it deposits the sand which it had in suspension to form "dune fields" which are aligned according to the direction of the prevailing wind.

The glaciers
The sculpting action of glaciers is today confined to regions with high mountains or at high latitudes. It is known however that long ago glaciers were much more widely distributed. The last Ice Age, during which much of North America and northern Europe were covered with ice, began about one million years ago. Among examples of the erosive power of glaciers are alpine or prealpine lake basins, cirques (basins of rock with vertical walls found in all the glacial mountain ranges) and the "U"-shaped valleys, so called owing to their typical cross section caused by the action of the channelled glacial mass (the picture on the left is of the St. Gottard valley). Deposits left behind by glaciers are called moraines.

The sea
The action of the sea is most clearly seen along its line of contact with the shore. Erosion is mainly caused by the action of the waves, whose considerable mechanical energy gradually wears away the rocky coast which can either appear even or indented according to the degree of disintegration of the rocks of which it is composed and the way in which the rocky strata present themselves to the erosive action of the sea (the photograph below shows a section of the south coast of Australia opposite Tasmania. Erosion has isolated several pinnacles called "The Twelve Apostles").

The works of man

Man has arrogantly included himself among those agents which modify the appearance of the surface of the Earth. He has built towns, he has woven a dense web of communication channels which crosses the rivers and mountains and he has replaced the forests with the type of agriculture necessary for his own existence. For centuries, man's intervention was on a fairly small scale, but from the beginning of the nineteenth century, with its enormous rate of development of technology and industry, and the growth of population and town planning, the effect of man on his natural environment became more significant and sometimes irreversible. We are now at a point in the history of mankind where, perhaps for the last time, we should reflect whether the name "sapiens" of which our species is so proud is deserved or not.

The soil
The soil consists of the very thin surface layer of the Earth's crust formed by the slow disintegration of the rocks, and it also contains organic substances and living organisms. Without the soil, any form of agriculture would be impossible. Solid waste matter constitutes one of the most worrying sources of pollution of the soil, particularly non-degradable substances such as some plastics.

The air
The gaseous envelope called the atmosphere which covers the Earth is formed of a mixture of gases. Oxygen makes combustion possible, including that occurring inside organisms (respiration); nitrogen supports the vigorous oxidising action of oxygen, while carbon dioxide is essential for chlorophyll photosynthesis, the method by which plants make food.
In the last ten years, man has accelerated the process of alteration of the atmosphere by introducing into it substances, in ever increasing quantities, which alter its composition such as sulphur dioxide, lead and unburnt particles originating mainly from domestic heating, vehicle exhausts and industrial installations (the photograph above shows the smoke from factories in Cleveland in the United States).

The water
The importance of water is obvious to everybody. Water is synonymous with life; without it those organisms which are composed of high percentages of water (in man, over 65% by weight) could not survive. Although water covers three quarters of the surface of the Earth, it is not an inexhaustible resource, especially when it is subjected to massive industrial pollution (the photograph on the right shows the effluents from a steelworks in Baltimore, USA), and pollution by sewage and agriculture which contributes to the destruction of both the animals and also the birds who live near water. *(Left:* bird killed by oil pollution.)

World atlas

North Pole

A R C T I C
O C E A N
Ellesmere
Queen Elizabeth Is.
Greenland
Magnetic Pole
Banks I.
Baffin Bay
C. Barrow
Beaufort Sea
Victoria I.
Boothia Pen.
Baffin I.
Melville Pen.
Davis Strait
ASIA
Bering Strait
Brooks Range
Great Bear L.
Mackenzie
Hudson Strait
Ungava Pen.
C. Farewell
Nunivak I.
Mt McKinley
Mt Logan
Great Slave L.
Hudson Bay
Belcher Is.
Labrador
Bering Sea
Gulf of Alaska
Coast Range
ROCKY MOUNTAINS
Yukon
Alexander Arch.
L. Winnipeg
Hudson Str.
7860
Aleutian Trench
Aleutian Is.
Vancouver I.
Great Plains
L. Superior
L. Huron
L. Michigan
L. Ontario
L. Erie
St Lawrence
G. of St Lawrence
Belle Isle Str.
Newfoundland
NORTH AMERICA
C. Sable
A T L A N
C. Cod
Missouri
Mississippi
C. Mendocino
Pikes Peak
Sierra Nevada
Whitney
6741
Colorado
Arkansas
Red R.
Mitchell
APPALACHIAN MTS.
C. Hatteras
Bermuda
Sargasso Sea
Hawaiian Islands
Midway I.
Guadalupe I.
Lower California
Gt. Plateau
Rio Grande
Eastern Sierra Madre
Mexican Plateau
Western Sierra Madre
Florida
6996
TROPIC OF CANCER
C. San Lucas
Gulf of Mexico
Bahamas
Greater Antilles
Hawaii
Johnston I.
G. of Campeche
Cuba
Jamaica
Puerto Rico
9220
Citlaltepetl
Yucatan
Hispaniola
Guadeloupe
Martinique
Revilla Gigedo Is.
G. of Honduras
Caribbean Sea
Lesser Antilles
Barbados
Tajumulco
Isthmus of Tehuantepec
Nicaragua L.
Pta. Gallinas
Trinidad
P A C I F I C
Clipperton I.
Chirripó
Lake Maracaibo
Orinoco
Guiana Highlands
Palmyra I.
Fanning I.
Isthmus of Panama
G. of Panama
Ileia
Llanos
Christmas I.
Galápagos Is.
Gulf of Guayaquil
Chimborazo
Amazon
Amazon
Marajó I.
Fernando de Noronha I.
Baker Is.
7251
EQUATOR
LONGITUDE WEST FROM GREENWICH
Japura
C. S. Roque
Phoenix I.
Malden I.
Starbuck I.
Huascarán
6768
Purus
Madeira
Selvas
Caatingas
São Francisco
Tokelau I.
Caroline I.
Marquesas Is.
SOUTH AMERICA
Andes
W. Samoa
O C E A N
Tonga Is.
(Friendly Is.)
Society Is.
Tahiti
Tuamotu Arch.
L. Titicaca
Illampú
Plateau of Mato Grosso
Brazilian Highlands
Pico da Bandeira
Bolivian Plat.
Tonga Trench
10882
Cook Is.
Tubuai Is.
TROPIC OF CAPRICORN
Paraná
C. Frio
Rapa
Pitcairn I.
Ducie I.
Sala-y-Gómez
Easter I.
S. Félix
S. Ambrosio
Gran Chaco
Pilcomayo
Paraguay
Paraná
Lagoa dos Patos
Kermadec Trench
10047
Kermadec Is.
Aconcagua
Pampas
Rio de la Plata
Juan Fernández Is.
G. of San Matias
Chatham Is.
Chiloé
Chonos Arch.
Patagonia
G. of San Jorge
Falkland Is.
South Georgia
8264
Str. of Magellan
Tierra del Fuego
C. Horn
Drake Passage
South Sandwich Is.
South Shetland Is.
South Orkney Is.
Antarctic Peninsula
ANTARCTIC CIRCLE
Charcot I.
Alexander I.
Weddell Sea
70
Ross Sea
Ellsworth L.
Coats Land
Byrd Land
South Pole

ATLANTIC OCEAN
Azores
C. St. Vincent
Madeira
Canary Is.
Mauritania
C. Blanco
C. Verde Is.
C. Verde
C. Palmas
Ascension
St. Helena
Tristan da Cunha
Gough I.

AVERAGE HEIGHT OF CONTINENTS

Arctic Circle
340
960
720
Tropic of Cancer
750
Equator
590
Tropic of Capricorn
340
Antarctic Circle
2200

Metres
HEIGHT
Over 3000
3000
1500
500
250
Sea level
0
Below sea level

DEPTH
0
150
3000
6000
Below 6000

COMPARISON OF WATER AND LAND AREAS AT VARIOUS LATITUDES

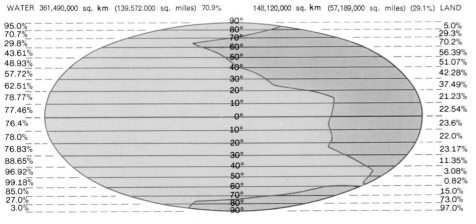

WATER 361,490,000 sq. km (139.572.000 sq. miles) 70.9%   148,120,000 sq. km (57,189,000 sq. miles) (29.1%) LAND

WATER	Latitude	LAND
95.0%	90°	5.0%
70.7%	80°	29.3%
29.8%	70°	70.2%
43.61%	60°	56.39%
48.93%	50°	51.07%
57.72%	40°	42.28%
62.51%	30°	37.49%
78.77%	20°	21.23%
77.46%	10°	22.54%
76.4%	0°	23.6%
78.0%	10°	22.0%
76.83%	20°	23.17%
88.65%	30°	11.35%
96.92%	40°	3.08%
99.18%	50°	0.82%
85.0%	60°	15.0%
27.0%	70°	73.0%
3.0%	80°	97.0%
	90°	

HYPSOMETRIC CURVE

(Average heights of land above and below sea level)

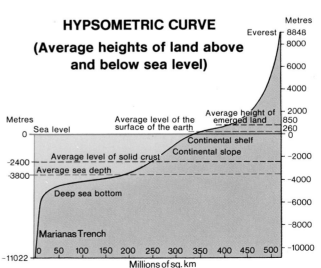

Copyright: Vallardi Ind. graf.

71

II

Map grid (top)
60 80 A 100 B 120 C 140 D 160 E 180 F 160 G 140 H 120 I 100

ARCTIC

Eurasia Basin
Severnaya Zemlya (North Land)
Lomonosov Ridge
Fletcher Ridge
Canada Basin
Novo Sibirskiye Ostrova (New Siberian Islands)
Chukchi Rise
Parry Is.
Banks I.
Victoria Island
De

Ob
Yenisey
Lena
Lake Baykal
Arctic Circle
Ostrow Vrangelya (Wrangel I.)
Yukon
Great Bear Lake
Great Slave Lake
Rocky Mountains

Lena
Amur
Sakhalin
St. Lawrence I.
Mt. McKinley 6196
Nunivak I.
Pribilof Is.
Kodiak I.
Alexander Archipelago
Queen Charlotte Is.
Vancouver I.
Great Bear Lake

Hwang Ho
Kuril Islands
Paramushir I.
Kommandorskiye Is.
Aleutian Is.
Aleutian Trench
North-East Pacific
Lake Superior

Hokkaido
Kuril-Kamchatka Trench -10542
North-West
Honshu
Japan Trench
Pacific Basin
Basin
-5697
-6800
Mt. Whitney •4418
Blanca Peak •4386
Lake Michigan

Yangtze Kiang
Ryukyu Is.
Okinawa -7507
Bonin Is.
Marcus-Necker Rise
Marcus-I. -7276
Midway I.
Hawaiian Islands
Murray Fracture Zone
Guadalupe I.
Tropic of Cancer
-10340

Taiwan
Batan I.
Volcano Is.
Wake-I.
Gardner Pinnacles
Kauai Oahu
Johnston
Hawaii
Revilla Gigedo Is.
Hainan
Babuyan-I.
Farallon
Mariana
PACIFIC
Clarion Fracture Zone
-6662
Luzon
Philippine Basin
Mariana Trench -8724
Guam
Marshall Islands
Clipperton I.
Guatemala Basin
Philippine Is.
Philippine Trench -10793
Eniwetok
Ralik Ratak Chain
Central Pacific Basin
Clipperton Fracture Zone
Cocos I.
Palau Is. -10497
Truk-I.
Kusaie
Makin
Gilbert Is.
Fanning Ridge -7315
Christmas I.
Equator
Galapagos Islands
Mindanao
Caroline Is.
MICRONESIA
Caroline Basin
MELANESIA
New Ireland
Naura
Arorae
Phoenix Is.
Jarvis I.
Isabela
Sulu Arch.
Talaud Is.
Molucca Is.
New Britain
Bismarck Arch.
Bougainville I.
Nanumea (Tuvalu Is.)
Gardner
Malden I.
Marquesas Is.
-5490
Peru Basin
Borneo
Celebes
New Guinea
Solomon Is.
Malaita
Ellice Is.
Tokelau
Manihiki
POLYNESIA
Sumatra
Ceram
Mukuoro
Santa Cruz I.
Wallis Is.
Savaii
Suwarrow
Flint
Pukapuka
Christmas
Java
Tanimbar
Aru
Timor
Louisiade Arch.
New Hebrides
Fiji Islands
Sámoa Is.
Society Is.
Tahiti
Cocos Is. -7455
Sumbawa
Sumba
Great Barrier Reef
Coral Sea Basin
New Caledonia
Loyalty Is. -7570
Tonga
Kermadec-Tonga Trench -10882
Cook Islands
Tubuai Is.
Oeno I.
Tropic of Capricorn
Norh-West Australian Basin -7001
Great Dividing Range
New Zealand Rise
Fiji Basin
Norfolk-I.
Gambier Is.
Pitcairn I.
Ducie I.
Sala-y-Gomez Reef
Easter I.
INDIAN
Australia
Mt. Kosciusko 2228
Murray
Lord Howe
Kermadec Is.
OCEAN
Rapa
Legouve Reef
Maria Theresa Reef -5578
Eastern Plateau
Diamantina Trench
South Australian Basin
North Island
East Pacific Ridge
South-East Indian Basin
Tasmania
East Australian Basin
New Zealand
South Island
Chatham Is.
South Pacific
East Pacific
Indian-Antarctic Ridge
Tasmania Ridge
Bounty Is.
Antipodes Is.
Ridge
-5399
Macquarie Ridge
Auckland Is.
Campbell-I.
South Pacific Basin
Antarctic Basin
INDIAN OCEAN
Macquarie Is.
Antarctic Circle

DEPTH Metres: 200 2000 4000 6000 over 6000

Scale 1: 85 000 000
0 500 1000 1500 2000 3000 4000 km

72

Mekong
Palawan
Mindanao
Hwang Ho
Mississippi

K 60 L 40 M 20 N O O 20 P 40 Q 60 R 80 S 100 T 140

~~~~~ Extreme Limit of Drift Ice
^^^^^ Average Limit of Drift Ice
^^^^^ Limit of Pack Ice

1
Franz-Joseph-Land

OCEAN

Lomonosov Ridge
Esmere I.

Spitsbergen

2

Murmansk Rise

Novaya Zemlya

Lena

Greenland

Greenland Basin

Bear I.

Kolguyev I.

Yenisey

Baffin Bay

Baffin Island

60

Jan Mayen I.

Norwegian Basin

Ural Mountains

Ob

Lake Baykal

Irtysh

Iceland

Faeroes
Shetland Is.

Volga

Aral Sea

3

British Isles

Reykjanes Ridge

Labrador Basin

North Atlantic Ridge

West European Basin

Mt.Blanc 4810

Alps

Danube

Caucasus 5633

Newfoundland

Lake Huron
Lake Ontario
Lake Erie

Newfoundland Basin

Iberian Basin

Corsica
Sardinia

Balearic Is.

Sicily

Crete Cyprus

Euphrates

Indus

Mt.Everest 8848

40

Azores

Madeira

High Atlas

4165

North American Basin

Bermuda I.

Canary Basin

Canary Is.

-6407

Ganges

4

-6996

Bahamas

Cuba
Greater Antilles
Jamaica

Hispaniola
Puerto Rico
-9219
-140

Cape Verde Is.

Niger

Nile

Socotra

Arabian Basin

Andaman Is.

Lakshadweep Is.

Sri Lanka
Nicobar Is.

20

Cape Verde Rise

Curaçao
Lesser Antilles
Guadeloupe
Dominica
Martinique
Barbados
Trinidad

Guiana Basin

Sierra Leone Basin

Guinea

Principe
São Tomé
Annobón

Somali Basin

Maldive Is.

5

-7730

St. Paul Rocks

Lake Victoria

-5358

Seychelles

Chagos Archipelago

0

pela

Amazon

Fernando de Noronha I.

Romanche Trench

Ascension I.

Angola Basin

Aldabra-I.

Farquhar Is.

Mid-

-216

Brazilian Basin

St. Helena

Comoro Is.

Madagascar

Mascarene Is.

-5386

Indian

Chile Basin

Trindade I.

South Atlantic Ridge

Réunion
Mauritius

Basin

20

A
n
d
e
s

-7973

-5755

-5630

Drakensberge

Mascarene Basin

Juan Fernandez Is.

an Ambrosio I.
an Felix I.

Aconcagua
6960

Rio Grande Rise

Orange

3650

Madagascar Ridge

INDIAN

Argentine Basin

Tristan da Cunha
Gough

Cape Basin

-5779

Madagascar-Indian Ridge

South-West Indian Basin

Amsterdam-I.
St. Paul I.

OCEAN

-2899

40

-6125

South Georgia Rise

Atlantic-Indian Ridge

Cape Rise

Agulhas Basin

Prince Edward Is.

Crozet Is.

Indian-Antarctic Ridge

Falkland Islands

Scotia Ridge

South Georgia

-8264

South Sandwich Islands

Bouvet I.

-2213

Kerguelen

Scotia Basin

-5859

Prince Edward Is.

Kerguelen-Gaussberg Ridge
Heard-I.

Indian-Antarctic Basin

South Shetland Islands

South Orkney Island

Atlantic-Indian-Antarctic Basin

8

ANTARCTIC

N O 9

80 K 60 L 40 M 20 Longitude West of Greenwich 20 P 40 Q 60 R 80 S 100 T

Scale 1:85 000 000

0 500 1000 2000 3000 4000 km

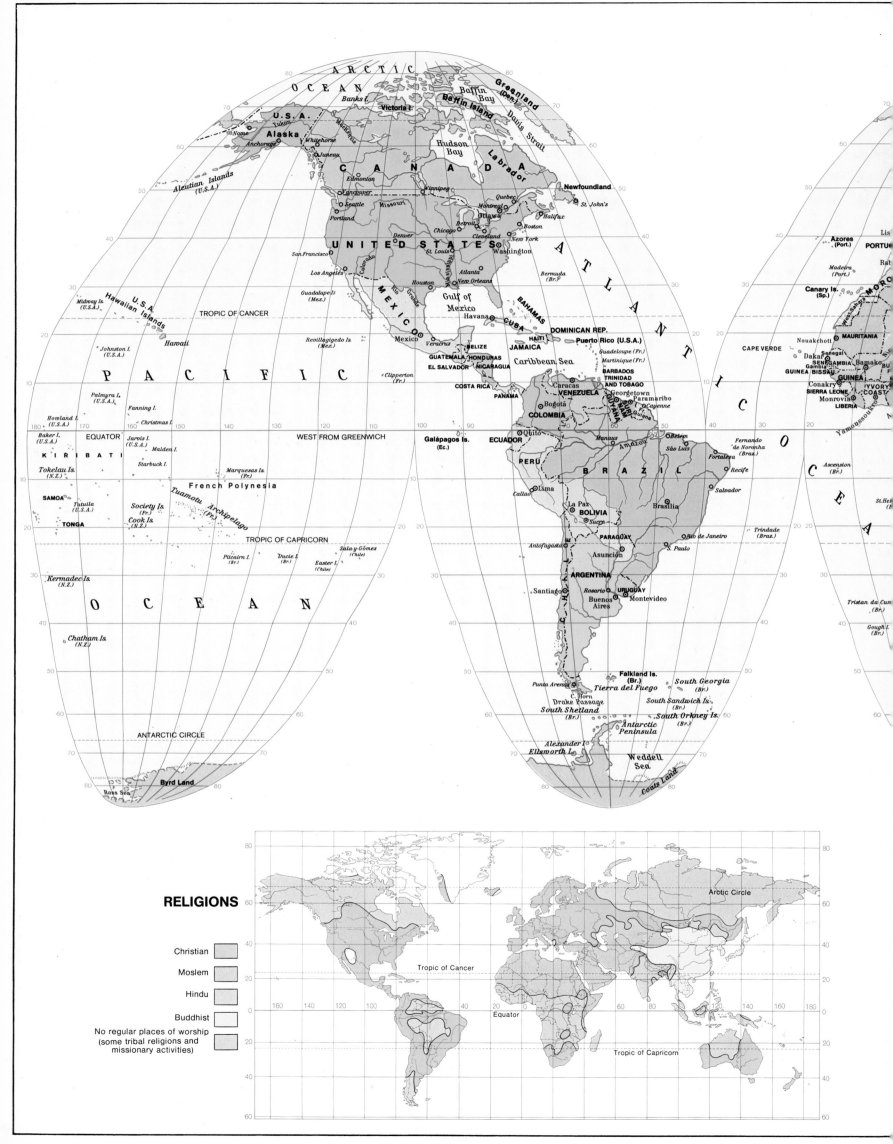

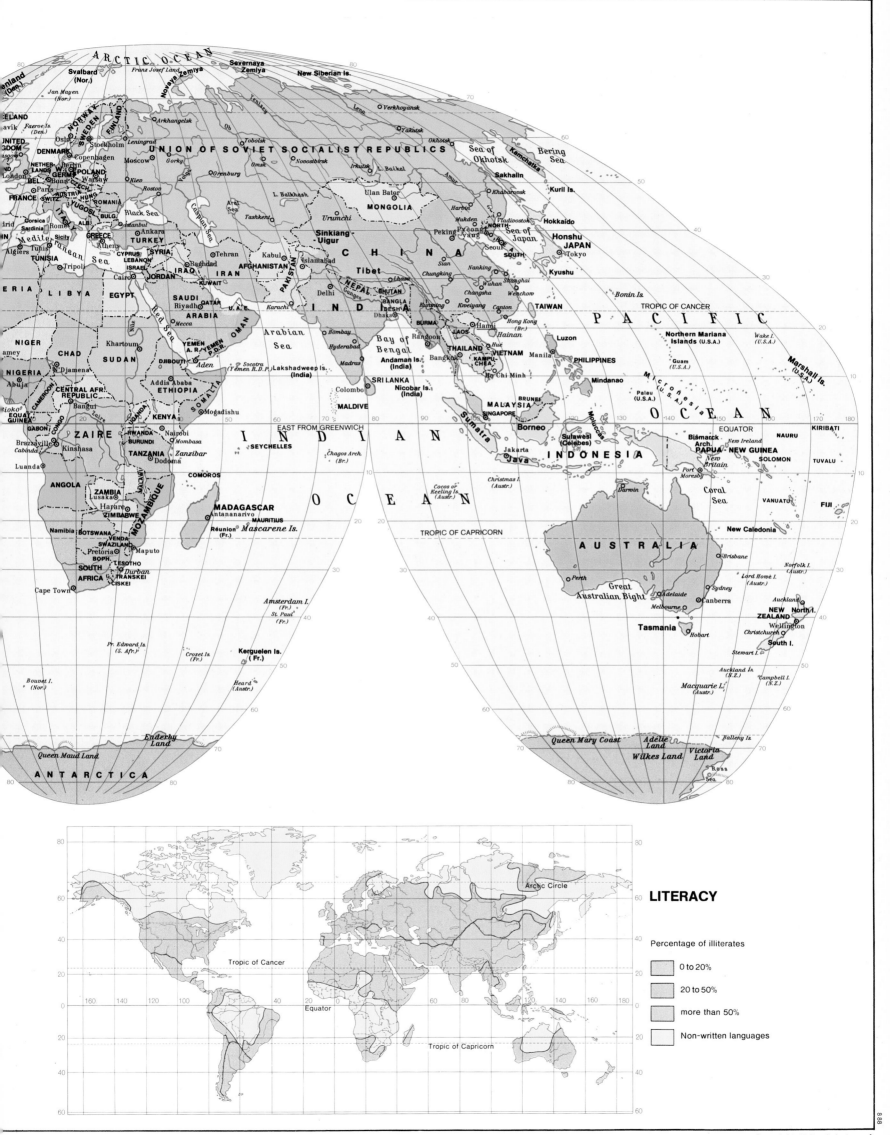

LITERACY

Percentage of illiterates

0 to 20%

20 to 50%

more than 50%

Non-written languages

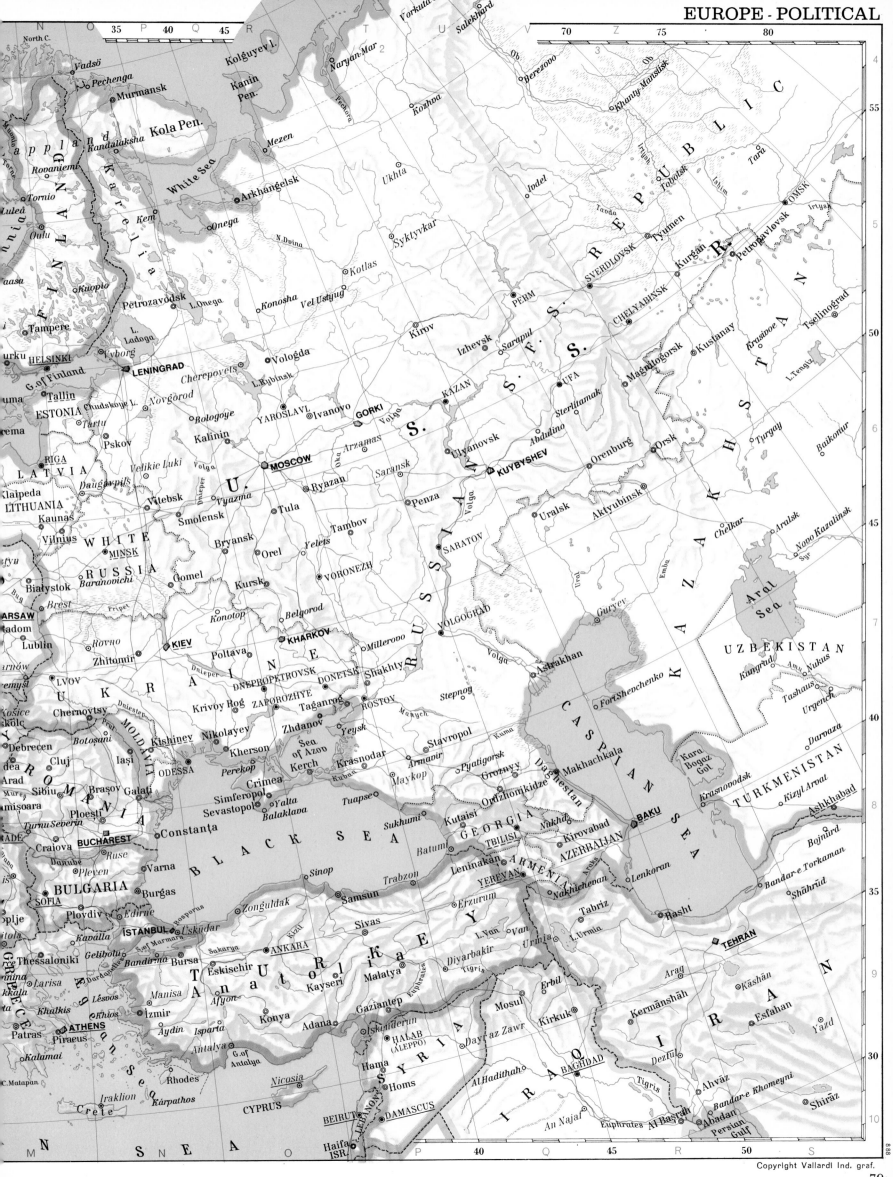

North C.

Vadsö
Pechenga
Murmansk

Kolgúyev I.
Kanin
Pen.

Naryan-Mar

Vorkuta
Salekhard

Ob
Berezovo

Khanty-Mansisk

Ob
Tara

Rozhoa

Ukhta

Iodel

Irtysh
Tobolsk

Ishim

OMSK
Irtysk

Kappland
Rovaniemi

Randalaksha
Kola Pen.

White Sea

Arkhángelsk

Onega

N.Dvina

Mezen

Syktyvkar

Kem

Taoda

Tyumen

Petropavlovsk

Tselinograd

Tornio
Luleå
Oulu

Karelia

Petrozavodsk
L.Onega

Konosha

Vel Ustyug

Kotlas

Kirov

PERM

SVERDLOVSK

CHELYABINSK

Krasnoe

Kustanay

L.Tengiz

Kuopio
Tampere
aasa
urku HELSINKI
Vyborg

L.
Ladoga

Cherepovets

Vologda

L.Rybinsk

Izhevsk
Sarapul

UFA

Magnitogorsk

Baikonur

G.of Finland
Tallin
Chudskoye L.
Novgorod

YAROSLAVL
Ivanovo
GORKI

KAZAN

Sterlitamak

K
A
Z
A
K
H
S
T
A
N

ESTONIA
Tartu
rema

LENINGRAD

Bologoye

Ulyanovsk

Abdulino

Orsk

Tyrgay

Pskov
Kalinin

S.

Arzamas

Volga

Turgay

RIGA
LATVIA

Velikie Luki

MOSCOW

Oka

Saransk

KUYBYSHEV

Orenburg

Uralsk

Aktyubinsk

Chelkar

Aralsk

Novo Kazalinsk

Klaipeda
Daugavpils

Vitebsk

Vyazma
Ryazan

Penza

U.

Volga

LITHUANIA
Kaunas

Smolensk

Tula

Tambov

Aral
Sea

Vilnius
MINSK

WHITE

Bryansk

Yelets

Saratov

S.
S.
F.
S.
R.

Syr

Białystok
RUSSIA
Baranovichi
Gomel

Orel

VOLGOGRAD

Ural

Emba

UZBEKISTAN

ARSAW
adom

Brest

Pripet

Kursk

Belgorod

R
U
S
S
I
A
N

Guryev

Kungrad
Amu
Nukus

Lublin
Rovno
Zhitomir
KIEV

Konotop

Poltava

KHARKOV

Millerovo

Volga

Astrakhan

Tashaus

Urgench

arnów
emyšl
LVOV

Chernovtsy

Dnieper

DNEPROPETROVSK

Shakhty

Volga

Krivoy Rog
ZAPOROZHYE

DONETSK

ROSTOV

Stepnoy

Manych

Fort Shevchenko

Darvaza

Košice
kolc

MOLDAVIA
Kishinev
Nikolayev

Zhdanov

Yeysk

Stavropol

Kuma

C
A
S
P
I
A
N

Kara
Bogaz
Gol

TURKMENISTAN

Kizyl Arvat

Ashkhabad

Debrecen
Cluj
Arad
mişoara

Iași

Kherson

Sea
of Azov

Krasnodar

Armavir

Pyatigorsk

Grozny

Makhachkala

Krasnovodsk

Bojnürd

ROMANIA

Botoșani

Galați

Perekop

Kerch

Kuban

Maykop

Dagestan

Ordzhonikidze

Bandar e Torkaman

Sibiu
Brașov

ODESSA

Crimea

Simferopol

Sukhumi

Kutaisi

GEORGIA

Nakha

BAKU

S
E
A

Turnu Severin
Craiova
BUCHAREST

Sevastopol
Yalta
Balaklava

Tuapse

Batumi

TBILISI

Kirovabad

Rasht

Ploesti
Ruse
Danube
Pleven
Varna

BLACK SEA

Leninakan
ARMENIA

Nakhichevan

Lenkoran

Shãhrüd

Mures
AZERBAIJAN

ADE
BULGARIA
SOFIA
Burgas

Sinop

Trabzon

YEREVAN

Erzurum

Tabriz

Araks

Plovdiv
Edirne

Samsun

Aras

Bosporus

Zonguldak

L.Van
Van

L.Urmia
Urmia

oplje

ISTANBUL
Üsküdar

Sakarya

Sivas

Diyarbakir

Tigris

I
R
A
N

TEHRAN

Kapalla
ila

Sea f Marmara

ANKARA

Kizil

T
U
R
K
E
Y

Anatolia

Malatya

Mosul

Erbil

Kirkuk

Kermanshah

Kāshān

Esfahan

Thessaloniki
Bandirma
Bursa
Eskisehir

Kayseri

Euphrates

Araq

Larisa
rmina
kkala
Manisa

Afyon

Konya

Gaziantep

Dayr az Zawr

Yazd

G
r
e
e
c
e

Khios
Izmir

Isparta

Adana

Iskenderun

HALAB
(ALEPPO)

BAGHDAD

Dezfūl

Patras
ATHENS
Piraeus

Aydin

Antalya

G.of
Antalya

Hama

Mosul

I
R
A
Q

Tigris

Ahvāz

Bandare Khomeyni
Abadan

Shiraz

Kalamai

C.Matapan

Iraklion
Kárpathos

Crete

Rhodes

Nicosia

CYPRUS

Homs

Al Hadithah

An Najaf

Euphrates
Al Basrah

Persian
Gulf

S
E
A

BEIRUT
LEBANON
DAMASCUS

SYRIA

Haifa
ISR.

Copyright Vallardi Ind. graf.

3

40 5 50 4 60 3 2 1 1 80

ATLANTIC OCEAN

Reykjavik
Iceland
Greenland
North Pole
4290
ARCTIC OCEAN
Jan Mayen 2545
3830
West Spitsbergen North East Land
Faeroe Is. 3970
Svalbard
Franz Josef Land
Komsomolets I.
Oct. Revolution I.
Bolshevik I.
C. Chelyuskin
Kotelny I. De Long Is.
New Siberian I.
British Isles
Ireland Shetland Is.
Bear I. Severnaya Zemlya
Taymyr Pen. Byrranga Mts.
Laptev Sea
Great Britain
North Sea
Norwegian Sea
North Cape Sea
Barents Sea
Novaya Zemlya
Kara Sea Bely I.
English Channel London Oslo **Scandinavia**
Lappland Kola Pen.
Kolguyev I. Kanin Pen. Pechora
Yamal Pen.
Gydan Pen.
Putorana Mts. 2037
Dublin Amsterdam Berlin Jutland Copenhagen Stockholm
G. of Bothnia **Finland**
White Sea
L. Ladoga Leningrad Lake Onega
Timani Ridge 1894
Narodnaya **West Siberian Plain**
Toz **Central Siberian Plateau**
Lisbon Bay of Biscay **Pyrenees**
Elbe Oder Warsaw **Baltic Sea** Riga Dvina
Valdai Hills 347
342
Uvaly
Lower Tunguska
Stony Tunguska
Iberian Peninsula
Togus Madrid Ebro Rhone 490 Rhine
Vistula Kiev **Ukraine** Dnepr Dniester
Central Russian Uplands
Volga Moscow 188
Kama Tobolsk Yeniseysk Angara
Barcelona Corsica **Apennines** Vienna Budapest 2305 **Carpathians** Danube
Don Volga 359
Ural Mountains
1638 Yamantau Ishim Omsk
Tomsk **Eastern Sayan** 454
Atlas Algiers Sardinia **Tyrrhenian Sea** Belgrade Rhodope 2925 Balkans
Black Sea
Volga Heights
Uralsk Ural
L. Chany 140 Barnaul **Western Sayan** 3491 Irkutsk
Tunisia Tunis Sicily 3263 Ionian Sea Pindus Mts. Athens Morea Crete Rhodes
Caucasus Elbrus 5633 Astrakhan Caspian Depression -28
Kirgiz Steppe
L. Tengiz **Kazakh Uplands** L. Zaysan **Belukha** 4506 **Altai** **Hangay Mts.** 4030 Ulan-Ba
Tripoli G. of Sidra Benghazi Bosporus 227 Istanbul Ankara **Pontine Mts.** Tbilisi Ararat 5165 Araks
Caspian Sea **Aral Sea** Mugunkun L. Balkhash 340 **Plateau of Mongol**
Tripolitania 3347 **Taurus Mts.** Cyprus 1953 **Anatolia**
L. Van L. Urmia 995 **Turanian Plain** Syrdarya
Tien Shan 5485 **Turfan Depression** Go
Mediterranean Sea Jerusalem Lebanon Mts. Damascus **Kurdistan** Euphrates Baghdad
Ustyurt Plateau 1880 Karakum **Kyzylkum** L. Issyk-Kul 1609 7439
Dzungaria Tarim
Fezzan **Libyan Desert** **Egypt** Cairo Sinai **Syrian Desert** **Mesopotamia** Tigris
Elburz Mts. 5604 Demavend Tehran **Plateau of Iran** Dashti-Kavir
Alai Ra. **Communism Peak** Kashgar **Tarim Basin** Lop Nor
Takla Makan Desert
Altyn Tagh **Nan Shan** **Tsaidam** Lanch
Kufra Oasis Tropic of Cancer 1934 J. Uwaynat L. Nasser 2nd Cat. 1st Cat. 397 Dead Sea -393 Baghdad
Zagros Mts. 4420 Dashti-Lut **Pamirs** 7700
Hari **Hindu Kush Ra.** 8611 **Karakoram Ra.** 7723 **Kunlun Shan** Koko Nor Hwang Ho
Bayan Kara Shan Yangtze-Kiang Minya
Nubian Desert 3rd Cat. 4th Cat. 5th Cat. 2187 **Nafud Desert** 1500 **Arabian Desert** Dahna Des.
Persian Gulf Qatar Kabul 1122 Khyber P. Helmand Indus
Plateau of Tibet Nam Tso Salween Mekong
Kordofan 6th Cat. Nile Riyadh **Red Sea** Mecca **Arabian Peninsula** Rub'al Khali
Makran **Baluchistan** 3107 Mascat G. of Oman **Trans-Himalaya** Mt. Everest 8847 Brahmaputra
Sudan Port Sudan Bahr el-Ghazal 2217 Khartoum Asmara Sana 2380
Oman Str. of Hormuz Karachi **Great Indian (Thar) Desert** Delhi Ganges **Himalaya** **Ganges Plain** Assam
Ras al-Hadd Ras Dashan 4620 3217 **Hadhramaut** Aden Al Masirah I.
Arhari Ra. 1721 **Aravalli Ra.** **Indus** **India**
Brahmaputra
Ethiopian Highlands Addis Ababa L. Tana **Danakil** Busin Djibouti G. of Aden
Kuria Muria Is. **Vindhya Mts.** Narmada **Satpura Ra.** Nagpur Mahanadi **Bengal** Calcutta Chittagong **Burma**
Arakan Yoma
4340 Hargeisa Socotra Ras Hafun **Arabian Sea**
G. of Cambay Bombay Godavari Hyderabad Krishna **Deccan** **Eastern Ghats** **Ganges Delta** Rangoon
Somali Plateau **Somali Peninsula** L. Kyoga L. Turkana 4321 Lugh Ganane Juba
Western Ghats Malabar Coast 2695 Coromandel Coast **Bay of Bengal** **Andaman Sea**
Andaman Is. Isthmus of Kra
L. Victoria 1134 Mt. Kenya 5199 Nairobi 5895 Kilimanjaro Shebell Mogadishu
5826 Lakshadweep Is. C. Comorin G. of Mannar Palk Str. **Sri Lanka** 2524 Pidurutalagala Dondra Head
Ten Degree Channel 4360 **Nicobar Is.** Phuket
Rungwe 2960 Pemba Zanzibar Dar es Salaam
Equator **Maldive Islands**
INDIAN OCEAN
3466 Simeulue Nias 5400 Mentaw
L. Malawi

Scale 1:34000000
0 250 500 750 1000 1250 1500 km
0 250 500 750 1000 St.mls.

F 40 G 50 H 60 I 70 L East from 80 Greenwich M 90 N

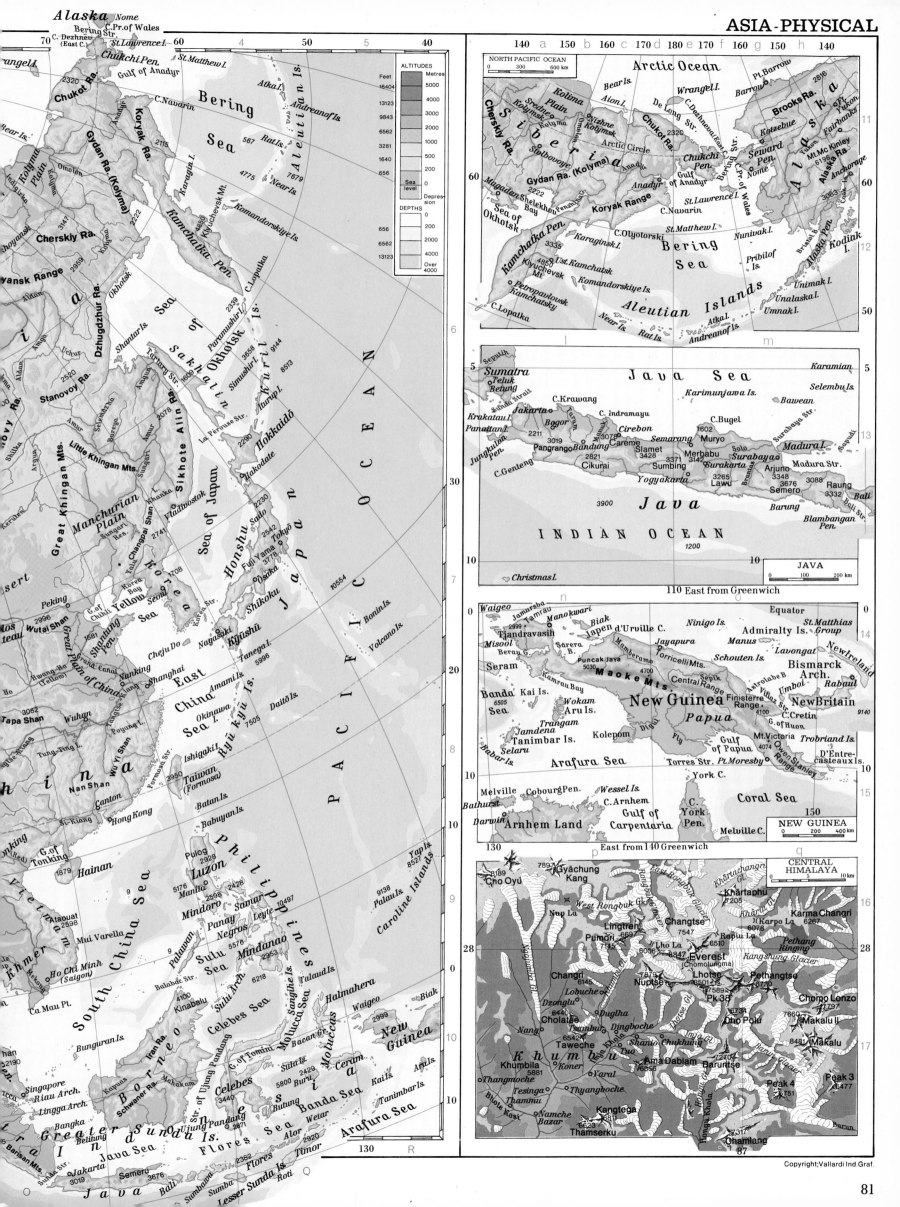

4

ATLANTIC OCEAN

ARCTIC OCEAN

Greenland (Den.)

ICELAND

North Pole

Jan Mayen (Nor.)

Norwegian Sea

West Spitsbergen

North East Land

Svalbard (Nor.)

Franz Josef Land

Komsomolets I.
Oct. Revolution I.
Bolshevik I.
Severnaya Zemlya

De Long Is.

New Siberian Is.

Reykjavik

Faeroe Is. (Den.)

Shetland Is.

Bear I.

North C.

Barents Sea

Novaya Zemlya

Kara Sea

Kotelnyi I.

C. Chelyuskin

Taymyr Pen.

Nordvik

Olenek

Khatanga

Anabar

Faroe

Outer Hebrides

IRELAND

UNITED KINGDOM

GLASGOW
EDINBURGH
Belfast
LIVERPOOL
BIRMINGHAM
LONDON
Plymouth
Le Havre

NORWAY
SWEDEN
FINLAND

Bergen
OSLO
Trondheim
Göteborg
STOCKHOLM
HELSINKI

Tampere
Oulu

Narvik

Murmansk
Kola Pen.
L. Onega
Petrozavodsk
Arkhangelsk
Mezen
Pechora
Kotlas
Syktyvkar

Vorkuta

Salekhard

Dikson

Dudinka

Turukhansk

Tazovskiy

Arctic Circle

PORTUGAL
LISBON
Oporto
La Coruña
Bilbao
Bordeaux

SPAIN
MADRID
BARCELONA
VALENCIA

FRANCE
PARIS
BRUSSELS
NETHER.
W. GERM.
HAMBURG
COPENHAGEN
DENMARK
Baltic Sea

Kaliningrad
LITHUANIA
LATVIA
RIGA
Tallin
ESTONIA

LENINGRAD
YAROSLAVL
MOSCOW
GORKIY
KAZAN
KIROV

UNION OF SOVIET SOCIALIST REPUBLICS

SIBERIA

PERM
SVERDLOVSK
Tyumen
Tobolsk
OMSK
NOVOSIBIRSK
Tomsk
Kemerovo
Novokuznetsk
KRASNOYARSK
Angara
Cheremkhovo
Irkutsk

MEDITERRANEAN

MOROCCO
Oran
ALGERIA
ALGIERS
TUNISIA
TUNIS

ITALY
ROME
NAPLES
MILAN
TURIN
GENOA
Florence
Sardinia
Sicily
PALERMO
MALTA

Corsica
Balearic Is.

AUSTRIA
SWITZ.
MUNICH
BERLIN
PRAGUE
CZECHOSLOVAKIA
POLAND
WARSAW
LODZ
KRAKOW

HUNGARY
BUDAPEST
YUGOSLAVIA
BELGRADE
ROMANIA
BUCHAREST
BULGARIA
SOFIA
ALBANIA

Minsk
White Russia
Vilnius
Gomel
Orel
Voronezh
KHARKOV
Kiev
Ukraine
DNEPROPETROVSK
ODESSA
Nikolayev
Sevastopol
Krasnodar

Penza
SARATOV
KUYBYSHEV
UFA
CHELYABINSK
Magnitogorsk
Kustanay
Pavlodar
Tselinograd
Semipalatinsk

KAZAKHSTAN

KARAGANDA
L. Balkhash
Balkhash

MONGOLIA

LIBYA
Tripoli
Benghazi

GREECE
ATHENS
Crete

TURKEY
ISTANBUL
ANKARA
Izmir
Konya
Adana
Kayseri

Black Sea
Samsun
Bursa
Constanta
Varna

Rostov
VOLGOGRAD
Astrakhan
Grozny
Baku
Tbilisi
YEREVAN
Georgia
Armenia
Azerbaijan

Caspian Sea

Aral Sea
UZBEKISTAN
TURKMENISTAN
Krasnovodsk
Ashkhabad
Bukhara
Samarkand
TASHKENT
ALMA ATA
Frunze
KIRGIZIA
Andizhan
TADZHIKISTAN
Dushanbe

Kzyl Orda

Urumchi
Turfan
SINKIANG-UIGUR
Kashgar
Khotan
Aksu

EGYPT
CAIRO
ALEXANDRIA
Suez
Asyut
Aswan
Libyan Desert

CYPRUS
Nicosia

LEBANON
BEIRUT
SYRIA
ALEPPO
Damascus
Homs
ISRAEL
Tel Aviv
Jerusalem
JORDAN
Amman

IRAQ
BAGHDAD
Basra
Mosul
Kirkuk

IRAN
TEHRAN
Tabriz
Mashhad
Esfahan
Shiraz
Kerman
Yezd
Ahvaz
Abadan
Kermanshah
Hamadan

AFGHANISTAN
Kabul
Herat
Kandahar
Kuldja

PAKISTAN
Peshawar
Rawalpindi
Islamabad
Quetta
LAHORE
Multan
Amritsar
Jammu
KASHMIR
Gilgit
Srinagar

Tibet
Lhasa
Shigatse
Gartok

CHENGTU

SUDAN
Khartoum
Omdurman
Port Sudan
Kassala
El Obeid
Atbara

SAUDI ARABIA
RIYADH
Mecca
Medina
Jidda
Buraida
Hail
Nafud
Rub al Khali

Red Sea

KUWAIT
BAHRAIN
Manama
QATAR
Doha
U.A.E.
Abu Dhabi

Persian Gulf
Bushir
Bandar Abbas
Zahedan

Tropic of Cancer

NEPAL
Katmandu
DELHI
AGRA
Bikaner
Jaipur
Jodhpur
BHUTAN
Punakha
Thimbu

INDIA
AHMADABAD
KANPUR
LAKHNAU
VARANASI (BANARAS)
Allahabad
Patna
Bareilly
Saharanpur

BURMA
Mandalay
Myitkyina
Lashio

ETHIOPIA
Addis Ababa
Asmara
Gondar
Harar
Hargeisa

DJIBOUTI

YEMEN ARAB REP.
San'a
Hodeida
YEMEN P. DEM. REP.
Aden
Mukalla

OMAN
Mascat
Sur
Al Masirah I.

Socotra (S. Yemen)

Kuria Muria Is.

Arabian Sea

HYDERABAD
Hubli
BOMBAY
PUNE
Sholapur
NAGPUR
Indore
Bhopal
Jabalpur
Vadodara (Baroda)
Diu
Jamnagar
Raipur
Ranchi
HOWRAH
CALCUTTA
BANGLADESH
DHAKA
Chittagong

Bay of Bengal

UGANDA
Kampala
KENYA
Nairobi
Lake Victoria
TANZANIA
Dodoma
Dar es Salaam
Zanzibar
Mombasa
L. Turkana

SOMALIA
Mogadishu
Berbera
Hobya
Ras Hafun

INDIAN OCEAN

MALDIVE
Male

Equator

DECCAN
HYDERABAD
BANGALUR
Vijayavada
Vishakhapatnam
Mangalur
Maisur
MADRAS
Pondicherry
Kozhikode
Tiruchirappalli
MADURAI
Trivandrum

COLOMBO
SRI LANKA
Jaffna
Kandy

Andaman Is. (Ind.)
Port Blair

Nicobar Is. (Ind.)

Banda Aceh (Kutaraja)

RANGOON

BANGKOK

MEDAN

Scale 1:34 000 000

0   250   500   750   1000   1250   1500 km
0   250   500   750   1000 St.mls.

East from 80 Greenwich

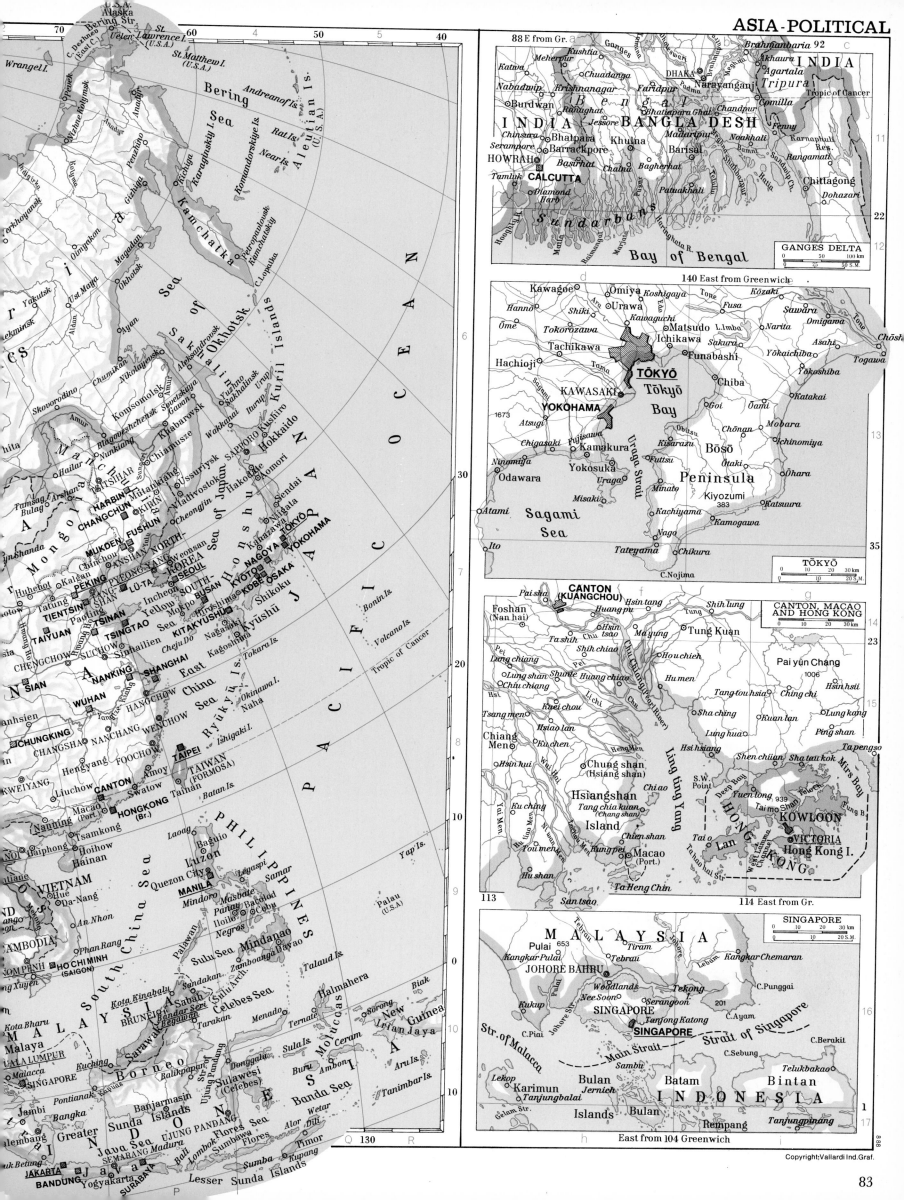

AFRICA-PHYSICAL

ATLANTIC OCEAN

Bay of Biscay
C. Finisterre
Cantabrian Mts. 5708
Pyrenees 3404
Iberian Peninsula
Lisbon
Madrid
Tagus
C. St. Vincent
Str. of Gibraltar
Tangier
Rabat
Madeira 1861 148
Er Rif
Maritime Atlas
High Atlas
Dj-Toubkal 4165
Anti Atlas
Canary Is.
Tenerife
Gr. Canaria
Fuerteventura
Ifni
C. Blanc
Dakhla
C. Vert
Dakar
St. Louis
Banjul
Gambia
Bissagos Is. 1515
Freetown 2100
Monrovia
C. Palmas

5365
Mt. Dore 1886
Mt. Blanc 4810
Jura
Alps
Rhône
Loire
Gironde
Bordeaux
Marseille
Genoa 2710
Apennines 2972
Corsica
Sardinia
Balearic Is.
Barcelona
Sa. Nevada 3478
Guadalquivir
Duero

Danube
Vienna
Plain of Hungary
Budapest
Drava
Sava
Belgrade
Transylvanian Alps
Carpathians
Dniester
Odessa
Danube
Dnieper
Sea of Azov
Don
Astrakhan
Volga
Aral Sea 68
Ustyurt Plateau

Dinaric Alps
Adriatic Sea
Venice
Vesuvius 2776
Tyrrhenian Sea
Rome
Ligurian Sea
3840
Balkans 2925
Olympus 2918
Pindus
Ionian Sea
Athens
Aegean Sea
C. Matapan
Crete 2456
Malta
C. Blanc
Tunis
Tunisia
Sicily
MEDITERRANEAN SEA

Black Sea 2211
Istanbul Bosporus
Ankara
Anatolia
Izmir
Taurus Mts. 3585
Cyprus 1953
C. Bon 4116 4482

Caucasus 5633
Elbrus
Lesser Caucasus
Ararat 5165
Pontine Mountains
L. Van
L. Urmia
Kurdistan
Tigris
Euphrates
Mesopotamia
Damascus
Baghdad
Lebanon Mts.
Jerusalem
Dead Sea
Syrian Desert
Basra
Al Jauf
Kuwait
Medina
Nafud Desert
Mecca
Arabian Peninsula
Dahna Des.
Riyadh
Persian G.
Shiraz
Tehran
Caspian Sea 995
Plateau of Iran
Zagros Mts. 4294
Namak
Elburz Mts.
-28 1880

Algiers
Atlas
Saharan Atlas
Chott Melrhir
Chott Djerid
Touggourt
Tripoli
G. of Gabès
Great Western Erg
Great Eastern Erg
Sfax
Sirte Dep. 837
Benghazi
G. of Sidra
Tobruk
Gharyan
Hamada
Sawknah
Fezzan
Murzuq
Ghat
Tademait Plateau
Erg Chech
Tanezrouft
Hoggar
Tahat 2918
Tassili-n-Ajjer 2254

Libyan Desert
Qattara Depression
Cairo
Suez Canal
Sinai Pen. 2637
Arabian Des.
Egypt
Asyut
Nile
Faráfra Oasis
1st. Cat.
Aswân
L. Nasser
Kufra Oasis
Wadi Halfa
2nd. Cat.
Nubian Desert
3rd. Cataract
J. Erba 2217
P. Sudan
J. Uwaynat 1934
4th. Cataract
Red Sea
Suakin
Medina
Mecca
Tropic of Cancer
Yemen
Hadhramaut
Rub' al Khali
Gulf of Aden
Socotra 5029
Ras Hafun
Aden 2408
Bab el Mandeb

Sahara
Adrar
Azaouad
El Djouf
Maritania
Tagant
Senegal
Tombouctou
Niger
Gao
Adrar des Iforas
Tamgak Mt.
Air
Agades
Ténéré
Bilma
Tibesti 3415
Emi Koussi
Ennedi
Bodélé Depression 1450
Ouadï
Darfur
J. Marra 3024
Kordofan
El Fasher
W. el Milk
5th. Cat.
6th. Cat.
Atbara
Khartoum
L. Tana
Abbay (Blue Nile)
Asmara 4620
Ras Dashan
Dahlak Arch.
Danakil Basin 3217
Somali Peninsula
Somali Plateau
Hargeisa
Ethiopian Highlands
Addis Ababa 4340
Harar

Sahel
Tagant
Niger
Bani
Niamey
Sokoto
Kano
Bornu
Lake Chad 240
Chad Basin
N'Djaména
Chari
Logone
Bahr el Ghazal
Sudan
Bahr el Arab
Bahr el Ghazal
White Nile
Sobat
Jebel (White Nile)

Fouta Djalon
Loma Mts. 1752
Guinea Highlands
Grain Coast
Nimba Mts.
Black Volta
L. Volta 1036
Upper Guinea
Ivory Coast
Gold Coast
Abidjan
Accra
Slave Coast
Lagos
Bight of Benin
Enugu
Sokoto
Benue
Adamawa Highlands 2040
Cameroons Mt. 4070
Sanaga
Bight of Biafra
Bioko
Principe
São Tomé
C. Lopez
Pagalu
Libreville
Equator 5212
Gabon
Ogooué

Ubangi Plateau
Bangui
Uele
Kotto
Zaire
Sangha
Zaire
Mbandaka
L. Mai Ndombe
Kasai
Sankuru
Zaire Basin
Lower Guinea
Brazzaville
Kinshasa
Ilebo
Kwango
Lulua
Kasai

Murchison Falls
L. Mobutu Sese Seko 619
Aruwimi
Ruwenzori 5119
Mt. Karisimbi 4507
L. Kivu
L. Tanganyika
L. Rutanzige
Mt. Elgon 4321
L. Kyoga
1134
East African Plateau
L. Victoria
Mt. Kenya 5199
Nairobi
Bukavu
Kilimanjaro 5895
L. Eyasi
L. Stefanie
Omo
L. Abaya
L. Turkana
Lugh Ganane
Mogadishu
Shabelle
Juba

Atlantic Ocean
Ascension I. 859
5704
5250
5212

Kwango
Lunda Plateau
Mitumba Mts.
Shaba
L. Upemba
Lubumbashi
L. Mweru
L. Bangweulu
Tanganyika
Rungwe 2960
Pemba
Zanzibar
Dar es Salaam
Mafia I.
Grande Comore
Comoro Arch.
C. d'Ambre
Aldabra Is.
Cosmoledo Is.
5069

Benguela 2615
Cuanza
Namibe
St. Helena 862
5250

Lungwebungu
Kasai
Kafue
Luangwa
Muchinga Mts.
Lake Malawi (Nyasa)
Luapula
Lunga
Moçambique
Tsaratanana 2880
4129

C. Frio
Ovamboland
Cunene
Namib Desert
Okavango (Okavango)
Etosha Pan
Brandberg 2606
Windhoek
4581
5830

Lusaka
Cabora Bassa L.
Kariba Lake
Victoria Falls
Zambezi
Mt. Mlanje 3003
Salisbury 2597
Beira
Zambezi Coastal Plain
Quelimane
Mozambique Channel
Madagascar
Ankaratra 2644
Antananarivo 5349
Antongil B.
Ste Marie
C. Ste. Marie

Damaraland 2333
Great Namaqualand 2202
Gt. Karas Mts.
Nossob
L. Ngami
Makarikari Salt Pan
Bulawayo
Rhodesian Uplands
Limpopo
Maputo
Maputo Bay
Kalahari Desert
Johannesburg
Pretoria
High Veld
Vaal
Drakensberg 3650
Durban
5360
5100
Tropic of Capricorn
700
5220
1372

Sneeu Berge
Great Karoo 2325
Nuweveld 2501
St. Helena B.
Cape Town
C. of Good Hope
C. Agulhas
False Bay
Algoa Bay
Port Elizabeth

INDIAN OCEAN

Tristan da Cunha Group
5375
1338
5457
1287
5536
5778
1646

Scale 1:34 000 000
0 250 500 750 1000 1250 1500 km
0 250 500 750 1000 St. mls.

ALTITUDES
Metres	Feet
4000	13123
3000	9843
2000	6562
1000	3281
500	1640
200	656
Sea level 0	0
Depression	

DEPTHS
0	0
200	656
2000	6562
4000	13123
Over 4000	

ATLANTIC OCEAN

Nantes Bordeaux Toulouse La Coruña Bilbao Oporto Valladolid ANDORRA MADRID LISBON PORTUGAL SPAIN Palma VALENCIA BARCELONA Balearic Is. Seville Cartagena Gibraltar (Br.) Tangier Rabat Fès Melilla Marrakech

FRANCE LYON SWITZ. Bern MILAN TURIN GENOA Nice Po Corsica Sardinia ITALY ROME NAPLES Cagliari Palermo Sicily Messina MEDITERRANEAN SEA

GERM. MUNICH AUSTRIA VIENNA BUDAPEST HUNGARY Trieste ZAGREB YUGOSLAVIA BELGRADE ROMANIA Cluj BUCHAREST Kishinev ODESSA U. Rostov S. Astrakhan Aral Sea

Black Sea Sevastopol Constanța SOFIA BULGARIA İSTANBUL Thessaloniki Bursa ANKARA Samsun Ordzhonikidze Georgia TBILISI Azerbaijan BAKU Krasnovodsk Turkmenistan S. S. R.

GREECE ATHENS İzmir Konya TURKEY Adana Kayseri Erzurum YEREVAN Tabriz L.Van L.Urmia Rasht Ashkhabad

Crete Rhodes Nicosia CYPRUS BEIRUT LEBANON DAMASCUS SYRIA Mosul Kermänshäh Esfahan IRAN TEHRAN

Madeira (Port.) Canary Is. (Sp.) Tenerife Las Palmas Gr. Canaria El Aiún ALGIERS TUNIS Annaba Constantine Bizerta Sfax Tripoli Sirte Benghazi Tobruk ALEXANDRIA CAIRO Pt.Said Suez Tel Aviv Jerusalem ISR. Amman JORDAN Al Başrah KUWAIT El Kuwait Abadan Shiräz BAHRAIN Riyadh QATAR Persian Gulf

MOROCCO ALGERIA Tripolitania Cyrenaica LIBYA EGYPT SAUDI ARABIA

Sidi Ifni Abadla Aïn Sefra Djelfa Biskra Touggourt Ghadames Tummo Savknah Kufra Oasis Al Jawf Siwa El Faiyum Asyut Qena Aswan L.Nasser Wadi Halfa Buraida Medina Mecca Jidda

Western Sahara Tropic of Cancer Dakhla Fderik C.Blanc Atar Nouakchott St.Louis C.Vert Dakar Senegal Tindouf Adrar Ft.Flatters Djanet Ghat Djado Bardai Djado Tamanrasset Taoudenni Araouane Ouallata Kiffa Kayes

MAURITANIA MALI NIGER CHAD SUDAN ERITREA YEMEN

Faya Largeau Fada El Fasher Omdurman Khartoum Kassala Asmara Wad Medani Massawa Hodeidah San'a P.D.R. of YEMEN Mukalla Aden G. of Aden Socotra C.Guardafui

Dongola Abu Hamed Atbara Port Sudan

SENEGAMBIA Banjul GAMBIA GUINEA-BISSAU Bissau Bissagos Is. Conakry SIERRA LEONE Freetown LIBERIA Monrovia Greenville

Niger Kaolack Kita Siguiri Bamako Sikasso Bobo Dioulasso BURKINA FASO Ouagadougou Kandi Niamey Sokoto Tahoua Agadès Zinder N'Guigmi Maq L.Chad N'Djamena Maiduguri Kano Kaduna Abuja NIGERIA IBADAN LAGOS Porto Novo Cotonou Maroua Am Timan Abéché Nyala Kodok Wau Bahr el Arab El Obeid Kordofan Gondar Dessye Debra Markos Djibouti DJIBOUTI Berbera Hargeisa Eil

IVORY COAST Bouaké GHANA Kumasi ACCRA TOGO Lomé BENIN Ogbomosho Enugu PtHarcourt CAMEROON Yaoundé Douala Bata EQUAT. GUINEA Malabo Bioko CENTRAL AFRICAN REPUBLIC Bangui Fort Archambault Ouanda Djalé L.Turkana Moyalé ETHIOPIA ADDIS ABABA SOMALI REP. Mogadishu Merca Kismayu

Gulf of Guinea S.TOMÉ AND PRÍNCIPE São Tomé Libreville GABON CONGO Brazzaville KINSHASA Matadi ZAIRE UGANDA Kampala L.Victoria KENYA Nairobi Mombasa SEYCHELLES

Equator Annobón P.Gentil Pointe Noire Cabinda (to Angola) L.Mai Ndombe (Lake Leopold II) Kisangani L.Albert L.Edward RWANDA Kigali BURUNDI Bujumbura Kananga Kindu Bukavu L.Kivu Mwanza Arusha Tabora TANZANIA Dodoma Dar-es-Salaam ZANZIBAR Mafia I.

ATLANTIC OCEAN Ascension (Br.) St.Helena (Br.) Luanda Malange Dundo ANGOLA Lobito Benguela Namibe Lubango ZAMBIA Lusaka MALAWI Lilongwe Zomba Blantyre MOZAMBIQUE Nampula Mocuba Quelimane COMOROS Aldabra Is. Cosmoledo Is. Antsiranana C.d'Ambre Mahajanga Maroantsétra MADAGASCAR Toamasina Antananarivo

L.Kariba Harare ZIMBABWE Bulawayo Masvingo Beira Inhambane Toliary Fianarantsoa Manakara C.Ste.Marie

Tsumeb Grootfontein NAMIBIA Windhoek Walvis Bay Lüderitz Tropic of Capricorn Kalahari Desert BOTSWANA Gaborone Transvaal Pietersburg Messina SWAZILAND Maputo Mozambique Channel

INDIAN OCEAN SOUTH AFRICA Kimberley Johannesburg PRETORIA Natal Maseru LESOTHO Pietermaritzburg Durban Bloemfontein Orange Cape Province Worcester East London Port Elizabeth CAPE TOWN C.of Good Hope C.Agulhas TRANSKEI CISKEI

Tristan da Cunha (Br.) Gough I. (Br.)

Scale 1:34000000
0 250 500 750 1000 1250 1500 km
0 250 500 750 1000 St.mls.

10 West from Greenw. 0 East from Greenw. 10 20 30 40

Mascarene Islands
Port Louis MAURITIUS
St.Denis St.Pierre Réunion (Fr.)

ASIA

ARCTIC OCEAN

Greenland Sea
Jan Mayen
Shetland Is.
Orkney Is.
Faeroe Is.
Iceland

North Pole

C. Morris Jesup
N.E. Cape
King Frederik VIII Land
King Oscars Fjord
Scoresby Sound
Denmark Strait

Aion I.
Wrangel I.
Chukchi Pen.
C. Dezhneva (East C.)
Bering Strait
C. Lisburne
C. Prince of Wales
Seward Pen.
Nome
Nunivak I.

Greenland

Mt Forel

U.S. Range
Axel Heiberg I.
Sverdrup Is.
Ellef Ringnes I.
Pr. Patrick I.
Queen Elizabeth Islands
Parry Is.
Ellesmere I.
Bathurst I.
Melville I.
N. Magnetic Pole
Devon I.
Lancaster Sd.
Somerset I.
Prince of Wales I.
Boothia Pen.

Beaufort Sea
C. Barrow
Mackenzie Bay
Banks I.
Amundsen G.
Victoria I.
King William I.
G. of Boothia

Brooks Ra.
Yukon
Alaska
Alaska Range
Mt. McKinley
Kenai Pen.
Kodiak I.
Aleutian Is.
Alaska Pen.
Bristol Bay
Gulf of Alaska
Mt St. Elias
Mt Logan

Bering Sea
St. Lawrence I.
St. Matthew I.
Pribilof I.
G. of Anadyr
C. Navarin

Mackenzie Mts.
Franklin Mts.
Great Bear Lake
Arctic Circle
L. Garry
Barren Grounds
Dubawnt L.

Baffin Bay
Baffin Island
Foxe Basin
Melville Pen.
Pr. Charles I.
Nettilling L.
Southampton I.
Foxe Channel

Davis Strait
Godthåb
Julianehåb
C. Farewell

Coast Range
Juneau
Alexander Arch.
Queen Charlotte Is.
Vancouver I.
C. Flattery

Great Slave Lake
L. Athabasca
Reindeer Lake
Churchill
Southern Indian L.

Canadian Shield
Hudson Bay Lowland
Hudson Strait
Resolution I.
Ungava Pen.
Ungava Bay
George
Hebron

Labrador

Churchill Pk.
Peace
Athabasca
N. Saskatchewan
S. Saskatchewan
Nelson

Hudson Bay
Churchill
Coats I.
Belcher Is.
James Bay
Severn
Rupert

Portland Promontory
L. Minto
Hamilton
L. Melville

Newfoundland
St. John's
Anticosti I.
G. of St. Lawrence
C. Race
Grand Banks

ROCKY MOUNTAINS
Mt. Robson
Columbia
Columbia Plateau
Blue Mts.
Cascade Range

Great Plains
Lake Winnipeg
Winnipeg
L. Manitoba

Great Bear Lake

Laurentian Plateau
Quebec
Gaspé Pen.
Pr. Edward I.
Nova Scotia
B. of Fundy
Sable I.

C. Mendocino
Mt. Shasta
Sierra Nevada
Coast Range
San Francisco
Pt. Concepción
Los Angeles
San Diego
Mt. Whitney
Death Valley
Great Basin
Wasatch Ra.
Great Salt Lake
Yellowstone National Park
Snake
Gannett Pk.
Bighorn Mts.
Black Hills
Front Range
Denver
Mt. Elbert
Colorado Plateau
Grand Canyon
Blanca Pk.

Missouri
Platte
Kansas
Arkansas
Red
Ozark Plateau

Interior Lowlands

L. Superior
L. Michigan
L. Huron
Georgian B.
L. Erie
L. Ontario
Chicago
Niagara
Ottawa
Boston
New York
Long I.
C. Cod
Allegheny Mts.
Appalachian Mts.
Mt. Mitchell
Piedmont Plat.
Washington
Chesapeake Bay
C. Hatteras
New England
Mt Washington

PACIFIC OCEAN

Lower California
Guadalupe I.
Sebastian Vizcaino Bay
Cedros I.
Tropic of Cancer
Alijos Rock
C. San Lucas
Tres Marias Is.
Repillagigedo Is.
C. Corrientes

Western Sierra Madre
Eastern Sierra Madre
Mexican Plateau
Llano Estacado
El Paso
Pecos
Rio Grande
Gila
Salton S.
Colorado
Brazos

Gulf Coastal Plain
New Orleans
Mississippi Delta
Savannah
Apalachee Bay
Florida
C. Canaveral
Miami
C. Sable
Florida Strait

Gulf of Mexico
Corpus Christi Bay
Havana
Cuba
I. de Pinos

Bahama Islands
Andros
Gr. Inagua I.

Southern Sa. Madre
Colima
Popocatepetl
Citlaltépetl
Orizaba
Mexico
Tampico

Gulf of Campeche
Yucatán
Gulf of Honduras
Cayman Is.
Jamaica

ATLANTIC OCEAN
Bermuda Is.

Greater Antilles
Hispaniola
Puerto Rico
Windward Passage
Central Cordillera

Caribbean Sea

Isthmus of Tehuantepec
G. of Tehuantepec
Tajumulco
San Salvador
G. of Fonseca
Honduras
C. Gracias a Dios
L. Nicaragua
Mosquitos
Isthmus of Panama
Darien
G. of Panama
Chiriqui
Cocos I.
Clipperton I.
Galápagos Is.
Isabela I.

Sierra Nevada de Santa Marta
G. of Venezuela
Curaçao
Caracas
Pta. Gallinas
Maracaibo
Cord. de Mérida
Bogotá
Western Cord.
Eastern Cord.
Nev. de Huila
ANDES
Quito
Chimborazo
Amazon
Orinoco
Meta
Guaviare
Caquetá
Putumayo

Equator

Scale 1:34 000 000
0 250 500 750 1000 1250 1500 km
0 250 500 750 1000 St.mls.

West from 100 Greenwich

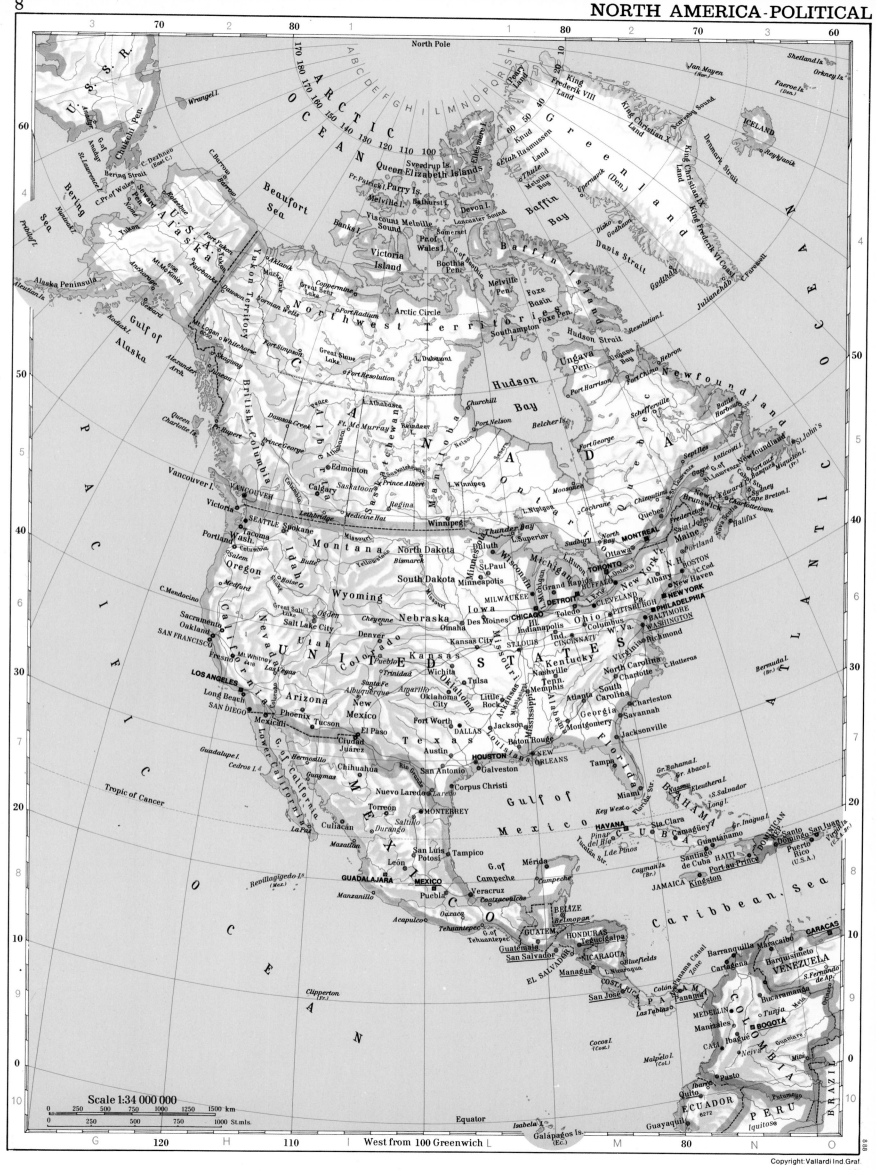

Scale 1:34 000 000

| 0 | 250 | 500 | 750 | 1000 | 1250 | 1500 km |
| 0 | 250 | 500 | 750 | 1000 St.mls. |

West from 100 Greenwich

SOUTH AMERICA PHYSICAL

Gulf of Mexico
Florida
C.Sable
Miami
Gr. Abaco I.
Bahamas
Cat.I.
Long I.
Andros Is.
Florida Strait
Havana
Acklins I.
Cuba
Gr. Inagua I.
I.de Pinos
Cayman Is.
Hispaniola
Jamaica
Greater Antilles
Puerto Rico
Virgin Is.
Leeward Is.
Caribbean Sea
Guadeloupe
Lesser Antilles
Martinique
Barbados
Grenada
Windward Is.
Margarita
Trinidad
C.Catoche
Yucatán
Gulf of Honduras
Honduras
C.Gracias a Dios
Vol.Tajumulco
S.Salvador
G.of Fonseca
L.Managua
L.Nicaragua
San Andrés
Pta. Gallinas
Guajira Pen.
Paraguaná Pen.
G.of Venezuela
Bonaire
Curaçao
Sa.Nevada de Santa Marta
Maracaibo
Caracas
Cord.de Mérida
Coast Ranges
Isthmus of Panama
Darien
Volcán Irazu
Azuero Pen.
G.of Panama
Magdalena
Apure
Llanos
Orinoco Basin
Meta
Orinoco
Georgetown
Guiana Highlands
Roraima
Sierra Pacaraima
Sa. Parime
Sa. Tumucumaque
Cayenne

ATLANTIC OCEAN
Tropic of Cancer

Cocos I.
Malpelo I.
Western Cord.
Central Cord.
Eastern Cord.
Tolima
Bogotá
Huila
Guaviare
Orinoco
Branco
Serra Imeri
Equator
Isabela I.
Sta. Cruz I.
Galápagos Is.
Volcán Cayambe
Quito
V.Cotopaxi
Chimborazo
Guayaquil
G.of Guayaquil
Pta. Pariñas
Maynas
Marañón
Caquetá
Napo
Putumayo
Japurá
Negro
Amazon
Manaus
Belém
Marajó I.
Pará
St.Peter and St.Paul Rocks
Equator

Amazon Basin
Selvas
Caatingas
Pta. Aguja
Lobos Is.
Western Cord.
Eastern Cord.
Montaña
Huascarán
Ucayali
Juruá
Purus
Madeira
Roosevelt
Salto Augusto
Valdés Pires
Capoeiras Falls
Tapajós
Xingu
Tocantins
São Luis
Parnaiba
Rocas I.
Fernando de Noronha
C.São Roque
C.Branco
Recife
Borborema Plateau
Jaguaribe

Lima
Madre de Dios
Mamoré
Guaporé
Serra dos Parecis
Bananal I.
R.das Mortes
Araguaia
Sertão
São Francisco
Salvador
Cordilleras
L.Titicaca
Illampu
La Paz
Sajama
Coropuna
Yungas
R. Grande
Plateau of Mato Grosso
Corumbá
Sa. Geral de Goias
Brasília
Campos
Brazilian Highlands
Pico da Bandeira
Jequitinhonha
L.Poopó
Bolivian Plateau
Gran Chaco
Sa. de Maracaju
Paraguay
Paraná
Paranaiba
Grande
Tocorpuri
Tropic of Capricorn
Antofagasta
Atacama Desert
V.Llullaillaco
P.San Francisco
Ojos d.Salado
Tucumán
Pilcomayo
Asunción
Iguaçu Falls
Iguaçu
Itatiaia
C.Frio
Rio de Janeiro
São Paulo
Sa.do Mar
Trindade I. Is.
Martin Vaz
S. Félix I.
S. Ambrosio I.
Salinas Grandes
Córdoba
Sa. de Córdoba
L.Mar Chiquita
Salado
Entre Ríos
Uruguay
Paraná
Porto Alegre
Lagoa dos Patos

Pampas
Juan Fernández I.
Aconcagua
Valparaíso
Vol.Maipo
Rosario
Buenos Aires
Montevideo
River Plate (Río de la Plata)
L.Mirim

Coast Ranges
Andes
Salado
Colorado
Bahía Blanca
Blanca Bay
R.Negro
Valdivia
Tronador
L.Nahuel Huapi
G.of San Matías
Valdés Pen.
Rawson
Chiloé I.
Patagonia
Chubut
Chonos Arch.
S.Valentín
G. of San Jorge
C.Tres Puntas
Taitao Pen.
Patagonian Cordillera
Chico
Wellington I.
Colorado

ATLANTIC OCEAN

Grande Bay
Queen Adelaide Archipelago
Punta Arenas
Sta. Inés I.
Tierra del Fuego
Strait of Magellan
Falkland Is. (Islas Malvinas)
I. de los Estados (Staten I.)
Shag Rocks
South Georgia
C.Horn
Drake Passage
South Sandwich Is.

PACIFIC OCEAN

ALTITUDES	
Metres	Feet
5000	16404
4000	13123
3000	9843
2000	6562
1000	3281
500	1640
200	656
Sea level	0
Depression	

DEPTHS	
0	
200	656
2000	6562
4000	13123
Over 4000	

Scale 1:34 000 000

0   250   500   750   1000   1250   1500 km
0   250   500   750   1000 St.mls.

West from Greenwich

Gulf of Mexico

UNITED STATES
Tampa
Gr. Bahama I.
Miami
Gr. Abaco I.
Florida Str.
Nassau
S. Salvador or Watling I.
HAVANA
Sta. Clara
CUBA
I. de Pinos
Camagüey
Mérida
Cayman Is. (Br.)
Santiago de Cuba
HAITI
Port-au-Prince
DOMINICAN REP.
Santo Domingo
S. Juan
Virgin Is. (U.S.A.-Br.)
JAMAICA
Kingston
Puerto Rico (U.S.A.)

Tropic of Cancer

ATLANTIC

MEXICO
BELIZE
Belmopan
GUATEMALA
HONDURAS
Tegucigalpa
San Salvador
EL SALVADOR
NICARAGUA
Bluefields
Managua
L. Nicaragua
COSTA RICA
San José

Caribbean Sea

Guadeloupe (Fr.)
DOMINICA
Martinique (Fr.)
SAINT LUCIA
BARBADOS
GRENADA
Margarita
Port of Spain
TRINIDAD AND TOBAGO

Lesser Antilles
Greater Antilles

Curaçao (Neth.)
Bonaire (Neth.)
G. of Venezuela

Panama Canal Zone
BARRANQUILLA
Maracaibo
CARACAS
Valencia
Cartagena
Colón
PANAMA
Panamá
G. of Panama
Barquisimeto
Cumaná
Maracaibo
S. Cristóbal
S. Fernando de Apure
Orinoco
Ciudad Bolívar
Georgetown
Paramaribo

MEDELLÍN
Bucaramanga
VENEZUELA
GUYANA
Cayenne
SURINAM
FRENCH GUIANA
Manizales
BOGOTÁ
S. Fernando de At.
COLOMBIA
CALI
Buenaventura
Neiva
Guaviare
Roraima
Cocos I. (Cost.)
Malpelo (Col.)
Popayán
Mitú
Tumaco
Pasto
Uaupés
Amapá
Macapá
Mouths of the Amazon

Quito
ECUADOR
Napo
Putumayo
Negro
Moura
Óbidos
Marajó I.
BELÉM
São Luís
St. Peter and St. Paul Rocks (Braz.)
Equator
Isabela I.
Sta. Cruz I.
Galápagos Is. (Ec.)
GUAYAQUIL
Cuenca
Iquitos
Leticia
Manaus
Santarém
Pará
Itaituba
Parnaíba
FORTALEZA
Rocas I.
Fernando de Noronha (Braz.)
Piura
Marañón
Amazon
Madeira
Tapajós
Caxias
Teresina
Maranhão
Iguatu
Natal
Chiclayo
Cajamarca
Cruzeiro do Sul
Juruá
Purus
Humaitá
Xingu
Carolina
Piauí
Campina Grande
João Pessoa
Trujillo
Porto Velho
Madeira
Tocantins
Marabá
RECIFE
Cerro de Pasco
Rio Branco
PERU
Guajará Mirim
BRAZIL
Conceição do Araguaia
Porto Nacional
São Francisco
Juàzeiro
Maceió
Riberalta
Rondônia
Guaporé
Barra
Aracaju
Callao
LIMA
Huancavelica
BOLIVIA
Magdalena
Trinidad
Mato Grosso
Bananal I.
Paranã
Bahia
SALVADOR
Pisco
Ica
L. Titicaca
La Paz
Cochabamba
Santa Cruz
Mato Grosso
Cuiabá
Goiânia
Brasília
Piraporа
Diamantina
Caravelas
Teófilo Otoni
Ilhéus
Arequipa
Puno
Oruro
Sucre
Puerto Suárez
Corumbá
Araguaia
Minas Gerais
Uberaba
Teófilo Otoni
Arica
L. Poopó
Potosí
Paraguay
Campo Grande
Ribeirão Preto
Uberaba
BELO HORIZONTE
Iquique
Uyuni
PARAGUAY
Pto. Casado
Bauru
Juiz de Fora
Vitória
Calama
Embarcación
Pilcomayo
Concepción
Paraná
Campinas
Campos
Tropic of Capricorn
Antofagasta
Jujuy
Asunción
S. PAULO
RIO DE JANEIRO
Niterói
Trindade (Braz.)
Martin Vaz Is. (Braz.)
Salta
Villarrica
Santos
Tucumán
Resistencia
Encarnación
CURITIBA
Paranaguá
Copiapó
Santiago del Estero
Corrientes
Blumenau
S. Félix I.
S. Ambroso I. (Chile)
Catamarca
Paraná
Passo Fundo
Florianópolis
La Serena
La Rioja
Sta. Maria
PÔRTO ALEGRE
CÓRDOBA
Santa Fé
Concordia
Rivera
Lagoa dos Patos
Juan Fernández Is. (Chile)
San Juan
Paraná
Paysandú
Pelotas
Valparaíso
ROSARIO
URUGUAY
Rio Grande
Mendoza
Mercedes
Rocha
L. Mirim
SANTIAGO
Talca
San Rafael
Mercedes
BUENOS AIRES
MONTEVIDEO
CHILE
Malargüe
Santa Rosa
La Plata
River Plate (Rio de la Plata)
Concepción
Chillán
Tandil
ARGENTINA
Neuquén
Bahía Blanca
Mar del Plata
Temuco
Zapala
Negro
Blanca Bay
Puerto Montt
S. Carlos de Bariloche
Viedma
G. of San Matías
Chiloé I.
Esquel
Chubut
Chonos Arch.
Pto. Aisen
Comodoro Rivadavia
Taitao Pen.
Deseado
Pto. Deseado
Chico
Santa Cruz
Falkland Is. (Islas Malvinas) (Br.)
Grande Bay
Rio Gallegos
Stanley
Str. of Magellan
Str. of Magellan
Tierra del Fuego
Shag Rocks (Br.)
Punta Arenas
I. de los Estados
Ushuaia
C. Horn
South Georgia (Br.)

Drake Passage

South Sandwich Is. (Br.)

PACIFIC OCEAN

ATLANTIC OCEAN

Scale 1:34 000 000
0   250   500   750   1000   1250   1500 km
0   250   500   750   1000 St. mts.

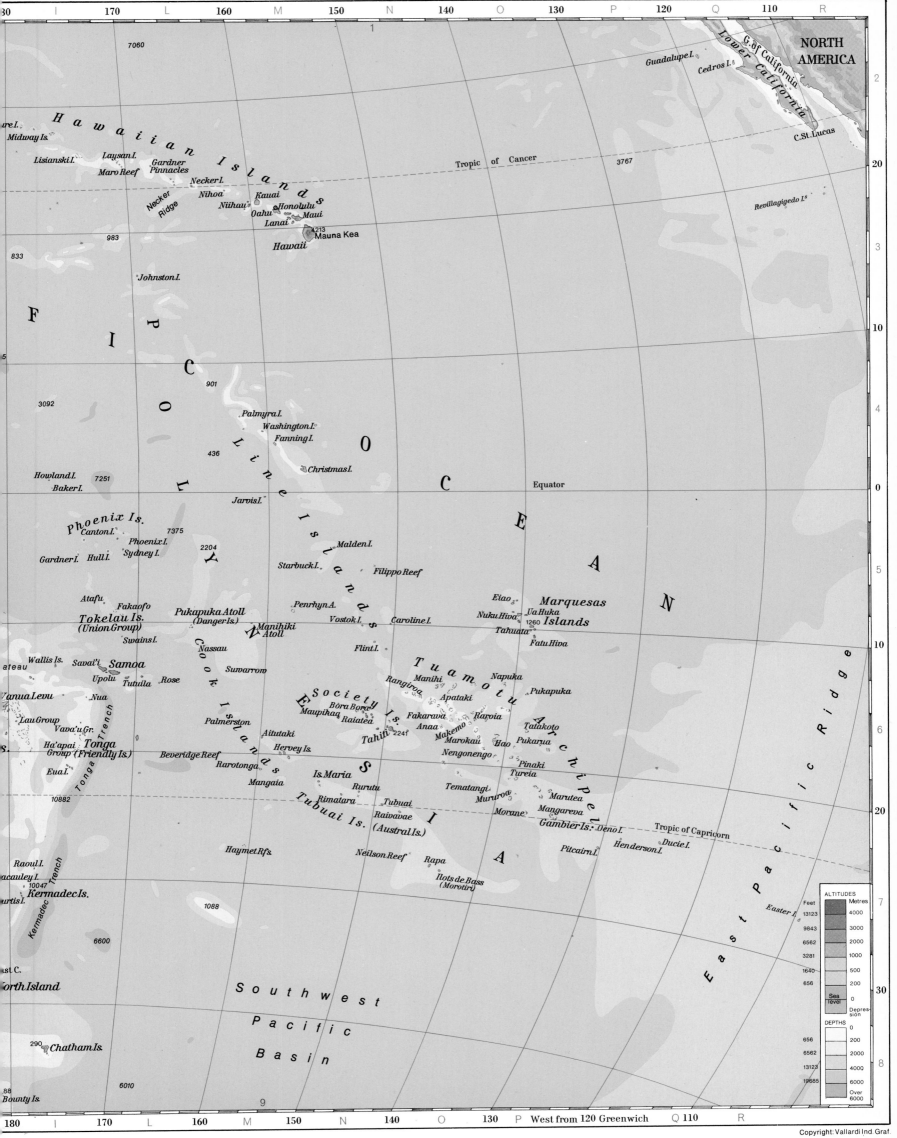

NORTH
AMERICA

G. of California

Lower California

Guadalupe I.
Cedros I.

C. St. Lucas

Hawaiian Islands

7060

Cure I.
Midway Is.
Lisianski I.
Laysan I.
Gardner Pinnacles
Maro Reef
Necker I.
Nihoa
Necker Ridge
Kauai
Niihau
Oahu *Honolulu* *Maui*
Lanai
4213
Mauna Kea
Hawaii

Tropic of Cancer
3767

Revillagigedo I.ˢ

983
833

Johnston I.

F

I

C

O

C

E

A

N

901

3092

Palmyra I.
Washington I.
Fanning I.

436

Christmas I.

Howland I.
7251
Baker I.

Jarvis I.

Equator

Phoenix Is.
Canton I.
7375
Phoenix I.
2204
Sydney I.
Gardner I. *Hull I.*

Malden I.

Starbuck I.
Filippo Reef

Eiao
Marquesas
Nuku Hiva *Ua Huka*
1260
Tahuata **Islands**
Fatu Hiva

Atafu
Fakaofo
Tokelau Is.
(Union Group)
Swains I.
Pukapuka Atoll
(Danger Is.)
Manihiki Atoll
Nassau

Penrhyn A.
Vostok I. *Caroline I.*

Flint I.

Wallis Is.
Savai'i **Samoa**
Upolu
Tutuila *Rose*
Suvarrow

Rangiroa *Manihi*
Napuka
Pukapuka
Society Is.
Bòra Bòra
Maupihaa *Raiatea*
Apataki
Fakarava *Raroia*
Makemo *Takaroto*
Anaa *Marokau* *Pukarua*
Hao

Vanua Levu
Nua
Lau Group
Vava'u Gr.
Ha'apai **Tonga**
Group *(Friendly Is.)*
Eua I.

Palmerston
Aitutaki
Hervey Is.
Tahiti
224f
Nengonengo
Pinaki

C
Beveridge Reef
Rarotonga
Mangaia
Is. Maria
Rurutu
Tureia
Tematangi *Mururoa* *Marutea*
Morane *Mangareva*
10882
Rimatara *Tubuai*
Raivavae
Tubuai Is.
(Austral Is.)
Gambier Is.
Oeno I.

Tropic of Capricorn

Ducie I.
Henderson I.

Raoul I.
Macauley I.
10047
Kermadec Is.
Curtis I.

Haymet Rfs.
Neilson Reef
Rapa
Ilots de Bass
(Morotiri)

Pitcairn I.

Easter I.

1088

6600

East C.
North Island

South west

Pacific

Basin

290 *Chatham Is.*

88
Bounty Is.
6010

East Pacific Ridge

ALTITUDES		
Feet		Metres
13123		4000
9843		3000
6562		2000
3281		1000
1640		500
656		200
Sea level		0
	Depression	

DEPTHS	
656	200
6562	2000
13123	4000
19685	6000
	Over 6000

West from 120 Greenwich

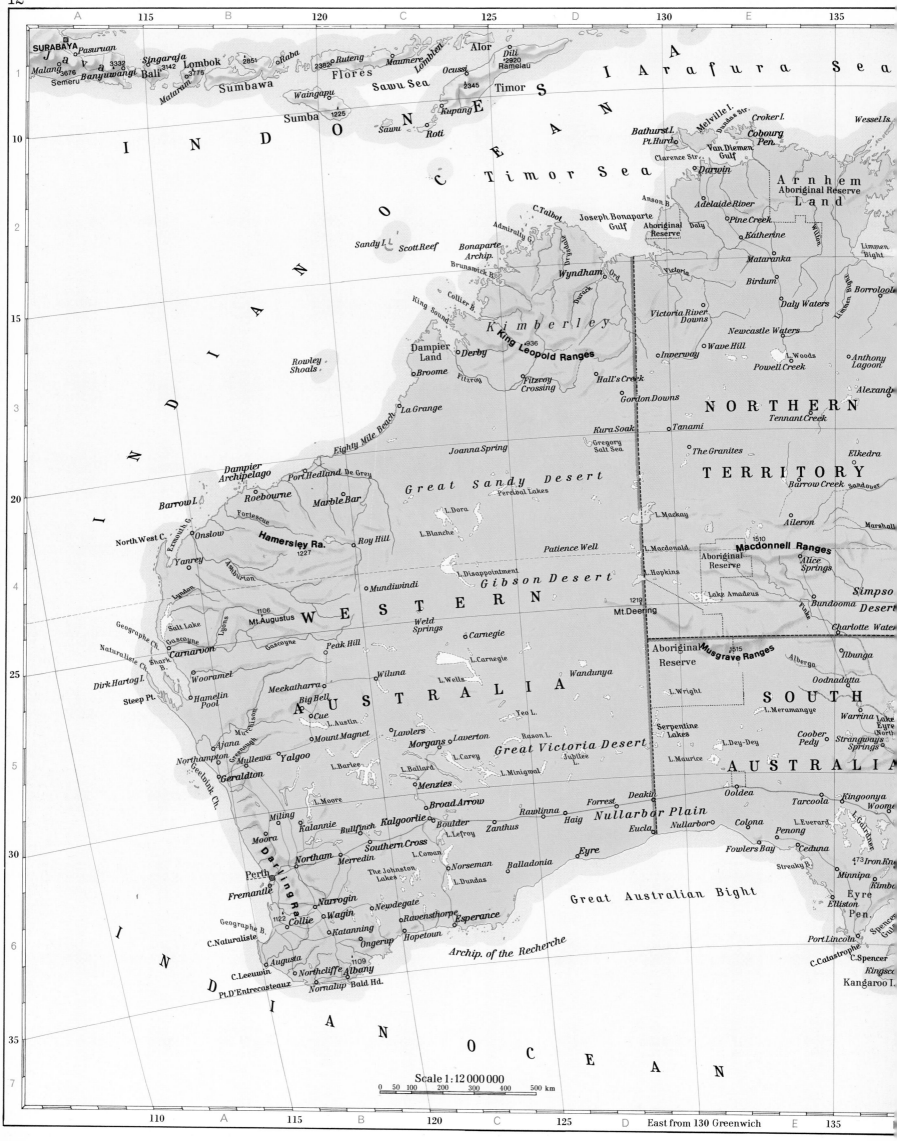

12

SURABAYA
Pasuruan
Java
Malang
Semeru 3676 Banyuwangi Bali 3142 Mataram 3775 Lombok 2851 Raba
Singaraja 3332
Sumbawa
Waingapu
Sumba 1225
Sawu
Roti
Kupang
Ruteng 2382 Flores Maumere Lomblen Alor
Sawu Sea
Ocussi 2345 Dili 2920 Ramelau
Timor
Maumere

Alor

I N D O N E S I A   Arafura Sea

I N D I A N   O C E A N

Timor Sea

Melville I. Dundas Str. Croker I.
Bathurst I. Cobourg Pen. Wessel Is.
Pt. Hurd Van Diemen Gulf
Clarence Str.
Darwin
Arnhem
Aboriginal Reserve
Land
Anson B. Adelaide River
Daly Pine Creek
Aboriginal Katherine
Reserve Mataranka
Limmen
Bight
Victoria Birdum
Daly Waters Borroloola
C. Talbot
Joseph Bonaparte
Gulf
Admiralty G.
Sandy I. Scott Reef
Bonaparte
Archip.
Brunswick B.
Wyndham Ord
Victoria River
Downs
Newcastle Waters
Collier B.
King Sound 936 Inverway Wave Hill L. Woods Anthony
Lagoon
K i m b e r l e y King Leopold Ranges Powell Creek
Dampier Derby
Land
Broome Fitzroy
Fitzroy
Crossing Hall's Creek
La Grange Gordon Downs
N O R T H E R N
Alexand
Eighty Mile Beach Kura Soak Tanami Tennant Creek
Joanna Spring Gregory
Salt Sea The Granites Elkedra
T E R R I T O R Y
Dampier Port Hedland De Grey
Archipelago G r e a t S a n d y D e s e r t Barrow Creek Sandover
Barrow I. Roebourne Percival Lakes
Marble Bar L. Dora Aileron
Fortescue L. Mackay Marshall
North West C. L. Blanche
E. mouth G. Onslow Roy Hill L. Macdonald Macdonnell Ranges 1510
Hamersley Ra. Patience Well Aboriginal Alice
Yanrey 1227 L. Hopkins Reserve Springs
Ashburton L. Disappointment G i b s o n D e s e r t Lake Amadeus Simpso
Lyndon Mundiwindi 1219 Bundooma Deser
Mt. Deering
1106 W E S T E R N Charlotte Water
Geographe Ch. Mt. Augustus Weld
Salt Lake Gascoyne Springs Carnegie Musgrave Ranges 1515
Carnarvon Lyons L. Carnegie Aboriginal Alberga Ilbunga
Naturaliste Ch. Gascoyne Peak Hill Reserve
Shark Wooramel L. Wells L. Wright Oodnadatta
B. Wiluna Wandunya S O U T H
Dirk Hartog I. Meekatharra L. Meramangye Warrina Lake
Steep Pt. Hamelin Big Bell Yeo L. Serpentine Coober Strangways Eyre
Pool Cue A U S T R A L I A Lakes L. Dey-Dey Pedy Springs North
L. Austin Lawlers Laverton L. Maurice A U S T R A L I A
Ajana Mullewa Mount Magnet Morgans Rason L. Jubilee L. Maurice Ooldea
Northampton Greenough Yalgoo G r e a t V i c t o r i a D e s e r t Tarcoola Kingoonya
Geraldton L. Barlee L. Carey Deakin Colona Woome
Mullewa L. Ballard Menzies Rawlinna Forrest L. Everard Iron Kn
L. Moore Broad Arrow Haig N u l l a r b o r P l a i n 473
Miling Kalannie Kalgoorlie Boulder Eucla Nullarbor Colona Penong Minnipa Kimb
Moora Bullfinch Zanthus Fowlers Bay Ceduna Eyre
Northam Southern Cross L. Lefroy Eyre Streaky B. Elliston Pen.
Perth Merredin L. Cowan Port Lincoln Spence
Fremantle Darling Ra. The Johnston Norseman Balladonia C. Catastrophe C. Spencer
Lakes Narrogin L. Dundas Great Australian Bight Kingsc
Geographe B. 1122 Wagin Newdegate Kangaroo I.
C. Naturaliste Collie Katanning Ravensthorpe Esperance
Augusta Ongerup Hopetoun Archip. of the Recherche
C. Leeuwin Northcliffe Albany 1109
Pt. D'Entrecasteaux Nornalup Bald Hd.

I N D I A N   O C E A N

Scale 1:12 000 000
0 50 100   200   300   400   500 km

Kolepom I.
Merauke
Irian Jaya
L. Saru
PAPUA-NEW GUINEA
Fly
Gulf of Papua
Kerema
Tauri
Morobe
C. Ward Hunt
Buna
Mt. Victoria 4074
Port Moresby
Trobriand Is.
Tufi
Collingwood
Goodenough I.
Fergusson I.
D'Entrecasteaux Is.
Normanby I.
Abau
Samarai
Banks I.
Torres Strait
Prince of Wales Island
C. York
Endeavour
Somerset
C. Arnhem
Cape York
Wenlock
Moreton
Iron Range
Coral Sea
Groote Eylandt
Gulf of Carpentaria
Aurukun
Archer
Coen
Peninsula
Princess Char.
C. Melville
Osprey Reef
Sir Edward Pellew Group
Coleman
Mitchell River
Mitchell
Musgrave
Laura
C. Flattery
Cooktown
Bougainville Reef
Mornington I.
Calvert Hills
Wellesley Is.
Bentinck I.
Karumba
Staaten
Galbraith
Walsh
Port Douglas
Cairns
Holmes Reefs
Burketown
Gilbert
Normanton
Croydon
Einasleigh
Chillagoe
Frere
Herberton
Mt. Bartle Frere 1612
Innisfail
Willis Group
Flinders Reefs
Leichhardt
Flinders
Iffley
Forsayth
Einasleigh
Hinchinbrook I.
Ingham
Lihou Reefs and Cays
Gregory
Dobbyn
Camooweal
Cloncurry
Woolgar
Charters Towers
1277
Townsville
Ayr
Bowen
Austral Downs
Mount Isa
Cloncurry
Richmond
Flinders
Pentland
Burdekin
Ravenswood
Proserpine
Marion Reef
Duchess
Selwyn
Hughenden
Mount Douglas
Mackay
Swain Reefs
Middleton
Winton
Muttaburra
Aramac
Birimgan
St. Lawrence
Broad Snd.
Boulia
L. Galilee
Saumarez Reefs
QUEENSLAND
Barcaldine
Jericho
Emerald
Marlborough
C. Manifold
Wreck Reefs
Bedourie
Barcoo
Blackall
Springsure
Rockhampton
Yeppoon
Capricorn Ch.
Birdsville
Windorah
Yaraka
Tambo
Mount Morgan
Curtis I.
Gladstone
Betoota
Cooper's Cr.
Thomson
Theodore
Tropic of Capricorn
L. Machattie
Adavale
Taroom
Eidsvold
Bundaberg
Sandy C.
Sturt Desert
Quilpie
Injuing
Mitchell
Roma
Miles
Proston
Hervey Bay
Fraser or Gt. Sandy I.
Eromanga
Charleville
Condamine
Maryborough
Thargomindah
Barcoo
St. George
Glenmorgan
Gympie
Nambour
Cunnamulla
Warwick
BRISBANE
Ipswich
Moreton I.
Hungerford
Dirranbandi
Goondiwindi
Southport
North Stradbroke I.
Pokataroo
Mungindi
Murwillumbah
Wanaaring
Bourke
Walgett
Moree
Lismore
Brewarrina
Narran L.
Inverell
Glen Innes
Clarence
Grafton
Byrock
Namoi
Narrabri
Barraba
Armidale
Coff's Harbour
Coonamble
NEW SOUTH WALES
Tamworth
Kempsey
Nyngan
Cobar
Dubbo
Muswellbrook
Taree
Wilcannia
Condobolin
Parkes
Orange
Maitland
Newcastle
Ivanhoe
Tottenham
Bathurst
Broken Hill
Menindee
Lachlan
Cowra
SYDNEY
Wollongong
Mingary
West Wyalong
Liverpool
Parramatta
Peterborough
Hay
Griffith
Goulburn
Nowra
Port Pirie
Murrumbidgee
Temora
Cootamundra
Wagga Wagga
Canberra
AUSTRALIAN CAPITAL TERRITORY
Cooma
ADELAIDE
Morgan
Waikerie
Renmark
Mildura
Deniliquin
Albury
Bright
Bega
Victor Harbour
Patchewollock
Kerang
Wangaratta
Kosciusko 2229
Bombala
Echuca
Bendigo
Mansfield
Bombala
VICTORIA
Ararat
Ballarat
Australian Alps
Bombala
Orbost
C. Howe
Mount Gambier
Portland
Hamilton
MELBOURNE
Geelong
Dandenong
Sale
Bairnsdale
Warrnambool
Colac
Port Phillip
Wonthaggi
Port Albert
Timboon
C. Otway
Wilson's Promontory
King I.
Bass Strait
Flinders I.

Scale 1:12 000 000
0 50 100 200 300 400 500 km

INDIAN OCEAN
PACIFIC OCEAN
Great Barrier Reef
Great Dividing Range
New England Ra.
Grey Range
Flinders Range
Grey Range

Tasmania inset:
Mount Gambier
Hamilton
MELBOURNE
Geelong
Dandenong
Phillip Bay
Orbost
Bairnsdale
C. Howe
Portland
Warrnambool
Timboon
Sale
Port Albert
C. Otway
Wonthaggi
Wilson's Promontory
King I.
Flinders I.
Bass Strait
Furneaux Group
C. Grim
Stanley
Burnie
Banks Str.
Cape Barren I.
Marrawah
Devonport
Eddystone Pt.
Zeehan
Mt. Ossa 1586
Great L.
1573
Launceston
St. Marys
Campbell Town
Queenstown
Brighton
New Norfolk
Hobart
Tasman Pen.
Port Davey
Storm B.
Bruny I.
South East C.
0 50 100 200 300 km

Sydney inset:
Riverstone
Hornsbury
Newport
St. Marys
Blacktown
Narrabeen
Deewhy
Brookvale
Manly
Parramatta
Granville
Fairfield
Port Jackson
SYDNEY
Liverpool
South Cr.
RANDWICK
Glenfield
Botany
Ingleburn
Kogarah
Rockdale
Botany Bay
Campbelltown
Sutherland
Cronulla
Port Hacking
Waterfall
National Park
Appin
Stanwell Park
Cataract Res.
Cordeaux Res.
Bulli
Mt. Kembla 534
Wollongong
Port Kembla 151
0 5 10 20 km

New Zealand inset:
Three Kings Is.
C. Maria van Diemen
North Cape
Awanui
Opua
Whangarei
Dargaville
Great Barrier I.
North Island
Devonport
Mercury Is.
AUCKLAND
Coromandel
Thames
Manukau
Hamilton
Bay of Plenty
East C.
Taumarunui
Rotorua
Raukumara Mts.
N. Taranaki Bight
Matata
1709
New Plymouth
C. Egmont 2520
L. Taupo
Gisborne
Mt. Egmont
Ruapehu 2797
Mahia Pen.
S. Taranaki Bight
Kaimanawa Mts.
Hawke Bay
Wanganui
Napier
C. Farewell
Takaka
Tasman Mts.
Hastings
Palmerston North
Tasman Bay
Karamea Bight
Nelson
1769
Masterton
Hutt
Wellington
Greymouth
C. Foulwind
Glenhope
Buller
Picton
Blenheim
D'Urville I.
Cook Strait
C. Palliser
Wharanui
Westport
Kaikoura Ra. 2336
NEW ZEALAND
Hokitika
Ross
Southern Alps
Wiau
Parnassus
Rangiora
Pegasus Bay
Mt. Cook 3764
Methven
Christchurch
Banks Peninsula
3495
Fairlie
Canterbury Bight
L. Tekapo
Timaru
3030
L. Wanaka
Waitaki
South Island
1858
Cromwell
Oamaru
Resolution I.
West C.
L. Wakatipu
Te Anau
Nightcaps
Gore
Dunedin
Stewart I.
Southwest C.
Foveaux Strait
Bluff
Invercargill
Tasman Sea
Pacific Ocean
0 50 100 200 300 km

East from 170 Greenwich

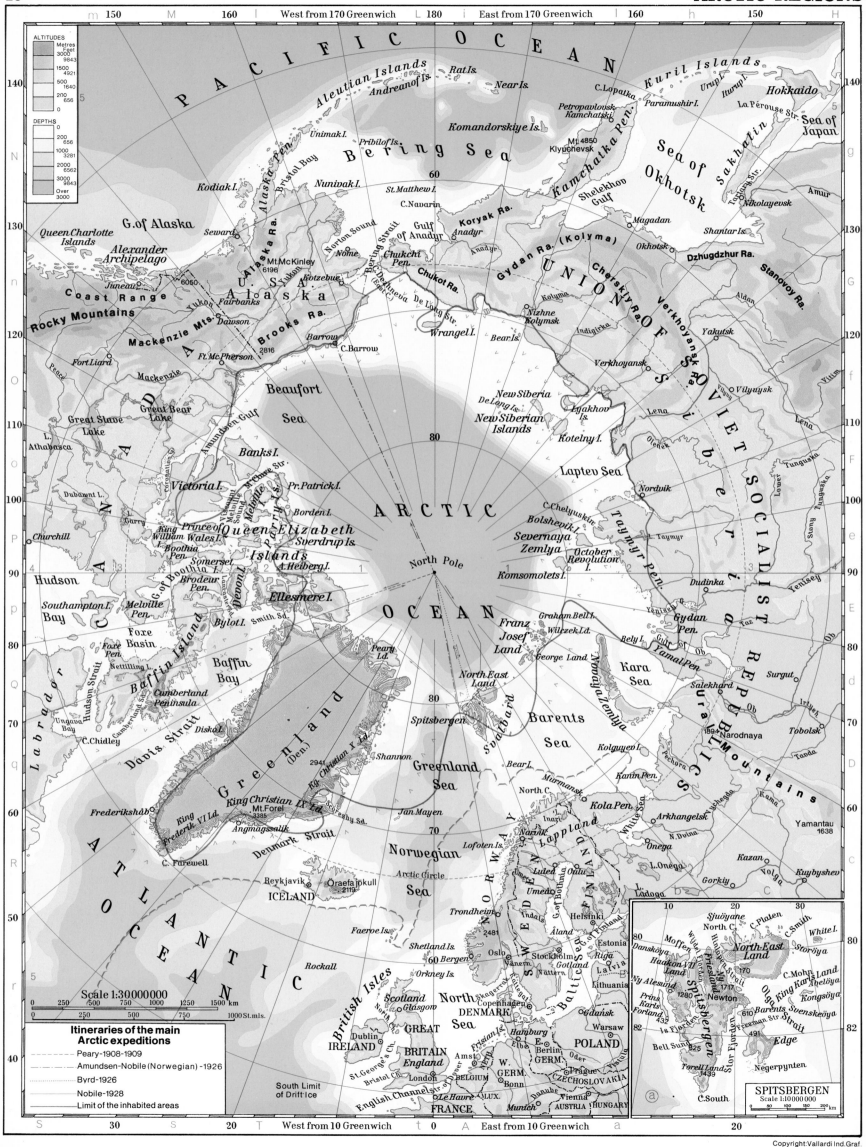

m 150   M 160   West from 170 Greenwich   L 180   East from 170 Greenwich   160   150   H

ALTITUDES
Metres	Feet
3000	9843
1500	4921
500	1640
200	656

DEPTHS
0	0
200	656
1000	3281
2000	6562
3000	9843
Over 3000	

PACIFIC OCEAN

Aleutian Islands
Andreanof Is.
Rat Is.
Near Is.
Unimak I.
Pribilof Is.
Komandorskiye Is.
C. Lopatka
Kuril Islands
Urup I.
Iturup I.
Paramushir I.
La Pérouse Str.
Hokkaido
Petropavlovsk-Kamchatski
Sea of Japan

Bering Sea

Kodiak I.
Nunivak I.
St. Matthew I.
Mt 4850 Klyuchevsk
Sakhalin
Sea of Okhotsk
Tatarsky Str.
Nikolayevsk
Amur

G. of Alaska
Queen Charlotte Islands
Alexander Archipelago
Seward
Bristol Bay
C. Navarin
Koryak Ra.
Gulf of Anadyr
Anadyr
Shelekhov Gulf
Magadan
Shantar Is.
Okhotsk
Dzhugdzhur Ra.
Stanovoy Ra.

Coast Range
Rocky Mountains
Juneau
Mt McKinley 6196
6050
Kotzebue
Nome
Norton Sound
Bering Strait
Chukchi Pen.
C. Dezhneva (East C.)
Chukot Ra.
Gydan Ra. (Kolyma)
Cherskiy Ra.
Verkhoyansk Ra.
UNION OF SOVIET

Fort Liard
Mackenzie Mts.
Fairbanks
Alaska Ra.
Dawson
Brooks Ra.
2816
C. Barrow
Barrow
De Long Str.
Wrangel I.
Bear Is.
Kolyma
Nizhne Kolymsk
Indigirka
Verkhoyansk
Yakutsk
Vilyuysk
Aldan
Vitim

Peace
Mackenzie
Great Bear Lake
Ft. McPherson
Yukon
Beaufort Sea
De Long Is.
New Siberia
New Siberian Islands
Lyakhov Is.
Kotelny I.
Lena
Olenek
Nordvik
Laptev Sea

Great Slave Lake
L. Athabasca
Dubawnt L.
Banks I.
Victoria I.
M'Clure Str.
Melville I.
Pr. Patrick I.
Borden I.
ARCTIC
L. Taymyr
Tunguska
Lower Tunguska

Churchill
L. Garry
King William I.
Prince of Wales I.
Boothia Pen.
Queen Elizabeth Islands
Sverdrup Is.
A. Heiberg I.
North Pole
Komsomolets I.
C. Chelyuskin
Bolshevik I.
Severnaya Zemlya
October Revolution I.
Graham Bell I.
Wilczek Ld.
Dudinka
Yenisey

Hudson
Southampton I.
Melville Pen.
G. of Boothia
Somerset
Boothia I.
Devon I.
Ellesmere I.
Brodeur Pen.
Bylot I.
Smith Sd.
OCEAN
80
Franz Josef Land
George Land
Novaya Zemlya
Gydan Pen.
Yamal Pen.
Gulf of Ob
Salekhard
Ob
Surgut
Irtysh
Tobolsk
Taz

Foxe Basin
Netilling L.
Foxe Pen.
Baffin Island
Baffin Bay
Peary Ld.
North East Land
Spitsbergen
Svalbard
Barents Sea
Bear I.
Kara Sea
Kolguyev I.
1894 Narodnaya
Pechora
Taoda

Labrador
Ungava Bay
Hudson Strait
Cumberland Peninsula
Cumberland Sd.
Davis Strait
Disko I.
2941
Greenland (Den.)
Shannon
Greenland Sea
Jan Mayen
Murmansk
North C.
White Sea
Kanin Pen.
Arkhangelsk
N. Dvina
Onega
Kama
Yamantau 1638

C. Chidley
Frederikshåb
King Frederik VI Ld.
King Christian IX Ld.
Mt. Forel 3385
Kg. Christian X Ld.
Scoresby Sd.
70
Lofoten Is.
Lappland
Kola Pen.
L. Onega
Kazan
Volga
Gorkiy
Kuybyshev

ATLANTIC
Angmagssalik
Denmark Strait
Norwegian Sea
Narvik
SWEDEN
FINLAND
Inari
L. Ladoga
Reykjavik
Öraefa jökull 2119
ICELAND
Arctic Circle
Trondheim
Umeå
G. of Bothnia
Helsinki
Estonia
Riga
Latvia
Lithuania

OCEAN
Faeroe Is.
Shetland Is.
Bergen
Oslo
Stockholm
Åland
Gotland
Baltic Sea

Rockall
Orkney Is.
Scotland
Glasgow
North Sea
Skagerrak
Kattegat
Copenhagen
DENMARK
Gdansk
Warsaw
POLAND

British Isles
IRELAND
Dublin
St. George's Ch.
GREAT BRITAIN
England
London
Bristol Ch.
English Channel
Le Havre
FRANCE
Amsterdam
BELGIUM
LUX.
W. GERM.
Bonn
E. GERM.
Berlin
Hamburg
Frisian Is.
Elbe
Oder
Prague
CZECHOSLOVAKIA
Munich
Danube
Vienna
AUSTRIA
HUNGARY

South Limit of Drift Ice

Scale 1:30000000
0 250 500 750 1000 1250 1500 km
0 250 500 750 1000 St. mls.

Copyright: Vallardi Ind. Graf.

Itineraries of the main Arctic expeditions
- – – – Peary-1908-1909
- –·–·– Amundsen-Nobile (Norwegian)-1926
- ········ Byrd-1926
- ——— Nobile-1928
- ——— Limit of the inhabited areas

SPITSBERGEN inset:
10 20 30
Sjuøyane
North C.
C. Platen
C. Smith
White I.
Danskøya
Moffen
Hinlopen Strait
170
North East Land
Storøya
Hadkon VII Land
Friesland
1717
C. Mohn
Olga King Karls Land
Ny Ålesund
1280
Spitsbergen
Newton
Abeløya
Prins Karls Forland
432
Barents Svenskøya
Kongsøya
Is Fjorden
Stor Fjorden
610
Freeman Str Strait
491
Bell Sd.
825
Edge
Torell Land
1439
C. South
Negerpynten

SPITSBERGEN
Scale 1:10000000
0 50 100 150 200 km

m 30 M 20 West from 10 Greenwich L 0 East from 10 Greenwich 20 h 30 H

Stations for scientific researches
- Argentina
- Australia
- Chile
- France
- United Kingdom
- New Zealand
- South Africa
- United States
- U.S.S.R.

Northern limit of drift ice
Average limit of drift ice
Limit of pack ice

ATLANTIC OCEAN

Bouvet I.
(Nor.)

Prince Edward I.
(S. Afr.) Marion Is.

40 40

N g

50 60

Antarctic Circle

Traversay Is.
South
Sandwich
Islands

Grytviken

South
Georgia
Shag Rocks

Scotia Sea
Falkland Is. Dependency

South Orkney Islands

Orcadas
Laurie I.
Coronation I.
Signi Is.

Falkland Is.
(Islas Malvinas)

SOUTH AMERICA

n G

50 50

Sanae 70

Princess Martha Coast Princess Astrid Princess Ragnhild Coast
Coast

Lazarevskaya

Lützow-Holm Bay Amundsen Bay

Prince
Harald Coast

Pr. Olaf
Coast

C. Ann
Proclamation I.

Mt. Christensen

Enderby
Land

Kemp
Coast

Colbeck
Arch.

Edward VIII Bay

Mac
Robertson
Land

Douglas Is.

C. Darnley
Mackenzie Bay

Amery
Ice Shelf

Prydz Bay

Davis

Ingrid Christensen
Land

Leopold and
Astrid Coast

Gaussberg

Wilhelm II Coast

Queen
Mary
Coast

Drygalski I.

Davis Sea
Masson I.
Shackleton
Ice Shelf

Mt. Amundsen

Mill I.

Bowman I.

Vincennes Bay

Budd
Coast

Knox Coast

C. Poinsett

Sabrina
Coast

Banzare
Coast

Paulding B.

C. Goodenough
Porpoise Bay

Elephant I.
South
Shetland
Islands

King George I.
Joinville I.
Hope Bay
Esperanza
Bernardo O'Higgins
Ross I.
Teen. Matienzo

Cap. A. Pratt
Pres. Pedro
Aguirre Cerda
Decepción

Brandsfield Str.

Halley

Weddell
Sea

Queen Maud Land

2717
Ritscher Upland
4200

Wohlthat
Mts.

3426

Antarctic
Peninsula

Palmer
Land

Graham Land

Larsen Ice Shelf

Gen. Belgrano

Ellsworth

Luitpold Coast
Caird Coast
Coats Land

Theron Mts.

Pres. G. gonzales Videla
Argentina
Anvers I.
Biscoe Is.

Palmer Arch.

Adelaide I.

Adelaide

Marguerite
Bay

Fossil Bluff

George VI Sound

Dyer
Plateau

Wilkins Coast

Alexander I.

Charcot I.

Ashley Snow I.

Joerg
Plateau
2896

Fitchner
Ice
Shelf

Berkner I.

Edith Ronne Land

Pensacola
Mountains
3658

American
Highland

3353
Pr. Charles Mts.

2646

2260

1216

371

Bellingshausen
Sea

Peter I st I.

Thurston I.

C. Flying Fish

Eights Coast

Robert English Coast

Ellsworth Land

Hudson
Mts.

Ellsworth
Mts.
5139

Vinson
Massif

ANTARCTICA

4267

Thiel Mts.
2812

South Pole
2800

Amundsen-Scott

Polar

Sub-Glacial

Basin

Queen Maud Ra.

2

e

P E

90 90

Amundsen
Sea

Martin
Pen.

Pine I. Bay

Byrd
Land

Walgreen Coast

Byrd

Sub-Glacial

Basin

3022

Hollick Kenyon
Plateau

3932

Horlick

Mt. Nansen

Queen
Alexandra Ra.

Mt. Markham

Wilkes

Sub-Glacial

Basin

C. Dart

Mt. Sidley
Mt. Siple
4575

4221

Rockefeller
Plateau

3496

Shackleton Inlet

Ross Ice Shelf

3609

Mt. M'Clintock

q D

Wrigley G.
Hobbs Coast

Cruzen I.

Edsel Ford Ra.

Rockefeller
Mts.

Edward VII
Pen.

Roosevelt I.
Little America
Ice Barrier

Moore
Embayment

Mt. Erebus
Ross I.
McMurdo
Scott

Prince Albert Mts.

Terra Nova b 2774

Kay Is. Mt. Levick

Victoria Land

Coulman I.

C. Adare
Hallett

Mt. Sabine
3850

Adelie
Land

George V
Coast

Dumont D'Urville

Oates Coast

Robertson B.

C. North
Rennick B. C. Hudson

South Magnetic
Pole

R C

Scott I.

Balleny
Islands

Antarctic Circle

Macquarie Is. Macquarie Is.

r C

PACIFIC OCEAN

ROSS Sea

INDIAN OCEAN

Wilkes Land

AUSTRALIA

Tasman Sea

Campbell I.

Auckland Is.

Antipodes
Islands

Bounty Is.

Stewart I. a

South C.

Tasmania

NEW ZEALAND East from 160 Greenwich B

150 S 160 T West from 170 Greenwich t 180 A

ALTITUDES
Metres	Feet
3000	9843
2000	6562
1000	3281
Sea level	0
Depression

DEPTHS
0	
1000	3281
2000	6562
3000	9843
4000	13123
5000	16404
Over 4000	

Itineraries of the main Antarctic expeditions
- Cook-1773-1775
- Gauss-1901-1902
- Scott-1903-1911-1913
- Amundsen-1911
- Ellsworth's flight-1935
- Hillary-Fuchs-1957-1958

Scale 1:30 000 000
0 250 500 750 1000 1250 1500 km
0 250 500 750 St.mls.

Geographical terms

Avalanche

Ammonite

Anticyclone

Anticline

Aa A particular type of lava flow which, when solidified, has a rough, slaggy appearance. The term is of Hawaiian origin.

Ablation Loss of thickness and surface area of part of a glacier caused by melting, evaporation or separation of icebergs along the coast. In the last case, the word "calving" is used to describe this phenomenon.

Alluvial cone Fan-shaped accumulation of sand and gravel deposited by a river when the gradient decreases. Typical examples are the Alpine cones at the mouths of the secondary valleys in the main valleys.

Alluvium All the debris and material deposited by rivers. It is composed of silt, sand and gravel and can form cones, alluvial plains and deltas.

Ammonite A fossil mollusc with a spiral shell especially common in rocks of the Mesozoic era, varying in size from a few centimetres to around two metres. By the end of the Mesozoic era ammonites were extinct; they have become used as dating fossils.

Andesite An igneous rock usually formed where the Earth's crust is sinking into the magma below. It takes its name from the Andes where it has been specially studied.

Anticyclone Area of high atmospheric pressure surrounded by areas of lower pressure; the weather is generally settled, calm and warm in summer, calm and cold (or cloudy) in winter. In the northern hemisphere one of the largest and most stable anticyclones is that of the Azores.

Anticline Structure of stratified rock folded upward by tangential or vertical forces acting on the Earth's surface; an anticline may be more or less flat on one side. The anticline does not always result in raised ground; in fact eroded anticlines frequently result in valleys.

Antipodes Points which are diametrically opposite each other on the surface of the Earth. For example, Spain is at the antipodes of New Zealand.

Archipelago At first this term meant a sea with many islands grouped closely together. Nowadays the word is used to describe the islands themselves, for example, the Azores Archipelago.

Ash The small particles of lava emitted from a volcano during an eruption; they can be carried enormous distances by the wind.

Atmosphere The gaseous envelope surrounding the Earth. The atmosphere does not have a well defined boundary; its thickness is always greatest around the Equator and least at the poles. It is divided into different layers, including the troposphere and the stratosphere which are distinguishable by their different physical characteristics. The troposphere is composed of nitrogen (78%), oxygen (21%), carbon dioxide (0.03%) and other rare gases, to which is also added water vapour.

Atoll A coral reef found in the Pacific Ocean with a circular or elliptical shape containing a lake. Its characteristic shape is due to the growth of corals around an island which is slowly sinking.

Avalanche Mass of snow or ice falling down a slope. It can occur in winter (when fresh, light snow slides on old snow) or in spring as a result of thawing.

Barchan A sand dune of the typical sickle shape, common in deserts where the wind blows from a constant direction; its height can exceed thirty metres. Occasionally barchans are found in isolation, but they are more often grouped together to form a sea of sand.

Barrier reef A reef of coral stretching parallel to the coast and separated from it by a lagoon. The most famous is the Great Barrier Reef on the north-east coast of Australia, more than 1,900 km in length.

Basalt A dark-coloured igneous rock comprised mainly of minerals of the felspar group. This rock most frequently forms wide lava flows and is often found in the form of hexagonal columns.

Batholith A large mass of intrusive igneous rock, usually granite, which has penetrated through existing rocks and has then solidified. The shape seen today is the result of erosion. Mont Blanc is a batholith.

Bathyal An adjective used to describe the underwater environment adjacent to the continental shelf and situated between 200 and 2,000 metres in depth.

Bay An inlet in the shore of a sea or lake.

Caatinga Forest typical of the tropical areas of north-east Brazil. It is composed of vegetation capable of surviving in dry conditions and with very irregular rainfall, such as cactus, acacias and spurge.

Caldera Roughly circular depression with a diameter of several kilometres connected with volcanic activity. The caldera is formed by the destruction of the top of a volcanic peak by a particularly violent eruption, or by the sinking of the existing peak into the magma below.

Cambrian First period of the Palaeozoic or Primary era. Its beginning has been established at over 600 million years ago; invertebrate fossils are found in the rocks of this period.

Canyon A narrow, deep valley with a river flowing through it; it is typical of rather arid regions where the sides of the valley are not subjected to the action of flood water. There is thus a continuous deepening of the bottom of the valley caused by the action of the river while the sides remain steep. A classic example of this is the Grand Canyon in the United States.

Capital Principal city of a nation where the seat of government is situated; for example Rome, in Italy. In federal states the capital is not usually the most important and highly populated city, but is simply the seat of government; for example Washington, in the United States.

Carboniferous The fifth period of the Palaeozoic or Primary era between 350 and 270 million years ago. The name comes from the vast layers of fossil coal existing in the rocks of this period.

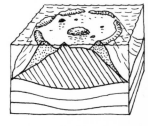

Atoll

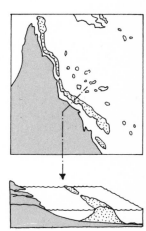

Barrier reef

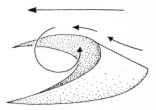

Barchan

Cumulus

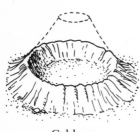

Caldera

Canyon

Cartography Work connected with the drawing of a map, from the surveying to the printing. The map shows, by means of special symbols, areas of various sizes from a few kilometres square to the entire world.

Cavern Underground cave especially common in limestone rocks, caused by the dissolving of the rock in the water which percolates through.

Cenozoic or Cainozoic The third geological era, also called the Tertiary era, whose duration has been calculated to be 65 million years. It includes four periods: Eocene, Oligocene, Miocene and Pliocene. Some authorities regard this era as including both the Tertiary and Quaternary eras.

Centrality Function exercised by a city in respect of the surrounding area; the centrality is measured on the basis of the quality and quantity of the services which the city (called the central place) can supply to the rest of the territory.

Chernozem Black soil especially common in parts of south-west Chernozem, Russia, Rumania and Hungary. Particularly rich in humus, it is a very fertile soil well suited to the cultivation of cereals.

Cirrus High cloud (between 6,000 and 12,000 m) consisting of crystals of ice and tuft-shaped; it is very thin and consequently does not exclude the light from the sun.

City An inhabited centre of some importance, either because of the number of inhabitants or the function (economic, political, religious, etc.), which places it above other nearby centres. The city may have one special function such as port or commercial centre; but most cities have many functions.

Clay Sedimentary rock formed by the cementation of very fine particles (muds); it is mainly composed of aluminium silicate derived from transformation of the minerals contained in different rocks. Clays may be classified according to the predominant mineral (such as kaolin) or according to the area where they are deposited (lake, sea, abyssal, etc.); red clays, for example, are formed from an abyssal deposit.

Cleavage Property possessed by some rocks to split along parallel planes in relation to the metamorphic pressure.

Cliffs Coast with steep vertical walls due to erosion by the sea. The form of the cliffs depends on the type of rock and whether there are fractures or stratification which encourage the work of destruction of the waves.

Climate The average atmospheric conditions which are typical of a fairly large region over a long period of time. Under the heading of climate are included characteristics such as temperature, precipitation and winds, and factors such as latitude, exposure, height, etc. Among the classifications most commonly used is that of Köppen who distinguishes five principal groups of climates in relation to the same number of types of vegetation.

Clouds Collection of water or ice particles formed by the condensation of water vapour and suspended in the atmosphere. Clouds are given different names such as cirrus, cumulus, stratus and nimbus according to their shape.

Coal A general term for combustible deposits formed from the accumulation of vegetable matter; this matter, covered with various sediments, was gradually decomposed by the action of the temperature and the pressure. Under the heading of coal are included peat, lignite and anthracite.

Conglomerate (Pudding-stone) Sedimentary rock composed of pebbles rounded by the action of water and cemented by various substances including calcium carbonate.

Continental drift Theory according to which the present-day continental masses originated from a single super-continent which broke up. The most famous upholder of this theory was Alfred Wegener who based it not only on the ability of the various continental coastlines to be fitted together, but also on similarities in geology and palaeontology.

Continental shelf Gently sloping area under the sea round the borders of continents. It is in fact the outer edge of the continent which is separated from the greatest ocean depths by the continental slope.

Contour line Line on a map joining points of the same height above sea level.

Conurbation Very large urban area consisting of a main inhabited centre and other smaller ones which have been absorbed by the main centre. The city of London, for example, with its smaller surrounding centres, forms the conurbation of Greater London.

Corrie A hollow surrounded by steep walls, of glacial origin. It is currently thought that the origin of the hollow is not only attributable to the erosion caused by the glacier (the corrie glacier) but also to the disintegration of the rock caused by the process of alternate freezing and thawing of melt water under the ice.

Crater Cavity at the summit of a volcano, usually circular, from which lava, ash and other volcanic material are emitted. Craters can also be produced by the impact of a meteorite.

Cretaceous The third period of the Mesozoic or Secondary era which covers the period from 130 to 70 million years ago. Among the plants appearing was the angiosperm, while the great reptiles of the Jurassic age disappeared.

Crevasse Fissure in the surface of a glacier caused by the variations in velocity of the glacial mass. According to their position, they can be longitudinal, transverse or marginal.

Cumulus Type of cloud extending upward with a flat base and rounded bulbous summit.

Current Movement of part of the sea in a permanent or seasonal manner. It is caused by various physical phenomena, such as differences in salinity and temperature in the water mass, wind action, etc. Among the best known is the Gulf Stream, which carries warm water from the Gulf of Mexico to the coasts of Western Europe.

Cyclone An area where the barometric pressure is low. There are two types: the depression of temperate latitudes, and a tropical depression with rotating winds and violent rain storms; at the centre of the cyclone is a small area of relative calm called the eye.

Deflation Effect of the wind blowing dust and sand from the ground for great distances. Typical of arid and coastal regions without vegetation. The material can be transported for many kilometres and accumulates in the form of dunes.

Delta Plain formed by material transported by a river to where it discharges into the sea, when the river slows down and loses

Cavern

Corrie

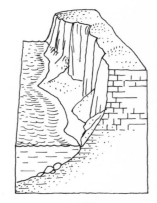

Cliffs

its carrying capacity. For a delta to be formed, the sea must not be able to carry away the sediment. Whenever that happens, an estuary instead of a delta is formed.

Density of population Ratio between the number of inhabitants in an area (country, region, community, etc.) and the unit measure of an area (in sq km). In practice it is the number of inhabitants per square kilometre.

Detritus Accumulation of material of various sizes (pebbles, sand, mud and clay) transported by various agents (water, glaciers and wind) and redeposited. Detritus found at the foot of cliffs is chiefly caused by fracturing of the rock by freezing water.

Devonian Fourth geological period of the Palaeozoic era, from 400 to 350 million years ago. It takes its name from Devon where many marine deposits have been found.

Diffluence Branching of a glacier across a low col into a neighbouring valley.

Dolomite Sedimentary rock formed from a double carbonate of calcium and magnesium, which occurs in sea water as a result of various chemical processes. Some mountain ranges are formed of it, the Dolomites being the most famous.

Dune Small hill or ridge of loose sand carried by the wind. They are found in deserts (like the Sahara) and along low and sandy shores. When they are shaped like a sickle, they are called barchans.

Crevasses

Earthquake Rapid vibration of part of the Earth's crust caused by movement along the margins of plates that form the crust. The movements are caused by a series of elastic waves which propagate in different directions. Earthquakes occur in the most tectonically unstable zones, especially along faults.

Ecology The study of the complex relationship between living things and their environment.

Eocene The first geological period of the Cenozoic or Tertiary era, from 70 to 40 million years ago; the flora and fauna were similar to those of the present day. Among the fossils nummulites are found.

Equator The great circle which divides the Earth into two hemispheres, the northern and the southern. It is the parallel of 0° of latitude.

Erg Area of the Sahara desert covered with sand and dunes.

Erosion The work of such agents as rivers, glaciers, wind and waves in shaping the surface of the Earth.

Erratic A mass of rock transported by glaciers and deposited after the glacier has melted, often at great distances from its place of origin.

Eruption The process by which volcanic material (lava, ash, gas) is emitted from the mouth of a volcano. An eruption can be calm or explosive.

Escarpment A range of hills typified by a distinct asymmetry of the slopes, one of which is very steep while the other has a much more gentle slope. The escarpment is usually caused by lithological factors (stronger rock strata lying on top of weaker strata) or tectonic factors (the presence of faults).

Estuary Mouth of a river shaped like a V with the vertex pointing upstream. A typical example is the Amazon estuary; the sediment carried down by the river is dispersed by the current.

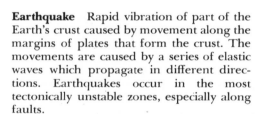

Delta

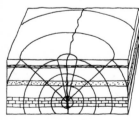

Earthquake

Fault Fracture of a rock mass with displacement of the two parts. It is caused by stretching or compression within the Earth's crust. It can be of various types: normal, reverse, thrust, etc.

Fjord Long, narrow inlet of the sea caused by submergence of a glacial valley. Typical of such coasts are those of Norway, Greenland and southern Chile. The fjords represent the valleys excavated by the Quaternary glaciers and gradually submerged.

Fog Condensed water vapour suspended in the lowest levels of the atmosphere; it is composed of minute water droplets in suspension and can seriously affect visibility.

Föhn A warm dry wind which blows from the mountains. The heating effect is due to the compression of the descending air mass. A typical föhn is that which blows down the north side of the Alps in spring and rapidly thaws the winter snows.

Fold Curvature of sedimentary rock caused by internal forces (for example, orogenesis). Folds which are curved upwards are called anticlines, while those which curve downwards are called synclines.

Fossil Trace or remains of animal or vegetable organism preserved in sedimentary rock. The fossils found in a particular geological period (dating fossils) are one of the methods of dating the rocks. The study of fossils is called palaeontology.

Freeze-thaw action Breaking up of rocks caused by continuous alternate freezing and thawing typical of elevated mountain areas. Water penetrates the cracks and expands when it freezes, resulting in considerable pressure on the rock which breaks up.

Front Term used in meteorology to describe the boundary between air masses of different characteristics, especially of temperature.

Gabbro A dark coloured igneous rock. It contains less than 55% silica and is therefore a basic rock. It consists mainly of plagioclase.

Geography The study of the relationship between man and his environment. Traditionally the subject has been divided into such branches as physical, economic and regional geography. In recent years a much more scientific approach to the subject has been taken.

Geology The study of the crust of the Earth and the natural processes which affect it. There are various branches, for example stratigraphy, palaeontology, applied geology, etc.

Geomorphology Study of the physical features of the Earth and the agents (such as water, ice and wind) that modify them.

Geosyncline Slowly sinking basin in the Earth's crust in which sediment is deposited. Compression of these sediments may uplift them to form mountains.

Geyser Violent emission of hot water and steam occurring intermittently through an aperture in the Earth's crust. It is part of so-called secondary vulcanism.

Glacial erosion The erosive action of a glacier on the rocks by smoothing, grinding and plucking. Owing to the weight and slow movement of the glacial mass, a polishing action may result on the underlying rock.

Glacier Ice mass found in a valley at high altitudes or high latitudes; it arises from the change of snow into ice and slowly moves towards lower altitudes.

Gneiss Metamorphic rock with a charac-

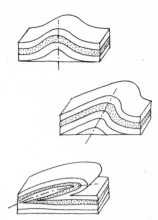

Fold

Erratic

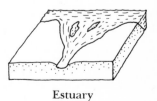

Estuary

teristic wavy striped appearance. Formed from the metamorphism of igneous rocks such as granite (orthogneiss) or sedimentary rocks (paragneiss).

Gondwanaland Great continental mass which, according to the theory of continental drift, comprised the southern part of the original super-continent called Pangaea. When it split up, it gave rise to the continents of Africa, India, some parts of South America and Australia.

Gorge Narrow, deep river valley with steep walls.

Granite Intrusive igneous rock with a characteristic granular appearance; it is composed of quartz, felspar and mica. It is often grey in colour, and has a high proportion of silica and is therefore an acid rock. The relatively large crystals result from slow cooling within the Earth's crust.

Grassland Regions where grass is the natural vegetation. A long dry season discourages tree growth though grazing animals such as bison or antelope may be an important factor.

Gravel Rounded pebbles deposited by a river.

Grotto A large cave formed by solution in limestone.

Gulf Very deep inlet or bay in the coast; for example the Gulf of Guinea or the Gulf of Carpentaria.

Günz The first of four great Pleistocene ice ages of the Quaternary era; the name comes from a small river in Bavaria where glacial deposits from this period were first identified.

Hamada Rocky desert, typical of vast areas of the Sahara and Australia.

Harmattan North-east wind which blows from the Sahara towards the coast of west Africa; it is a dry wind which may be hot and dusty.

Horst Stretch of land elevated with respect to the surrounding area and bordered by parallel faults. It is also called a block mountain.

Hot desert Regions with very little rainfall (less than 250 mm of rain per year) and hence very little vegetation. Temperatures are very high in the day (temperatures over 50° have been measured in the deserts) and the daily range of temperature is also significant. The largest desert is the Sahara in North Africa.

Hurricane Tropical cyclone of the West Indies and the Gulf of Mexico. It is accompanied by extremely violent winds and torrential rains.

Hydrography The study and charting of the water in the Earth's lakes, seas and rivers. Their distribution, properties and different uses are analysed.

Ice field Layer of floating ice covering the sea in the polar regions. It is caused by the freezing of sea water and the piling up of the ice sheets so formed, on top of which falling snow also accumulates. The whole gives rise to an irregular surface crossed by many channels.

Iceberg Large mass of floating ice originating from the Arctic or Antarctic glaciers; it is carried along by winds and sea currents and constitutes a severe danger to navigation. The submerged portion is always a great deal larger than the exposed portion.

Inselberg An isolated rocky hill with smooth rounded walls typical of desert or semi-desert areas. Often rises over 300 metres above the surrounding plain.

Inundation Flooding of normally dry areas by water from rivers, lakes or the sea. It most commonly occurs in the lower course of a river.

Irrigation Agricultural techniques for bringing water on to dry land to make it suitable for cultivation. The water may be brought to the fields through channels which catch the overflow from a river or can be brought up from wells or reservoirs.

Island Land completely surrounded by water. It is distinguished from a continent by its small size. The largest island in the world is Greenland with an area of over two million sq km.

Isobar Line on a map joining points with the same barometric pressure. The pressure is usually reduced to sea level before plotting; the unit of measurement is the millibar (mb).

Isotherm Line on a map joining points with the same temperature, usually reduced to mean sea level.

Isthmus A strip of land, usually quite narrow, which separates two seas and connects two continents or a peninsula to a continent.

Joint Fracture found in a rock mass without any displacement of the two parts concerned as in a fault. Joints are often transverse with respect to the rock strata and represent a line of weakness where erosion can attack easily.

Jurassic The second geological period of the Mesozoic or Secondary era, from 180 to 135 million years ago. The name comes from the Jura mountains. The dinosaurs evolved during this period.

Karst All those phenomena resulting from the solvent action of water on limestone rocks; the name comes from the Karst region of Yugoslavia where these phenomena are seen and have been specially studied. The principal features of karst regions are the lack of surface water and the presence of caves and sink-holes.

Laccolith Mass of solidified magma found at a shallow depth which has forced itself between the strata, arching the surface strata into a dome.

Lagoon Stretch of water along a shore; it is separated from the sea by small islands, a bar or a coral reef. Also the circular lakes situated within atolls are sometimes called lagoons.

Lake Cavity in the Earth's surface filled with water but without direct connection with the sea. Lakes can have various origins; they can result from the filling up of ancient glacial basins (glacial lakes), tectonic trenches (structural lakes), volcanic craters (crater lakes). There are also lakes caused by an obstruction such as a landslide or moraine.

Landslide A fall of rocks or earth along a slope. Landslides are often caused by water

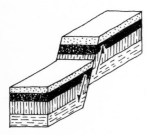

Normal fault

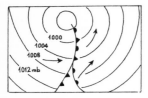

Front

Fjord

Fossil

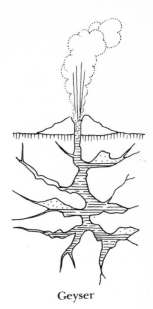

Geyser

Gorge

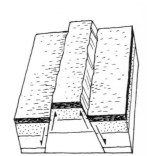

Horst

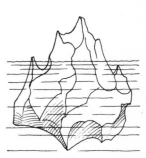

Iceberg

Inselberg

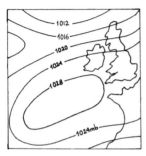

Isobars

Island

Glacial lake

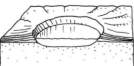

Crater lake

(from rain or the melting of snow) penetrating the soil or the rock strata. The force of gravity then overcomes the adhesion of the rocks.

Laterite Layer of reddish clayey material originating from chemical changes in rock; it is typical of moist tropical climates. Laterites cover large areas of Africa, Brazil and India.

Latitude Angular distance of a point from the Equator, measured in degrees along the meridian passing through the point. The Equator is at 0° latitude and the poles are at 90°.

Lava Magma which flows from the Earth's surface in liquid form. It can be rich in silica and can solidify rapidly without flowing large distances (acid lava), or it can flow a long way before solidifying (basic lava).

Limestone Sedimentary rock composed mainly of calcium carbonate; it may be of chemical or organic origin. Associated with magnesium carbonate (dolomite) it may form extensive mountain ranges such as the Dolomites.

Loess Very fine, fertile soil generally regarded as carried by the wind and coming from desert areas or from glacial and fluvioglacial deposits. Thick layers of loess are found in north-west China and also in Europe where it derived from the edge of former ice sheets.

Longitude Angular distance of a point from the prime meridian (the Greenwich meridian, passing through London) measured along the parallel which passes through that point.

Magma Molten material found below the Earth's surface at very high temperatures. When magma solidifies below the Earth's surface it forms intrusive magmatic rocks (for example granite); when it reaches the surface it is turned into lava which gives rise to effusive magmatic rocks.

Mangrove Type of tropical tree which lives in marshy regions where the roots are continually submerged by the tides. They form dense forests as, for example, along the Amazon or Niger deltas.

Mantle Intermediate shell of the Earth between the crust and the molten core. Its existence is shown by the study of earthquake shock waves. It extends from 2,900 km to 6,300 km from the centre of the Earth.

Marl Rock composed of clay and limestone in equal proportions.

Marsh Area partly or wholly covered with water and vegetation consisting mainly of water-loving plants like reeds. The water may come from springs or the sea.

Meander Curve in a river flowing on a plain or even in an enclosed valley (in the latter case the meander is called incised). The term comes from the river Meander in Asia Minor.

Megalopolis A vast almost continuous urban area formed from the expansion of several cities and possessing a very large population. The Atlantic coast of the United States is an example of this.

Meridian Great circle passing through both the poles; starting from the prime or Greenwich meridian which is the 0° meridian, longitude is measured up to 180° East or West.

Mesozoic The second geological era (it is also called the Secondary era) from 220 million to 70 million years ago. It includes the Triassic, Jurassic and Cretaceous periods.

Metamorphism Process by which existing rocks undergo significant changes of their physical and chemical nature. These changes are caused by high temperatures and pressures within the Earth's crust and give rise to the metamorphic rocks.

Migration Dispersal of people within the boundaries of their own country or outside it. When they move outside it is called emigration, when people move into a country from outside it is called immigration. Economic factors are usually the cause of these movements.

Mindel Second of the four great ice ages of the Quaternary era which has left recognisable fluvioglacial deposits.

Mineral Homogeneous substance of natural origin forming part of the Earth's crust; the aggregation of various minerals forms the rocks. Minerals usually have a crystalline structure.

Miocene Third geological period of the Secondary or Cenozoic era, from 25 to 11 million years ago. The most intense phases of the great upheavals which gave rise to the Alps occurred during this period.

Monoculture Method of cultivation based on growing one kind of crop only (for example rice in the monsoon regions). Clearly this type of production is very susceptible to market fluctuations and can produce rapid impoverishment of the soil.

Monsoon Seasonal wind in south-east Asia which blows from the continent towards the sea in winter and from the sea towards the land in summer. This change in direction is due to the changing temperature and pressure gradients of the air masses over the land and over the sea with the changing seasons.

Moor Countryside typified by vegetation such as heather, broom, bilberry and specialised plants which can thrive on ill-drained land.

Moraine Accumulation of detritus carried and deposited by a glacier. The rocky fragments which fall on the surface of a glacier or which the glacier itself tears from its rock bed are carried along and then deposited in the valley in the form of a lateral, terminal or medial moraine.

Mountain Prominence with typically steep sides and summit and climatic changes between the base and the summit. By convention, uplands over 600 m in height are considered mountains. The word mountains also means the area where these peaks are situated.

Mountain pastures Pastures at high altitudes used by cattle during summer; they are usually located at the edges of glacial valleys where the slope is reduced and plateaux form.

Nappe A huge fold resulting from Earth movements in which the rock may be folded on top of itself and thrust forward for several miles.

Nation Body of people united by a common language, civilisation and history, which often congregates in one independent State.

National park Area reserved for the conservation of flora, fauna and natural countryside. The first national park was Yellowstone in the United States made in 1872.

Nomad Person with no fixed dwelling

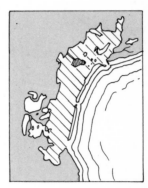

Lagoon

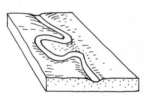

Meander

place who is continuously on the move in order to find new pastures for his livestock. Nomadic peoples are much less numerous today.

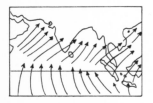

Winter monsoon

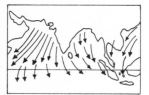

Summer monsoon

Oasis Area in the desert with springs or wells which provides sufficient water for the growth of vegetation and for man's survival. The term applies particularly to the deserts of North Africa.

Ocean Vast area of the Earth's surface covered with water which surrounds the continents. The oceans cover about three-quarters of the Earth's surface. The largest ocean is the Pacific with over 166 million sq km.

Ocean ridge Underwater ridge rising from the ocean bed. The most typical is the mid-Atlantic ridge which runs parallel to the continents. According to recent theory, the ridges are proof of the origin of the continents.

Ocean trench Long narrow depression in the ocean bed situated close to archipelagos at a depth greater than 5,000 m. The deepest trenches are found in the Pacific Ocean (Mariana Trench, over 11,000 m deep, Philippine Trench, 10,800 m, etc.).

Oil Mixture of hydrocarbons, not only liquid but solid and gaseous. The liquid part which is usually given this name is extracted from the earth by drilling. The crude oil is progressively distilled and produces a very wide range of products essential for the present-day economy, such as petrol and lubricating oils.

Oligocene Second geological period of the Cenozoic or Tertiary era during which the sea covered a large part of central Europe. Important phases of the Alpine orogenesis occurred.

Orogenesis All those phenomena leading to the compression and upheaval of parts of the Earth's crust and thus the formation of new mountain ranges. In the European region there have been at least three orogeneses (the Caledonian, the Hercynian and the Alpine), but the most impressive example is the most recent, the Alpine orogenesis.

Moraine

Palaeozoic The first of the so-called geological eras, from 600 to 225 million years ago and comprising six periods (Cambrian, Ordovician, Silurian, Devonian, Carboniferous and Permian).

Pampas Vast prairie in South America typical of Argentina and Uruguay. At the present time it is partly used for the growing of crops such as cereals and alfalfa, the remainder is traditionally given over to rearing livestock.

Pangaea According to the theory of the origin of the continents, this was a single huge super-continent from which the present-day continents were formed as it split up. Following the first separation Gondwanaland was formed in the south and Laurasia in the north.

Parallel Line parallel to the Equator; each parallel is a minor circle compared to the Equator which is a great circle situated at 0° latitude. Latitude is measured north and south starting from the Equator.

Pass Passage through a mountain range connecting two valleys. It is usually located at a particularly weak point where erosive forces have been able to operate with the most markedly effective results.

Peneplain Almost flat region whose actual shape is due to the action of agents of erosion over a great period of time.

Permafrost Permanently frozen soil typical of the tundra. Thawing can occur during the summer, but this only affects the surface. Frost heaving may litter the surface with stones.

Permian Sixth geological period of the Palaeozoic or Primary age from 270 to 225 million years ago. The name comes from the Russian city of Perm where rocks belonging to this period are found. The Hercynian orogenesis was completed during the Permian age.

Plain Large area of flat land; the term is also used for areas with gentle undulations but without any significant projections or depression. The North European Plain provides a good example of a plain.

Plateau Flat area situated at great heights bordered by steep slopes or mountain ranges. It may have various origins, tectonic, residual, volcanic.

Pliocene Fourth geological period of the Cenozoic or Tertiary era, from 1.8 to 7 million years ago. The boundary with the next period, the Pleistocene which started the Quaternary era, has not been well defined by the various authorities.

Podsol A type of soil which formed in cold, damp regions with vegetation consisting of moorland and conifers. The surface layer is sandy with an ash grey layer beneath. It is strongly leached. Podsol is found in the moorland and coniferous forest areas of western and northern Europe.

Polder Land usually reserved for agriculture and lying below sea level. It is formed from stretches of reclaimed coastal land and is enclosed by dykes. They are typical of the Low Countries where the largest Polder, the Zuider Zee, covers over 2,000 sq km.

Pole Each of the two ends of the Earth's axis constitutes one geographical pole. The magnetic poles do not coincide with the geographical poles but are located to the north of mainland Canada and in South Victoria Land (Antarctica).

Pond A small lake sometimes artificially constructed in order to water stock.

Porphyry An igneous rock with large crystals such as quartz and orthoclase embedded in a fine grained substance. The term is also used to mean rocks of the granite type formed from magma which has solidified at a shallow depth.

Port Place along the coast where ships can tie up and shelter from the seas while loading and unloading. Behind the port there is usually a settlement of variable size closely involved with the surrounding region.

Precambrian (era) Includes the very long period of time between when the Earth's crust first solidified (more than three thousand million years ago) up to the Palaeozoic era. The remains of algae and invertebrates belonging to this era are found.

Projection Technique by means of which the spherical surface of the Earth can be represented on a geographical map with as little distortion as possible. Cylindrical and conical projections are often used in atlases.

Quaternary Fourth of the geological eras beginning one million, eight hundred

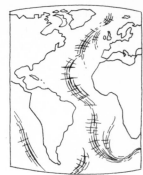

Ocean ridge

Pangaea

Pass

thousand years ago. It is divided into two periods: Pleistocene and Holocene. The first period is notable for a great expansion of the glaciers which covered over 44 million square kilometres of the Earth's surface.

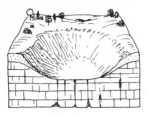

Sink-hole

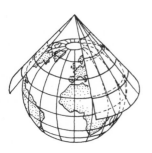

Conical projection

Cylindrical projection

Rapids Stretch of a river where the current is rapid and violent caused by an outcrop of hard rock or increase in the slope of the river bed; it is not necessary for there to be a sharp change in the slope, which would result in a waterfall.

Reclamation Those activities by means of which land is made suitable for agriculture. For example, reclamation can constitute drainage of flooded land like marshy plains (the Pontine Marshes in Italy) or areas covered with shallow sea water (Dutch polders).

Reg Means a desert of gravel and stones as opposed to sand (erg) and rock (hamada). It is synonymous with serir. This second name is used in Libya and in Egypt, while reg is used in Algeria.

Rendzina Type of dark coloured soil found in limestone terrain. It is found in some parts of England and the United States owing to the moist temperate climate.

Ria Long, narrow coastal inlet resulting from the submersion of a river valley under sea water. Rias are common on the coast of south-west Spain, in Britain and in Ireland.

Riss Third of the four great ice ages of the Quaternary era between the Mindel-Riss and Riss-Würm interglacial eras. The glaciers probably reached their greatest extent during this period.

River General term meaning a perennial water course fed by minor streams as well as by rainfall, springs, glaciers or lakes. The river flows by gravity towards the sea, a lake or a larger river. The longest river in the world is the Nile (6,650 km).

River bed Bed normally occupied by a river or stream.

Rocks Aggregate of minerals formed naturally and making up part of the lithosphere. Rocks are classified as follows, according to their origin: igneous (caused by the cooling and solidification of magma); sedimentary (formed by the consolidation of materials of various origins carried by agents such as rivers, the wind, and deposited in the seas or continental areas); metamorphic (caused by change resulting from high pressures and temperatures in existing rocks).

Run-off Quantity of water running down the slope or along a river, due to precipitation or the melting of snow. The run-off depends on the steepness of the slope, the type of rock and the presence or lack of vegetation and evaporation.

Sand Substance composed of minute grains, mainly of quartz. The size of the grains must be between 0.02 and 2 mm.

Sandstone Sedimentary rock of various colours (from brown to red and yellow) composed of cemented and compacted sand. They are classified according to their mineralogical composition, the size of the particles and the position where they are found. The latter may be continental or marine.

Savannah Type of grassland typical of tropical areas. Here are found tall grasses

with trees and scattered shrubs, such as the baobab or the euphorbia. From the climatic point of view it represents the transition between the desert and the rain forests.

Scale Ratio between the distance measured on a map and the corresponding distance on the ground. It can be expressed as a segment of a given length (linear scale) or as a fraction (representative fraction). For example, a scale of 1:25,000 means that each centimetre on the map corresponds to 25,000 cm, or 250 km on the ground.

Sea General term meaning the body of salt water surrounding the land and divided into oceans and smaller seas.

Serac Block of ice in the shape of a tower or spire sometimes tens of metres in height, found glaciers. They are formed when crevasses cross each other.

Sial Rocky substance forming the surface layer of the Earth's surface. The rock is of the granite type mostly composed of silica (Si) and alumina (al).

Silurian Third geological period of the Palaeozoic or Primary era from 440 to 400 million years ago. Among typical fossils found are trilobites and graptolites.

Sima Rocky substance formed from silica (Si) and magnesia (ma) which is found below continental masses of sial. The bed of some oceans is formed of sima.

Sink-hole Funnel or bowl shaped depression typical of karst regions. Caused by dissolving of the limestone rock by rain water.

Slate Metamorphic rock formed from muddy deposits (clay) subjected to pressure within the Earth's crust. It has the property of being easily split into sheets and is often used for covering roofs.

Snow Solid precipitation caused by water vapour passing into the solid state owing to the low temperature. Minute crystals of ice form which gather together in the characteristic star shape.

Snow basin The place where a glacier starts as a result of accumulation of snow from snow storms or avalanches. When the accumulation exceeds the melting, the front of the glacier advances.

Soil Thin surface layer of the Earth's crust consisting of chemically changed rock particles, organic material and living organisms. Soil is essential for the cultivation of crops.

Solifluction Relatively rapid movement of saturated soil downslope. It is common in mountains and in high latitudes when the surface of the ground thaws and slides over the underlying ground which is still frozen.

Spring Point where water flows naturally from the ground. Its location and flow depend on the arrangement of the permeable and impermeable rock strata and the amount of rainfall or snow melt.

Stalactite Deposit in the shape of a sharp cone or veil which hangs from the roof of a cave. It is formed from the calcium carbonate contained in the water which filters through fissures in the cave.

Stalagmite Column shaped deposit rising from the floor of a cave; formed by drops falling from the roof to the floor which are rich in calcium carbonate.

Stratification Characteristic of sedimentary rocks which appears as strata of various thicknesses. The strata are often distinguishable by their different colours and composition.

Swallow-hole Cavity in limestone rocks caused by solution in rain water or by the collapse of a subterranean vault.

Ria

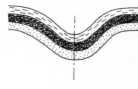

Syncline

Stalagmite

Stalactite

Tides

Terrace

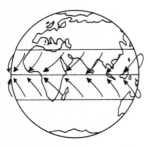

Trade winds

Syncline Rock strata folded downwards. It may form a basin as in the London basin. However, the compression in the bottom of the syncline makes the rock there very strong. After millions of years only the bottom of the syncline may survive erosion, thereby forming a mountain.

Taiga Evergreen coniferous forest found in the climatic zone south of the tundra in Siberia. The name is applied to similar forests in Scandinavia and North America where the winters are also very severe and the summers short and cool.

Terrace Step which breaks the evenness of a slope. Alluvial terraces are found along valleys and are the remains of former flood plains into which rivers have cut down with new energy when there has been, for example, a fall in sea level.

Tides Periodical movement of the waters of the oceans and seas due to the attraction of the Sun and the Moon; alternate raising and lowering of the sea level occurs four times a day. Least noticeable in enclosed seas such as the Mediterranean, the tides can reach considerable heights in deep bays on coastlines of the open ocean.

Tectonics That branch of geology which studies those movements that cause folds and faults in the Earth's crust.

Trade winds Winds which blow towards the Equator from about latitude 30°; in the northern hemisphere they blow from the north-east, in the southern from the south-east. Their principal characteristic is their constant direction which is useful when sailing in the world's oceans.

Tropic Each of the two parallels situated at 23° 30'; the one to the north is called the Tropic of Cancer and the one to the south is called the Tropic of Capricorn. Between them lies the so-called tropical zone.

Trough (glacial) U-shaped valley of glacial origin, as opposed to the V-shaped valley formed by a river.

Tuff Rock formed by volcanic ash cemented together and compacted; tuff is defined as a pyroclastic deposit.

Tundra The area between the polar regions of permanent ice and snow to the north and the coniferous forest regions to the south. The typical vegetation consists of dwarf bushes, lichens and mosses. The summers are short and the mean temperature in the warmest month does not exceed 10°C.

Uvala Hollow in limestone ground larger than a sink-hole; formed by the merging of several sink-holes.

Valley Elongated depression between two slopes; a river usually flows through a valley. Valleys with a U-shaped cross section are usually glacial in origin while those with a V-shape are formed by rivers.

Vauclusian spring Spring fed by the surfacing of an underground stream especially in karst country where the limestone lies on a layer of impervious rock. A zone of springs may result along the margin of the limestone.

Village A settlement which is smaller in size than a town. They are usually centres of agriculture and trade.

Volcano Prominence in the Earth's crust, usually conical in shape, formed by material erupted from a fissure in the crust. Volcanoes can be either active, dormant or extinct. Volcanic areas are usually to be found associated with the major earthquake areas.

Wadi Dry river bed typical of desert regions. Only after intense rain does a stream flow for a short time.

Water meadow Grassland which can be irrigated to give a strong growth of grass even in dry seasons.

Waterfall Fall made by a river course on reaching a sharp change in level, usually due to a tough rock outcrop. The highest falls in the world are the Angel Falls in Venezuela (980 m).

Watershed Also called a divide, this separates the various drainage basins. It can consist of a well-defined line, like a mountain ridge, or of an irregular region of limited height.

Wave Fluctuation in the surface of seas or lakes usually caused by the action of the wind. In waves on the open sea, which can reach heights of over ten metres, the water particles execute a circular motion and there is no forward movement of water but simply rotation of the water particles.

Würm The last of the four great ice ages of the Quaternary era which ended the Pleistocene period. After the Würm, the glaciers commenced a large scale shrinkage leading very gradually to the positions they occupy today.

Xerophilous Type of vegetation adapted to survive the climatic condition where there is a very low level of precipitation.

Zenith Point on the celestial sphere immediately above an observer.

Trough

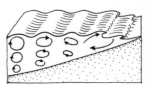

Wave

Volcano

Index to maps

Mamuk 3 I13
Managua 8 M8
Manakara 6 H8
Manama 4 GH7
Manaus 10 D4
Manchester F5
Manchuria 4 Q5
Manchuria Plain 3 Q5
Manda 6 G7
Mandalay 4 N7
Mangaia 11 L7
Mangareva 11 O7
Manheim 2 H6
Mani 11 M2
Manicoré 10 D4
Manifold C. 12 I4
Manihi 11 N6
Manihiki Atoll 11 LM6
Manila 4 P8
Manisa 2 N8
Manitoba 8 L4
Manitoba L. 7 I4
Manizales 10 C3
Manly 12 e10
Mannar, Gulf of 3 L9
Manokwari 3 n14
Manomo 6 F6
Mansfield 12 H7
Manuch 1 Q6
Manukau 12 g13
Manych Gudilo L. 1 Q6
Maoke Mts. n14
Mapia Is. 11 D4
Maputo 6 G8
Maputo Bay 5 G8
Maracaibo 10 C2
Maracaibo L. 9 C23
Marajo I. 9 EF
Maramba 6 F7
Maramao Piani 10 F4
Maranoa 12 H5
Marañón 9 C4
Marble Bar 12 B4
Mar Chiquita L. 9 D7
Marcus (Minami Tori Shima) 11 F2
Marcus-Necker Rise II DE4-5
Mar del Plata 10 E7
Maré 11 G7
Margarita 10 D2
Marguerite Bay 14 O3
Maria Is. 11 M7
Mariana Is. 11 E3
Mariana Trench II D5
Marianas Trench 11 E3
Mariato, Pta 7 M9
Maria van Diemen C. 12 f12
Marian Reef 12 I3
Maritime Atlas 1 GH8
Maritsa 1 N7
Marjata 4 a12
Markham Mt. 14 Bb2
Marlborough 12 H4
Marmara, Sea of 1 N7
Moroantsetra 6 H7
Marobe 12 H1
Marokau 11 N6
Maroua 6 E4
Maro Reef 11 I
Marquesas Islands 11 O5
Marra, Jebel 5 F4
Marrakech 6 C2
Marrawah 12 a9
Marree 12 F5
Marsabit 6 G5
Marsala 2 I8
Marseille 2 H7
Mar, Serra do 9 F6
Marshall 12 H7
Marshall Islands 11 G3
Martin Pen. 14 Qq2
Martin Vaz Is. 10 H6
Marutea 11 O7
Maryborough 12 I5
Masbate 4 Q8
Mascarene Basin QR7
Mascarene Is. 6 a10
Mascat 4 H-I7
Maseru 6 F8
Mashhad 4 H6
Masila, Wadi 3 G8
Massawa 6 GH4
Massif Central 1 G6-7
Masson 14 E3
Masterton 12 f14
Masurian L. Plateau 1 M5
Masvingo 6 G8
Matadi 6 E6
Matapan C. 1 M8
Mataram 12 B1
Mataranka 12 E3
Matla 4 a12
Mato Grosso 10 E5
Mato Grosso Plateau of 9 E5
Mato Grosso, St. 10 E5
Matsudo 4 d13
Matsuura 4 e13
Mathew 11 H7
Maumere 12 C1
Maun 6 F7
Mauna Kea 11 M3
Maupihaa 11 M6

Maurice L. 12 E6
Mauritania 6 B4
Mauritius 6 a10
Maykop 2 Q7
Maynas 9 C4
Ma yung 4 f14
Mayunga 6 H7
Mazatlan 8 I7
Mazar-i-Sharif 4 I6
Mazatlan 8 I7
Mbandaka 6 E5
McClintock Mt. 14 B-b2
McKinley Mt. 7 E3
M' Clure Str. 7 G2
Mecca 4 G7
Medan 4 N19
Medellin 10 C3
Medford 8 G5
Medicine Hat 8 I4
Medina 4 G7
Medjerda 1 H8
Meekatharra 12 B5
Meghna 4 b11
Meherpur 4 a11
Meknès 2 D9
Mekong 3 N6-7
Melanesia 11 DH4-6
Melbourne 12 G7
Mellish Reef 11 F6
Melville Bay 7 O2
Melville C. 12 G2
Melville I. (Austr.) 12 E2
Melville I. (Canada) 8 HI2
Melville Pen. 7 M3
Menado 4 Q9
Menam 4 N8
Mendocino C. 7 G5
Mendoza 10 D7
Menindee 12 G6
Menongue 6 E7
Menorca 2 GH8
Mentawai Is. 4 N10
Menzies 12 C5
Meramangye L. 12 E5
Merauke 12 FG1
Merauke R. 12 G1
Merbabu 3 m13
Merca 6 H5
Mercedes (Argentina) 10 D7
Mercedes (Uruguay) 10 E7
Mercury I. 12 h13
Mergui Archip. 4 N8
Merida 8 L7
Merida, Cord. de 9 C2-3
Merredin 12 B6
Merrick 1 F4
Mesopotamia 3 FG6
Messina (Italy) 2 I8
Messina (S. Afr.) 6 G8
Messina Str. 1 L8
Meta 9 CD3
Methven 12 g14
Metz 2 H6
Meuse 1 H5
Mexicali 8 H6
Mexican Plateau 7 I7
Mexico 8 IL7-8
Mexixo, Gulf of 7 LM7
Mexico Str. 8 IL7-8
Mezen 2 R2
Mezen (R.) I R2
Mezen Bay 1 Q2
Miami 8 M7
Michigan 8 M5
Michigan L. 7 5M
Micronesia 11 EH4-5
Middle Atlas 1 EF9
Middleton 12 G4
Middleton Reef 11 G7
Mid-Indian Basin II S6-7
Mid-Indian Ridge II R6-8
Midway Is. 11 I2
Milan 2 H6
Mildura 12G6
Miles12 I5
Mili 11 H4
Miling 12 I6
Milk, Wadi el 5 F4
Millerovo 2 Q6
Mill I. 14 d3
Milparinka 12 G5
Milwaukee 8 L5
Minami Tori-shima (Marcus) 11 F1
Minas Gerais 10 F5
Minato 4 d13
Mindanao 4 Q9
Mindoro 3 PQ8
Mingary 12 F6
Minho 1 E7
Minigwal L. 12 C5
Minneapolis 8 L5
Minnesota 8 L5
Minnipa 12 F6
Minorca 2 8G
Minsk 2 N5
Minto L. 7 N4
Minya Konka 3 O7
Miquelon I.8 P5
Mirim L. 9 E7
Mirs Bay 4 g15
Misaki 4 d13
Misoöl 3 n14
Mississippi 7 L5-6

Mississippi Delta 7 LM
Mississippi (St.) 8 LM6
Missouri 1 M7
Missouri (St.) 8 L5-6
Mitchell 12 H5
Mitchell, Mt. 7 M6
Mitchell (R.) 11 E6
Mitchell River 12 G3
Mitre I 11 H6
Mitteland Canal 1 HI5
Mitu 10 C3
Mitumba Mts. 5 F6
Mlanje Mt. 5 G7
Moara 4 e13
Moçâmedes 6 DE7
Mogadishu 6 H5
Mokpo 4 Q6
Moksa 1 Q5
Moldavia 2 N6
Mollendo 10 C5
Moluccas 3 Q10
Molucca Sea 3 Q9
Mombasa 6 H5
Monaco 2 H7
Mona Pass. 7 O8
Moncayo 1 F7
Monchique, Serra da I E8
Mongallo 6 F5
Mongolia 4 N-P5
Mongolia, Plateau of 3 O5
Mongu 6 F7
Monrovia 6 B5
Montana 9 C4-5
Montana (St.) 8 HI5
Monterrey 8 I7
Montevideo 10 E7
Montgomery 8 M6
Montluçon 2 G6
Montpellier 2 G7
Montreal 8 N5
Mozambique Channel 5 CH 7-8
Moora 12 I6
Moore L. 12 B5
Moosonee 8 M4
Mopti 6 C4
Morane 11 O7
Morava 1 M7
Moray Firth 1 F4
Morea 1 M8
Moree 12 H5
Morena, Sierra I EF8
Moreton 12 G2
Moreton I. 12 G5
Morgan 12 F6
Morgans 12 C5
Mornington I. 12 F3
Morobe 12 H1
Morocco 6 C3
Morondava 6 H7
Morris Jesup, C. 7 R1
Mortes, Rio dos 9 E5
Mortlock Is. 11 F4
Moscow 2 P4
Mosquito, Gulf of 7 M8
Mostaganem 2 F8
Mosul 4 G6
Mouila 6 E6
Moulmein 4 N8
Moulouya 1 F9
Mount Douglas 12 H4
Mount Gambier 12 F7
Mount Isa 12 F4
Mount Magnet 12 B5
Mount Morgan 12 H4
Moura 10 D4
Moyale 6 G5
Mozambique 6 H7
Mozambique Channel 5 GH7-8
Mozambique Coastal Plain 5 G7-8
Mozambique St. 6 G7
Mtwara 6 H7
Muang Ubon 4 O8
Muchinga Mts. 5 G7
Mui Varella 3 O8
Mukalla 4 H8
Mukden 4 Q5
Mulhouse 2 H6
Mull 1 E4
Mullewa 12 B5
Mulobezi 6 F7
Multan 4 L7
Mundiwindi 12 C4
Mungbere 6 F5
Mungindi 12 H5
Münster 2 H5
Muonio 1 M2
Mupuera 9 E4
Mur 1 L6
Murchison 11 B7
Murchison Falls 5 G5
Murcia 2 F8
Murcia (Region) 1 F8
Mures 1 M6
Murmansk 2 O2
Murmansk Rise II P2
Murray 12 H7
Murray Fracture Zone II GH4
Murrumbidgee 12 H6
Murtoa 12 G7
Mururoa 11 N7
Murwillumbah 12 I5

Muryo 3 m13
Murzuq 5 E3
Musala 1 M7
Musgrave 12 G2
Musgrave Ranges 12 E5
Muswellbrook 12 I6
Mutankiang 4 Q5
Muttaburra 12 G4
Muyunkum 3 I5
Mwanza 6 G5
Mweru L.5 F6
Myitkyina 4 N7

N

Nabadwip 4 a11
Nafud Desert 3 G7
Nagasaki 4 Q6
Nago 4 e13
Nagoya 4 R6
Nagpur 4 L7
Naha 4 Q7
Nahuel Huapi L. 9 CD8
Nairobi 6 G5
Nakhichevan 2 R8
Nakumanu 1. 11 F5
Namib Desert 5 E8
Nambour 12 I5
Namoi 12 H6
Nampula 6 G7
Namsos 2 I3
Nam Tse 3 N6
Nanchang 4 P7
Nancy 2 H6
Nang 3 p17
Nam hai (Foshan) 4 f14
Nanking 4 P6
Nanning 4 O7
Nansen Mt. 14 tA1
Nan Shan 3 NO6
Nantes 2 F6
Nanumea 11 H5
Nao, C. 1 G8
Napier 12 h13
Naples 2 G7
Napo 6 E4
Napuka 11 N6
Naracoorte 12 G7
Narayanganj 4 b11
Narbonne 2 G7
Narita 4 d13
Narmada 3 L7
Narodnaya 1 T3
Narokau 11 N6
Narrabeen 12 e10
Narrabri 12 H6
Narran L. 12 H5
Narrogin 12 B6
Narvik 2 L2
Naryan Mar 2 SV2
Nashville 8 M6
Nassau 8 N7
Nassau 1. 11 L6
Nasser L. 5 G3
Natal 10 G4
Natal (St.) 6 G8
Naturaliste C. 12 I6
Naturaliste Ch. 12 A4
Nauru 11 G3
N'Djaména 6 E4
Ndola 6 F7
Neagh L. 1 E5
Nebraska 8 I5
Necker I. 11 L2
Necker Ridge 11 L2
Nee Soon 4 h16
Negoiu Mt. 1 N6
Negro (Brazil) 9 D3-4
Negro (Uruguay) 9 E7
Negros 4 Q9
Neilson Reef 11 N7
Neisse 1 I5
Neiva 10 C3
Nejd 4 G7
Nelson 12 g14
Nelson (R.) 7 L4
Neman 1 M4
Nengengo 11 N6
Nepal 4 M7
Netherlands 2 GH5
Nettilling L. 7 N3
Neuquén 10 D7
Nevada 8 I6
Nevada, Sierra (Spain) I F8
Nevada, Sierra (U.S.A.) 7 GH6
Nevada de Sta. Marta, Sierra 9 C9
Nevers 2 G6
New Britain 11 F5
New Brunswick 8 O5
New Caledonia 11 G7
New Castle I F7
Newcastle (Australia) 12 I6
Newcastle (England) 2 F4
Newcastle Waters 12 E3
Newdegate 12 B6
New England NO5

New England Ra 11 EF7
Newfoundland 8 P5
Newfoundland Basin II M3
New Georgia 11 FS
New Guinea 11 DE5
New Hampshire 8 N5
New Hanover 11 F5
New Haven 8 N5
New Hebrides 11 GH6
New Hebrides Tr. 11 G6
New Ireland 11 F5
New Mexico 8 I6
New Norfolk 12 B9
New Orleans 8 N6
New Plymouth 12 g13
Newport 12 e10
New Siberia 4 S2
New Siberian Is. 4 RS2
New South Wales 12 GH6
New York 8 N5
New York (St.) 8 N5
New Zealand 11 GH8-9
New Zealand Rise II E7
N'Guigmi 4 E4
Ngura 6 E4
Niagara Falls 7 N5
Niamey 6 D5
Nias 3 N9
Nicaragua 8 M8
Nicaragua L. 7 M8
Nice 2 H7
Nicobar Is. 4 N9
Nicosia 2 O8
Niger (R.) 5 C4
Niger (St.) 6 DE3-4
Nigeria 6 DE4
Nightcaps 12 f15
Nihoa 11 L2
Niigata 4 R6
Nikolayev 2 O6
Nikolayevsk 4 R4
Nile 5 G3-4
Nimba Mts. 5 C5
Nimes 2 G7
Ninigo Group 11 E5
Ninomiya 4 d13
Nipigon, L. 7 M5
Nis 2 M7
Niteroi 10 F6
Ni wan Men 4 g15
Nizhne Kolymsk 4 V3
Noakhali 4 b11
Nojima C. 4 e13
Nome 8 C3
Nonouti 11 H5
Nordik 4 P2
Norfolk I. 11 G7
Norman 12 G3
Normanby I. 12 I1
Normandy I FG6
Normanton 12 G3
Norman Wells 8 F3
Nornalup 12 B6
Norrland 1 LB
Norrköping 2 L4
Norseman 12 C6
Northam 12 I6
Northampton 12 A5
North Atlantic Ridge II LM3-4
North Bay 8 N5
North C. (Antarctica) 14 a3
North C. (N.Z.) 11 H8
North Carolina 8 MN6
North Channel 1 E4
Northcliffe 12 B6
North Dakota 8 IL5
North East Cape 7 T1
North East Land 4 E2
North-East Pacific Basin II FG3-4
Northern Ireland 2 E5
Northern Territory 12 E3-4
North European Plain 1 H5-P3
North Island 11 I8
North Korea 4 Q5
North Magnetic Pole 7 IL2
North Minch I E4
North Pole 13 P1-E1
North Saskatchewan 7 H4
North Sea 1 G4-5
North Sporades I M8
North Stradbroke I. 12 I5
North Taranaki Bight 12 g13
North-West Australian Basin II AB6-7
North West C. 12 A4
North-West Pacific Basin II DE3-4
North West Highlands 1 E-EF4
North West Territory 8 GN3
Norway 2 HK1-3
Norwegian Basin II O2
Norwegian Sea 1 EH13
Norwich 2 G5
Nossob 5 EF8
Notec 1 L5
Nouakchott 6 B4
Novarin C. 3 V5

Novaya Zemlya 4 GH2
Novgorod 2 O4
Novi Sad 2 L6
Novo Kazalinsk 2 U6
Novokuznetsk 4 M4
Novosibirsk 4 M4
Nowra 12 I6
N. Sosva 1 U3
Nua 11 I6
Nubian Desert 5 G3-4
Nuevo Laredo 8 I7
Nüham 11 L2
Nui 11 H5
Nukha 2 R7
Nuku Hiwa 11 N5
Nukuoro 11 F4
Nukus 2 U7
Nullarbor 12 D6
Nullarbor Plain 12 D6
Nunivak I. 7 BC3
Nunkiang 4 Q5
Nuoro 2 H7
Nup La 3 p16
Nuptse 3 P17
Nuremberg 2 I6
Nuweveld 5 EF9
Nyala 6 F4
Nyasa (Malawi) L. 5 G7
Nyngan 12 H6

O

Oahu 11 M2
Oakland 8 G5
Oamaru 12 g14-15
Oami 4 e13
Oates Coast 14 aB2
Oaxaca 8 L8
Ob 1 Z3
Ob, Gulf of 4 L3
Obbia 6 H5
Obidos 10 E4
Obitsu 4 d13
Obshchiy Syrt 1 RS5
Ocussi 12 C1
Odowara 4 d13
Odense 2 HI4
Oder 1 L5
Odessa 2 O6
Odienne 6 C5
Oeno 11 I1 O7
Ogbomosho 6 D5
Ogden 8 H5
Ogoué 5 DE6
Ohara 4 e13
Ohio 7 M6
Ohio (St.) 8 M5
Oho Polu 3 pq17
Oimyakon 4 S3
Ojos del Salado 9 D6
Oka 1 Q4
Okavango (Cubango) 5 EF7
Okavango Smamps 5 F7
Okhotsk 4 S3
Okhotsk, Sea of 3 S4
Okinawa I. 4 Q7
Oklahoma 8 L6
Oklahoma City 8 L6
Oland 1 L4
Olbia 2 H7
Old Castile 1 EF7
Olekma 3 P4
Olekminsk 4 Q3
Olenëk 3 Q2
Oleron, Ile d' 2 F6
Oleron, I. d' I F6
Olsztyn 2M5
Olympus 1 M7
Omaha 8 L5
Oman 4 H7-8
Oman, Gulf of 3 H7
Omdurman 6 F4
Ome 4 D13
Omigawa 4 e13
Omiya 4 d13
Omo 5 G5
Omolon 3 T3
Omsk 4 L4
Ongerup 12 B6
Onega 2 P3
Onega, Gulf of 1 P3
Onega L. 1 P3
Onega R. 1 P3
Onslow 12 B4
Ontario 8 M4-5
Ontario L. 7 N5
Oodnadatta 12 E5
Ooldea 12 E6
Oporto 2 E7
Opua 12 g13
Oradea 2 M6
Oraefa jökull 1 C3
Oran 2 F8
Orange 12 H6
Orange (R.) 5 EF8
Orange Free State 6 F8
Orbost 12 H7
Ord 12 D3
Ordos Plateau 3 O6
Ordzhonikidze 2 Q7
Orebro 2 IL4
Oregon 8 G5
Orël 2 P5

Orenburg 2 T5
Orense 2 E7
Orinoco 9 D3
Orinoco Basin 9 D3
Orkney Is. 2 F4
Orleans 2 G6
Orsk 2 T5
Oruro 10 D5
Osaka 4 R6
Oslo 2 I3
Osprey Reef 12 H2
Ossa Mt. 12 b9
Ostend 2 G5
Ostersund 2 I3
Ostrava 2 L6
Otaki 4 e13
Otranto 2 L8
Otranto, Str. of I L8-9
Ottawa 7 N5
Ottawa 8 N5
Otway C. 12 G7
Ouadaï 5 EF4
Ouagadougou 6 C4
Ouanda Djalé 6 F5
Oued Zem 2 E9
Ouesso 6 E5
Oujda 2 N3
Oulu 2 N3
Oulu L. 1 N3
Oum er Rhia 1 E9
Outjo 6 E8
Ouyen 12 G7
Ovamboland 5 E7
Oviedo 2 E7
Owen Stanley Ra. II E5
Oxley 12 G6
Ozark Plateau 7 L6

P

Pacaraima, Sierra 9 D3
Pacific Ocean II DH5-7
Padang 4 N10
Padua 2 I6
Pagalu 5 D6
Pagan 11 E3
Paisha 4 f14
Pai yün Chang 4 g15
Pakistan 4 IL6-7
Palau Is. 11 D4
Palawan 4 P9
Palembang 4 O10
Palermo 2 I8
Palk Str. 3 MN8
Palliser C. 12 f14
Palma 2 G8
Palmas C. 5 C5
Palmer Arch. 14 O3
Palmer Land 14 n2
Palmerston 11 L6
Palmerston North 12 gf14
Palmyra I. 11 LM4
Palos C. 1 F8
Pamirs 3 L7
Pampas 9 D7
Pamplona 2 F7
Panama 8 MN9
Panama Canal Zone 8 M9
Panama, G. of 9 C3
Panama, Isthmus of 7 N9
Panay 4 Q8
Pangrango 3 I13
Panié Mt. 11 G7
Panjim (Goa) 4 L8
Panonian Basin 1 L6
Pantelleria 2 I8
Paoting 4 P6
Paotow 4 ON5-6
Papua, G. of 12 GH1
Papua-New Guinea 12 GH1
Parà 9 E4
Paracel Island 11 B3
Paracis, Serra dos 9 D5
Paraguana Pen. 9 D2
Paraguay 10 E6
Paraguay (R.) 9 E6
Paraiba 9 F4
Parakilna 12 F6
Paramaribo 10 E3
Paramushir I. 3 S4
Parana 10 F5
Paranà (R.) 10 ED6-7
Paranagua 10 F6
Paranaiba 9 F5
Paratoo 12 F6
Parece Vela 11 D2
Parinas 9 B4
Paris 2 G6
Paris Basin 1 g6
Parkes 12 H6
Parma 2 H7
Parnaib 10 F4
Parnaiba (R.) 9 F4
Parnassos 1 M8
Parnassus 12 g14
Paroo 12 G5
Parramatta 12 I6
Parry Is. 8 HK2
Passero C. 1 I8
Passo Fundo 10 E6
Pasto 10 C3
Pasuruan 12 A1
Patagonia 9 D7-8
Patagonian Cordillera 9 C8-9

Patchwollock 12 G7
Patience Well 12 D4
Patna 4 M7
Patos, Lagoa dos 9 EF7
Patras 2 M8
Patuakhali 4 b11
Pavlodar 4 L4
Paysandu 10 E7
Peace 7 H4
Peak 4 q17
Peak Hill 12 B5
Peary Land 8 RS1
Pechenga 2 O2
Pechora 1 T3
Pechora B 1 ST2
Pechora R. 1 ST2
Pecos 7 I6
Pécs 2 L6
Peebinga 12 G6
Pegasus Bay 12 b14
Pei 4 f15
Peking 4 P5
Pelotas 10 E7
Pemba 6 H7
Penang 4 N9
Pennines 1 F5
Pennsylvania 8 N5
Penong 12 E6
Penrhyn Atoll 11 M5
Pensacola Mountains 14 NM1
Pentland 12 H4
Pentland Firth 2 F4
Penza 2 R5
Penzance 2 E5
Penzhino 4 V3
Percival Lakes 12 CD4
Perekop 2 O6
Perigueux 2 G7
Perm 2 T4
Persian Gulf 3 GH7
Perth 12 I6
Perù 10 C4-5
Peru Basin II E5
Perugia 2 I7
Pescara 2 I7
Peshawar 4 L6
Peterborough 12 F6
Peter Ist. I. 14 P3
Pethang Ringmo 3 q16
Pethangtse 3 q17
Petropavlosk 2 V5
Petropavlosk-Kamchatskiy 4 T4
Petrosul 1 M6
Pevek 4 V3
Phan-Rang 4 O8
Philadelphia 8 N6
Philippine Basin II C5
Philippine Basin 11 D2
Philippines 4 Q8-9
Philippine Trench II C5
Philippine Trench 11 C3
Phnom Penh 4 O8
Phoenix 8 H6
Phoenix I. 11 I5
Phuket 3 N9
Piai C. 4 h16
Piave 1 I6
Picardy 1 G5
Picton 12 G14
Pidurutalagala 3 M9
Piedmont Plat.7 MN6
Pielinen L. 1 O3
Pietermaritzburg 6 G8
Pietersburg 6 F8
Pilcomayo 9 D6
Pinaki 11 O6
Pinar del Río 8 M7
Pindus Mts 1 M8
Pine Creek 12 E2
Pine I. Bay 14 Q2
Ping shan 4 g15
Pins Iles des 11 G7
Pirapora 10 F5
Piraeus 2 M8
Pisca 10 C5
Pitcairn 11 O7
Pittsburg 8 N5
Piura 10 B4
Plate R. (Rio de la Plata) 9 E7
Platte 7 L5
Pleven 2 N7
Ploesti 2 N6
Plovdiv 2 M7
Plymouth 2 F5
Plzen 2 I6
Po 1 I7
Podolian Upland 1 MN5-6
Pointe Noire 6 D6
Pointe S.W. 4 g15
Poitou 1 G6
Pokataroo 12 H5
Poland 2 LM5
Polar Sub-Glacial Basin 14 eE-dD
Polish Uplands 1 LM5
Poltava 2 O6
Ponape 11 E4
Pondicherry 4 M8
Pondoland 5 F8
Ponoi 1 PQ2
Pontianak 4 O10

Pontine Mts. 1 OP7
Poopo, L. 9 D5
Popayan 10 C3
Popocatépeti 7 IL8
Pori 2 M3
Porpoise Bay 14 c3
Porsanger Fj. 1 MN1
Port Adelaide 12 F6
Port Albert 12 H7
Port Amboin 6 E7
Port Augusta 12 F6
Port-au-Prince 8 N8
Port au Basques 8 P5
Port Blair 4 N8
Port Davey 12 b9
Port Douglas 12 H3
Port Gentil 6 D6
Port Hacking 12 e11
Port Harcourt 6 D5
Port Harrison 8 N4
Port Hedland 12 B4
Port Kembla 12 d11
Portland (Australia) 12 G7
Portland (Maine) 8 N5
Portland (Oregon) 8 G5
Portland Promontory 7 MN4
Port Lincoln 12 F6
Port Louis 6 a10
Port Moresby 12 H1
Port Nelson 8 L4
Port Nolloth 6 E8
Porto Aisén 10 C8
Porto Alegre 10 E6
Port of Spain 10 D2
Porto Nacional 10 F5
Porto Novo 6 D5
Porto Velho 10 D4
Port Phillip Bay 12 G7
Port Pirie 12 F6
Port Radium 8 H3
Port Said 8 G2
Port Sudan 6 G3
Portugal 2 E7-8
Potenza 2 L7
Potomar 7 N6
Potosì 10 D5
Powell Creek 12 E3
Poyang L. 3 P7
Poznan 2 L5
Prague 2 I6
Prairies 7 IL5-6
Pretoria 6 F8
Pribilof I. 7 C4
Prince Albert Mts. 14 Bb2
Prince Charles I. 7 N3
Prince Charles Mts. 14 f2
Prince Edward I. (Canada) 7 O5
Prince Edward I. (S.Afr.) 14 H5
Prince George 8 G4
Prince Harald Coast 14 H2
Prince of Wales, C. 7 C3
Prince of Wales I. 8 HI2
Prince of Wales I. 9 C9
Prince Olaf Coast 14 g3
Prince Patrick I. 8 G2
Prince Rupert 8 G4
Princess Astrid Coast 14 iI2
Princess Charlotte Bay 12 G2
Princess Martha Coast 14 IL2
Princess Ragnhild Coast 14 hH2
Principe & Sao Tome 6 D5
Pripyat Marshes 1 N5
Pripyat, R. 1 N5
Proclamation I. 14 G3
Prome 4 N8
Proserpine 12 H4
Proston 12 I5
Provence 1 H7
Prut 1 N6
Prydz Bay 14 F3
Pskov 2 N4
Puebla 8 L8
Pueblo 8 I6
Puerto Aisen 10 C8
Puerto Casado 10 E6
Puerto Deseado 10 D8
Puerto Montt 10 C8
Puerto Rico 8 O8
Puerto Suarez 10 D5
Pukapuka 11 O6
Pukapuka Atoll (Danger Is.) 11 L5
Pukarna 11 O6
Pulai 4 h16
Pulai (R.) 4 h16
Pulap 11 E4
Pulo Anna 11 D4
Pulong 3 P8
Pumori 3 p16
Puncak Jaya 3 n14
Punggai C. 4 i17
Puno 10 C5
Punta Arenas 10 C9
Purus 9 D4
Pusur 4 a11
Putorana Mts. 3 N3
Putumayo 9 C4
Pya L. 1 O2

Pyatigorsk 2 Q7
Pyeong Yang 4 Q6
Pyrenees 1 FG7

Q

Qatar 4 H7
Qena 6 G3
Quattara Depression 5 F2
Quebec (Prov.) 8 NO4
Quebec 8 N5
Queen Adelaide Arch. 9 C9
Queen Alexandra Ra. 14 B1
Queen Charlotte Is. 7 F4
Queen Elizabeth Is. 8 HN2
Queen Mary Coast 14 B3
Queen Maud Land 14 IH2
Queen Maud Ra. 14 Ss-Tt
Queensland 12 GH4
Queenstown 12 b9
Quelimane 6 G7
Quetta 4 I6
Quezon City 4 Q8
Quilpie 12 G5
Quito 10 C3

R

Raba 12 B1
Rabat 6 C2
Race C. 7 P5
Radom 2 M5
Raiatea 11 M6
Raimangal 4 a12
Raimer Mt. 7 G5
Raipur 4 M7
Raivavae 11 N7
Ralik Chain 11 G4
Ramapo Trench 11 E2
Ramelau 12 C1
Ramghat 4 a11
Ranchi 4 M7
Randwick 12 e10
Rangamati 4 b11
Rangiora 12 g14
Rangitaiki 12 h13
Rangoon 4 N8
Raoul I. 11 I7
Rapa 11 N7
Raratonga 11 L7
Raroia 11 N6
Ras al Hadd 3 H7
Ras Dashan 5 G4
Ras Hafun 5 I4
Rasht 4 H6
Rason L. 12 C5
Ratok Chain 11 H4
Raung 3 m13
Ravenstorpe 12 C6
Ravenswood 12 H4
Rawalpindi 4 I6
Rawlinna 12 C6
Real, Cordillera 9 CD5
Recherche Arch of 12 C6
Recife 10 G4
Red 7 L6
Red Sea 5 G34
Regensburg 2 I6
Reggio 2 L8
Regina 8 I4
Reims 2 G6
Rempang 4 i17
Reindeer L. 7 I4
Renmark 12 G6
Rennel 11 G6
Rennes 2 F6
Renniek Bay 14 a3
Resistence 10 E6
Resolution I. (Can.) 7 O3
Resolution I. (N.Z.) 12 f15
Reunion 6 a10
Revilla Gigedo Is.7 H8
Reykjanes Ridge II M2-3
Reykjavík 2 T3
Rey-Malabo 6 D5
Rezaiyeh 2 OR8
Rhine 1 H6
Rhodes 2 N8
Rhodesia (Zimbabwe) 6 FG7
Rhodesian Uplands 5 F7
Rhodope Mts. 1 MN7
Rhön 1 HI5
Riau Archipelago 3 O9
Ribeirao Preto 10 F6
Riberalta 10 D5
Richmond (Australia) 12 G4
Richmond (U.S.A.) 8 N6
Rifstangi 1 CD2
Riga 2 M4
Riga, Gulf of 1 N4
Rijeka 2 I6
Rimatara 11 M7
Rio de Janeiro 10 F6
Rio Gallegos 10 D9
Rio Grande de Santiago 7 I7
Rio Grande Rise II LM7
Ritscher Upland 14 iL2
Rivera 10 E7

Riverstone 12 d10
Riyadh 4 GT
Robert English Coast 14 Oo2
Robertson Bay 14 A2
Robson Mt. 7 GH4
Roca C. 1 E8
Rocas I 10 G4
Rocha 10 E7
Rockall 1 D4
Rockdale 12 e10
Rockefeller Mts. 14 Ss2
Rockefeller Plateau 14 rS2
Rockhampton 12 H4
Rocky Mountains 7 GH4-5-6
Roebourne 12 B4
Roma 12 H5
Romanche Trench II MN6
Rome 2 I7
Romania 2 MN6
Rondônia 10 D5
Rongbuck Glacier, East 3 p16
Rongbuck Glacier, West 3 p16
Rongelap 11 G3
Roosevelt 9 D4-5
Roosevelt I. 14 Tt2
Roper 11 D5
Roraima 9 D3
Roraima 10 D3
Rörö 2 I3
Rosa, Mte. 1 H6
Rosario 10 D7
Rose 11 L6
Ross 12 g14
Ross Ice Shelf 14 TA1
Ross I. 14 n3
Ross I. 14 Aa2
Ross Sea 14 Tt2
Rostock 2 I5
Rostov 2 P6
Rosvatn 1 I2
Rota 11 E3
Rotorua 12 h13
Rotterdam 2 G5
Rotuma 11 H6
Rouen 2 G6
Rovaniemi 2 N2
Rovno 2 N5
Rowley Shoals 12 B3
Roy Hill 12 C4
Ruapehu 12 h13
Rub'al Khali 3 GH7
Rubtsovsk 4 M4
Rufiji 5 G6
Rügen 1 I5
Rukwa L. 5 G6
Rungwe 5 G6
Rupert 7 N4
Rupiu La 3 q16
Rurutu 11 M7
Ruse 2 N7
Russian S.F.S. Republic 2 MZ2-6
Ruteng 12 C1
Ruvuma 5 G7
Rwanda 6 G5
Rybachi Pen. 1 O2
Rybinsk Reservoir 1 PQ4
Ryu kyu Is. 3 Q7
Ryukyu Trench 11 C2

S

Saarema 2 M4
Sabah 4 P9
Sabat 5 G5
Sebha 6 E3
Sabine Mt. 14 A2
Sable, C. (Canada) 7 O5
Sable, C. (U.S.A.) 7 M7
Sable I. 7 P5
Sabrina Coast 14 cD3
Sacramento 8 G5
Sadiya 4 N7
Sado 3 Q6
Safi 2 D9
Segami 4 d13
Sagami Sea 4 d13
Sahara 5 CF3
Saharan Atlas 5 D2
Saharanpur 4 L6
Sahel 5 C4
Saigon (Ho Chi Min) OP8-9
Saihut 4 H8
St. André C. 5 H7
St. Denis 6 a
St. Elias Mt. 7 E4
St. Étienne 2 G6
St. George 12 H5
St. George's Ch. I E5
St. Gotthard Pass 1 H6
St. Helena C7
St. Helena B. 5 E9
Saint John 8 O5
St. Laurence 12 H4
St. Laurence, Gulf of 7 O5
St. Laurence Is. 7 B3
St. Laurence (R.) 7 N5
St. Louis (Senegal) B4

St. Louis (U.S.A.) 8 LM6
St. Lucia 10 D2
St. Marie C. 5 H8
St. Marys 12 b9
St. Marys 12 d10
St. Mathias Group 11 F5
St. Mathieu Pte. 1 E6
St. Matthew I. 7 B3
St. Nazaire 2 F6
St. Paul 8 L5
St. Peter and St. Paul Rocks 10 GH3
St. Pierre 6 a
St. Quentin 2 G6
St. Vincent C. 1 E8
St. Vincent Gulf 2 F7
Saipan 11 E3
Sajama 9 D5
Sakarya 1 O7
Sakhalin 4 S4
Sakura 4 e13
Salado 9 D6-7
Salamanca 2 E7
Salazar 12 C1
Sale 12 H7
Salekhard 4 I3
Salem 8 G5
Salerno 2 G7
Salinas Grandes 9 D6
Salisbury 6 G7
Salpaus Selka 1 MN3
Salta 10 D6
Saltillo 8 I7
Salt Lake 12 A4
Salt Lake City 8 H5
Salto Augusto 9 E4
Salton Sea H6
Salum 6 F2
Salvador 10 G5
Salween 3 N6-7
Salzburg 2 I6
Samar 4 Q8
Samarai 12 HI2
Samarkand 4 I6
Sambu 4 h16
Samoa 11 I6
Samsum 2 P7
San'a 4 G8
S. Ambrosio I. 9 C6
San Antonio 8 L7
S. Carlos 10 D3
S. Carlos de Bariloche 10 C8
San Cristobal 10 C3
S. Cristobal I. 11 G6
Sandakan 4 P9
San Diego 8 G6
Sandover 12 F4
Sandwip Ch. 4 b11
Sandy C. 12 I4
Sandy I. 12 C6
S. Félix I. 9 B6
S. Fernando de Apure 10 D3
S. Fernando de Atabapo 10 D3
San Francisco P. 9 D6
San Francisco 8 G8
Sangha 5 E5
Sangihe Is. 3 Q9
San Jorge, G. of 9 D8
San Josè 8 M9
San Juan (Argentina) 10 D7
San Juan (Puerto Rico) 8 O8
S. Lucas C. 7 I7
San Luis Potosi 8 I7
San Marino 2 I7
San Matias, Gulf of 9 D8
San Rafael 10 D7
San Salvador 8 L8
San Salvador, I. 8 N7
San tsao 4 f15
S. Valentin 9 C8
Santa Clara 8 N7
Santa Cruz (Argentina) 10 D8
Santa Cruz (Bolivia) 10 D5
Santa Cruz I. 9 B4
Santa Cruz Is. 11 G6
Santader 2 F7
Santa Fé (Argentina) 10 D7
Santa Fé (U.S.A.) 8 I6
Sta-Ines I. 9 C9
Santa Isabel 11 G5
Santa Maria 10 E6
Santarem 10 E4
Santa Rosa 10 C7
Santiago 10 C7
Santiago de Cuba 8 N8
Santiago del Estero 10 D6
Santo Domingo 8 O8
Sao Francisco 10 F4
Sao Francisco (R.) 2 F5
Sao Luis 10 F4
Saône 1 H6
Sao Paulo 10 F6
Sao Roque C. 9 G4
Sao Tomé 5 D5
Sao Tomé and Príncipe 6 D5
Sapudi 3 m13
Sarajevo 2 L7
Sarapul 2 S4
Saratov 2 R5

111